Building Web Sites with XML

ISBN 0-13-086601-6

90000

9 780130 866011

⟨CFG OIM⟩ Charles F. Goldfarb Series on Open Information Management

"Open Information Management" (OIM) means managing information so that it is open to processing by any program, not just the program that created it. That extends even to application programs not conceived of at the time the information was created.

OIM is based on the principle of data independence: data should be stored in computers in non-proprietary, genuinely standardized representations. And that applies even when the data is the content of a document. Its representation should distinguish the innate information from the proprietary codes of document processing programs and the artifacts of particular presentation styles.

Business data bases—which rigorously separate the real data from the input forms and output reports—achieved data independence decades ago. But documents, unlike business data, have historically been created in the context of a particular output presentation style. So for document data, independence was largely unachievable until recently.

That is doubly unfortunate. It is unfortunate because documents are a far more significant repository of humanity's information. And documents can contain significantly richer information structures than data bases.

It is also unfortunate because the need for OIM of documents is greater now than ever. The demands of "repurposing" require that information be deliverable in multiple formats: paper-based, online, multimedia, hypermedia. And information must now be delivered through multiple channels: traditional bookstores and libraries, the World Wide Web, corporate intranets and extranets. In the latter modes, what starts as data base data may become a document for browsing, but then may need to be reused by the reader as data.

Fortunately, in the past ten years a technology has emerged that extends to documents the data base's capacity for data independence. And it does so without the data base's restrictions on structural freedom. That technology is the "Standard Generalized Markup

Language" (SGML), an official International Standard (ISO 8879) that has been adopted by the world's largest producers of documents and by the World Wide Web.

With SGML, organizations in government, aerospace, airlines, automotive, electronics, computers, and publishing (to name a few) have freed their documents from hostage relationships to processing software. SGML coexists with graphics, multimedia, and other data standards needed for OIM and acts as the framework that relates objects in the other formats to one another and to SGML documents.

The World Wide Web's HTML and XML are both based on SGML. HTML is a particular, though very general, application of SGML, like those for the above industries. There is a limited set of markup tags that can be used with HTML. XML, in contrast, is a simplified subset of SGML facilities that, like full SGML, can be used with any set of tags. You can literally create your own markup language with XML.

As the enabling standard for OIM of documents, the SGML family of standards necessarily plays a leading role in this series. We provide tutorials on SGML, XML, and other key standards and the techniques for applying them. Our books vary in technical intensity from programming techniques for software developers to the business justification of OIM for enterprise executives. We share the practical experience of organizations and individuals who have applied the techniques of OIM in environments ranging from immense industrial publishing projects to websites of all sizes.

Our authors are expert practitioners in their subject matter, not writers hired to cover a "hot" topic. They bring insight and understanding that can only come from real-world experience. Moreover, they practice what they preach about standardization. Their books share a common standards-based vocabulary. In this way, knowledge gained from one book in the series is directly applicable when reading another, or the standards themselves. This is just one of the ways in which we strive for the utmost technical accuracy and consistency with the OIM standards.

And we also strive for a sense of excitement and fun. After all, the challenge of OIM—preserving information from the ravages of technology while exploiting its benefits—is one of the great intellectual adventures of our age. I'm sure you'll find this series to be a knowledgeable and reliable guide on that adventure.

About the Series Editor

Dr. Charles F. Goldfarb invented the SGML language in 1974 and later led the team that developed it into the International Standard on which both HTML and XML are based. He serves as editor of the Standard (ISO 8879) and as a consultant to developers of SGML and XML applications and products. He is based in Saratoga, CA.

About the Series Logo

The rebus is an ancient literary tradition, dating from 16th century Picardy, and is especially appropriate to a series involving fine distinctions between things and the words that describe them. For the logo, Andrew Goldfarb incorporated a rebus of the series name within a stylized SGML/XML comment declaration.

The Charles F. Goldfarb Series on Open Information Management

As XML is a subset of SGML, the Series List is categorized to show the degree to which a title applies to XML. "XML Titles" are those that discuss XML explicitly and may also cover full SGML. "SGML Titles" do not mention XML per se, but the principles covered may apply to XML.

XML Titles

Goldfarb, Pepper, and Ensign
- SGML Buyer's Guide™: Choosing the Right XML and SGML Products and Services

Megginson
- Structuring XML Documents

Leventhal, Lewis, and Fuchs
- Designing XML Internet Applications

DuCharme
- XML: The Annotated Specification

Jelliffe
- The XML and SGML Cookbook: Recipes for Structured Information

McGrath
- XML by Example: Building E-commerce Applications

Goldfarb and Prescod
- The XML Handbook™ Second Edition

Floyd
- Building Web Sites with XML

SGML Titles

Ensign
- $GML: The Billion Dollar Secret

Rubinsky and Maloney
- SGML on the Web: Small Steps Beyond HTML

McGrath
- ParseMe.1st: SGML for Software Developers

DuCharme
- SGML CD

General Titles

Martin
- TOP SECRET Intranet: How U.S. Intelligence Built Intelink—The World's Largest, Most Secure Network

Building Web Sites with XML

■ Michael Floyd

Prentice Hall PTR, Upper Saddle River, NJ 07458
www.phptr.com

Library of Congress Cataloging-in-Publication Data

Floyd, Michael
    Building Web sites with XML / Michael Floyd.
       p. c m. -- (Charles F. Goldfarb series on open information management)
    ISBN 0-13-086601-6
       1. XML (Document markup language) 2. Web pages—Design. I. Title. II. Series
    QA76.76.H94 F58 1999
    005.7'2--dc21

                                                                99-051537

Editorial/Production Supervision: *Faye Gemmellaro*
Acquisitions Editor: *Mark L. Taub*
Editorial Assistant: *Michael Fredette*
Marketing Manager: *Kate Hargett*
Manufacturing Manager: *Alexis R. Heydt*
Cover Design: *Anthony Gemmellaro*
Cover Design Direction: *Jerry Votta*
Series Design: *Gail Cocker-Bogusz*

© 2000 Prentice Hall PTR
Prentice-Hall, Inc.
Upper Saddle River, NJ 07458

Prentice Hall books are widely used by corporations and government agencies for training, marketing, and resale.

The publisher offers discounts on this book when ordered in bulk quantities. For more information, contact: Corporate Sales Department, Phone: 800-382-3419; FAX: 201-236-7141; E-mail: corpsales@prenhall.com; or write: Prentice Hall PTR, Corp. Sales Dept., One Lake Street, Upper Saddle River, NJ 07458.

Printed in the United States of America

10 9 8 7 6 5 4 3 2

ISBN 0-13-086601-6

Prentice-Hall International (UK) Limited, *London*
Prentice-Hall of Australia Pty. Limited, *Sydney*
Prentice-Hall Canada Inc., *Toronto*
Prentice-Hall Hispanoamericana, S.A., *Mexico*
Prentice-Hall of India Private Limited, *New Delhi*
Prentice-Hall of Japan, Inc., *Tokyo*
Pearson Education Asia Pte. Ltd.
Editora Prentice-Hall do Brasil, Ltda., *Rio de Janeiro*

To the loving memory of Kimberly Rawlins

Contents

Foreword   xxi

Preface   xxiii

▌ Part One   XML, XSL, and Web Vocabularies   1

Chapter 1   Enabling Web Sites with XML   2

1.1 HTML and the Balkanization
     of the Web   4
1.2 Web Developer: Jack of All Trades   5
1.3 The Return to Spaghetti Code   6
1.4 The Evolution of XML   7

1.5 What Is XML and
What Can I Do with It?   8
1.6 Schemas, Vocabularies,
and DTDs   10
1.7 What About XSL?   12
1.8 XML and HTML: Peaceful
Coexistence   13
1.9 Conclusion   14
1.10 References   15

Chapter 2   XML, Web Style   16

2.1 HTML and Structured Documents   18
2.2 Structuring Your Documents   20
2.2.1 Navigating Your Web Site   21
2.2.2 An XML Database Example:
Creating a Product Directory   25
2.3 Conclusion   28

Chapter 3   Transforming XML   30

3.1 The XPath Data Model   32
3.2 Template Rules   35
3.3 Creating a Style Sheet   36
3.4 Patterns   38
3.4.1 Other Node Types   41
3.4.2 Comparing, Testing, and Other
Refinements   43
3.5 Templates   44
3.5.1 Creating Other Result Nodes   48
3.6 Expressions   49
3.6.1 Location Paths   50
3.6.2 Node-Set Expressions   52
3.6.3 String Expressions   54
3.6.4 Numbers   56

3.6.5 Booleans   57
3.6.6 Extension Functions   59
3.7 Additional Features   59
3.7.1 Conditional Processing   62
3.7.2 Sorting   63
3.8 Conclusion   64

Chapter 4   Web Vocabularies   66

4.1 Scalable Vector Graphics   68
**4.2 Synchronized Multimedia
      Integration Language**   73
4.3 XHTML   76
4.4 WDDX   77
4.5 Channel Definition Format   79
4.6 Java Speech Markup Language   79
4.7 MusicML   80
4.8 Other Vocabularies   81
4.8.1 Resource Description Framework   82
4.9 Conclusion   83
4.10 Resources   84
4.11 References   85

Part Two   Client-Side XML   87

Chapter 5   Document Object Model   88

5.1 Introduction to the DOM   90
5.1.1 The Document Interface   92
5.1.2 Node Interface   95
5.2 Direct Interfaces   99
5.2.1 Element Interface   100

5.2.2 The Attr Interface   101
5.2.3 The CharacterData Interface   102
5.2.4 Text Interface   102
5.2.5 Extended Interfaces   104
5.3 Conclusion   106

Chapter 6   XML and Internet Explorer   108

6.1 XML in Internet Explorer   110
6.1.1 Inline XML   111
6.1.2 XML Data Source Objects   113
6.1.3 Channel Definition Format   121
6.1.4 Open Software Description   128
6.2 DOM Extensions   134
6.2.1 Schemas   135
6.2.2 Data Types in Schemas   140
6.3 Closing Thoughts   143
6.4 References   143

Chapter 7   Projects for Internet Explorer   144

7.1 Accessing the Document Object   146
7.2 A Utility for
Documenting Structure   152
7.3 Web Site Navigation   159
7.4 A Quick and Dirty XML Validator   167
7.5 Supporting Internet Explorer 4   168
7.5.1 Loading a Document   169
7.5.2 Documenting Structure in IE4   171
7.6 Conclusion   179

Chapter 8   Presenting XML in the Client   180

8.1 Presentation Strategies   182
8.2 Selecting From Multiple Style Sheets   192

8.3 Presenting Data   196
  8.3.1 Filtering Your Result Set   200
  8.3.2 Searching   204
8.4 Conclusion   208

■ **Part Three**   Server Side XML   211

Chapter 9   XML on the Server   212

9.1 Solving the Basic Problem   215
9.2 Extending Web Servers   216
9.3 The XML::Parser Module   218
9.4 Server APIs   223
9.5 Java Servlets   224
9.6 Active Server Pages   225
9.7 Commercial XML Servers   225
  9.7.1 Bluestone XML-Server   226
9.8 Conclusion   229
9.9 Resources   230
9.10 References   230

Chapter 10   Serving XML Using Java Servlets   232

10.1 About Java Servlets   234
10.2 Cocoon: An XML-enabled
         Servlet for Apache   235
  10.2.1 Installing Cocoon   236
  10.2.2 Working with Cocoon   237
  10.2.3 Generating XML Dynamically   238
10.3 Building Your Own XML Server   243
  10.3.1 Java Development Kit   244
  10.3.2 Adding a Servlet Engine   246

10.3.3 The XML Processor   248
10.3.4 Adding an XSL Processor   249
10.3.5 XML Enabler   251
10.4 Java ProjectX   252
10.5 Conclusion   253
10.6 Resources   253
10.7 References   254

Chapter 11   XML and Active Server Pages   256

11.1 Introducing Active Server Pages   258
11.1.1 Creating Active Server Pages   259
11.1.2 Adding Script to Server Pages   262
11.1.3 XML and ASP   264
11.1.4 Scripting XML with ASP   266
11.1.5 Processing XML on IIS   267
11.1.6 Threading Models   270
11.1.7 Sending XML from the Client   271
11.2 XML and Database Development   273
11.2.1 The Flat-File Database   273
11.2.2 Connecting to ODBC Data Sources   277
11.2.3 Making the Connection   278
11.3 Building a Document From a Query   279
11.4 Conclusion   283

Part Four   XML and Web Development   285

Chapter 12   Supporting Forms in XML   286

12.1 Extensible Forms
        Description Language   288
12.1.1 Setting Options   292

12.2 The <compute> Element   294
12.3 XML Forms Architecture   297
12.4 Conclusion   299

Chapter 13   Schemas in XML   300

13.1 What Exactly Are Schemas?   302
13.2 Defining Schemas   303
  13.2.1 Refining the Content Model   307
  13.2.2 Defining Attributes   308
  13.2.3 Putting It All Together   310
13.3 Conclusion   311
13.4 References   312

Chapter 14   An XML-Based
                 Web Site   314

14.1 Site Design   315
14.2 Serving It Up   318
  14.2.1 Toc.xml   320
  14.2.2 Homepage.xsl   321
14.3 Linked Pages   330
14.4 Conclusion   331

Appendix A   Just Enough XML   332

A.1 The Goal   334
A.2 Elements: The Logical Structure   335
A.3 Unicode: The Character Set   337
A.4 Entities: The Physical Structure   338
A.5 Markup   340
A.6 Document Types   342
  A.6.1 Document Type Definitions   342

A.6.2 HTML: A Cautionary Tale   343
A.6.3 Declaring a DTD   344
A.7 Well-Formedness and Validity   345
A.8 Hyperlinking and Addressing   347
A.9 Stylesheets   349
A.10 Programming Interfaces and Models   350
A.10.1 Parsing   350
A.10.2 APIs   351
A.11 Conclusion   353

Appendix B   Document Type Definitions   354

B.1 Declaring Use of a DTD   356
B.2 DTD Syntax   356
B.2.1 Element Type Declarations   356
B.2.2 Content Specifications   357
B.2.3 Occurrence Indicators   357
B.3 Attribute List Declarations   358
B.3.1 Anatomy of an Attribute List Declaration   358
B.3.2 Attribute Defaults   358
B.3.3 Enumerated Lists   359
B.3.4 Notation Attributes   359
B.3.5 Entity Attributes   359
B.4 Notations   359
B.4.1 Example   360
B.5 Anatomy of an Entity   360

Appendix C   Cascading Style Sheet Properties   362

Index   405

Foreword

It is undoubtedly content, community, and commerce that make people want to surf the Web, and bandwidth that makes the experience endurable—or even pleasant, if you have enough of it.

But the ingredient that makes it all possible is the work of the Web developer—a job title that didn't even exist five years ago.

Like the proverbial "Jack of all trades," the Web developer is part programmer, part content creator, part designer, part system integrator, and part administrator. But unlike Jack, who was master of none of his trades, today's Web developer is the master of a wide repertoire of tools and technologies.

And now the Web developer must add yet another—XML, the Extensible Markup Language.

XML is quite different from the developer's familiar scripting and programming languages. XML *describes* data, rather than instructing a system on how to process it. As a result, while XML provides powerful capabilities for data integration and data-driven styling, it also introduces new processing paradigms and requires new ways of thinking about Web development.

Fortunately, Michael Floyd has long experience in guiding Web developers through the complexities of new technologies. He is the founder of *Web Techniques* magazine and the author of its acclaimed *BeyondHTML* column. Michael also practices what he preaches—and teaches in this book—as you can see by visiting his leading-edge Web site at www.beyondhtml.com.

Developers will appreciate Michael's focus on the bottom line: how to put XML, XSLT, DOM, schemas, and related technologies to work—right now—with currently available tools. This immensely practical and helpful book will have you quickly *Building Web Sites with XML!*

Charles F. Goldfarb
Saratoga, CA
December, 1999

Preface

The time was early 1997, and the place was the Sixth International World Wide Web Conference. I was sitting at a courtyard table at the Santa Clara, California, conference trying to grab a free meal as journalists are known to do. Across from me was a product manager from a French-based company, Grif, extolling the marvels of a new markup language, XML.

It was, literally, a far cry from the Fifth International World Wide Web Conference I had attended a year earlier in Paris. Then, there was talk of putting full SGML on the Web. But there were enormous hurdles to overcome. SGML was too bloated with options for the Web. It sported features that had more to do with large-scale document management than individual Web page publishing. Worse, full SGML was very complex compared to HTML, which is just a single application of SGML. Let's face it, the reason for HTML's success is largely thought to be its simplicity.

In 1996, XML was a non-story. Yet, in one short year it had become one of the hottest topics within the Web community. As the Editor in Chief of *Web Techniques* magazine, I was attending this '97 conference with an eye toward securing an XML columnist for our monthly publication. Grif was one of the early companies involved in XML development and possessed the talent we were looking for. I didn't want a theorist. I was looking for a practitioner. Unfortunately, Grif was on XML's event horizon: a black hole sucking everything in its path. I would have to find my columnist elsewhere.

Little did I know at the time that within 12 months I would resign my post as the magazine's editor and become that columnist.

Meeting Charles

Four months into the Beyond HTML column, I noted from a message in the newly-formed XML news group that Charles F. Goldfarb would be giving a talk at our local Computer Literacy book shop. Charles, the inventor of SGML, was out promoting his latest book, *The XML Handbook*. I decided that an interview with the father of markup languages would fit nicely into the column, so I contacted him to make the arrangements. He graciously accepted.

In preparing for the interview, I learned that it was he who coined the term "markup language." I also learned that in 1969 Charles, leading a small team at IBM, developed a language called GML (Charles is the "G" in GML). Of course, I knew he created SGML in 1974, but I also learned that he wrote the first SGML parser, ARC-SGML. Charles also worked to turn SGML into the ISO 8879 standard, and he serves as its editor.

My interview with Charles was delightful. He was extremely approachable, and his answers were insightful. In querying him about document exchange versus data exchange, Charles responded that:

> "These are all documents in the sense of the way that word is used in the dictionary. It's recognizing that XML is a data representation that has the characteristics of a document.

That's where the real power comes in, because you can process it as data—you can parse it and extract the data—or you can present it the way you would a document. And you can do both of those in the same application at the same time. That's the real breakthrough."

Charles and I stayed in touch over the following months, and it wasn't long before he suggested that I write a book for his series. Needless to say, I was honored. During those months we tossed around several ideas. We knew that XML was quickly spreading beyond the confines of the Web. As such, XML's roots in Web development were being left behind. My background with *Web Techniques* set up the perfect match to write *Building Web Sites with XML*. So, with a nod of approval from Charles, my journey began.

About the Journey

Building Web Sites with XML explores the technologies, tools, and most importantly, the techniques required to build cutting-edge Web sites using XML, Extensible Stylesheet Language (XSL), and the Document Object Model (DOM). The book introduces XML concepts with expanded coverage of the latest XSL Transformation language, then shows Web designers, Web application developers, and Webmasters how they can use XML to enhance the look and feel, interoperability, operation, and maintenance of their Web sites. This is not a theoretical discussion of XML, nor is it a case study of someone else's project. This book presents hands-on techniques that Web developers can immediately use to enhance their Web sites. Most importantly, the book presents this information in a concise, straightforward manner that doesn't cloud the practical application of XML with esoteric theory.

Goals for This Book

One of my goals in writing this book has been to recognize and address all Web developers—from authors and designers comfortable in the ways of HTML and JavaScript, to Web application developers using industrial strength languages like Java and C++. At the same time, it is not my intention to obscure important XML topics with esoteric programming details. Therefore, the primary language used in this book is JavaScript. This choice should make programming, particularly as it relates to the DOM, approachable to non-programmers while giving seasoned developers enough detail to apply XML to their discipline.

An additional goal of this book is to remain platform neutral. Therefore, you will find coverage of both Unix and Windows NT, Apache and Internet Information Server, Java Server Pages and Active Server Pages. Thus, you will be able to find hands-on information that you can apply to your existing arrangement, regardless of the platform, software, and tools you are using. One caveat, of course, is client-side processing. At the time of this writing, only Internet Explorer provides sufficient XML support to warrant coverage in this book. Therefore, this book uses Internet Explorer 5 solely for its browser platform. However, it shows how you can use server-side processing to process XML for display in any browser, no matter what its capabilities are.

Another goal is to provide all of the information you will need to create real-world XML applications. In particular, the first half of this book provides in-depth coverage of XML, the DOM, and XSL. Later parts of the book cover XML schemas and Document Type Definitions (DTDs). The book includes numerous tables for easy reference. So, while the focus of this book is on Web-based applications, you should find it to be a valuable resource in much of your XML-related development.

In addition, applications and examples are included to walk you step by step through the process of creating and processing XML.

Examples show how you can transform and render XML using XSL, search and sort XML data, populate tables with XML data streams, create XML-based navigation schemes, and more. Unlike other books, the tools and techniques presented here cover both server- and client-side processing of XML data.

As a final goal, this book covers all of the tools you will need to create real-world XML applications. In particular, this book presents tools for Java servlet and CGI programmers, ASP developers, and JavaScript scripters. The book walks you through the steps of installing these tools on both the development and server platforms so that you can create your own development environment and build solutions for delivering XML.

How to Use This Book

This book is organized into four parts. Part 1 covers general XML topics, including XSL, the DOM, and Web-based vocabularies, and gives a quick review of XML markup. Part 2 covers XML in the browser, while Part 3 presents solutions for delivering XML from the Web server. Part 4 covers extended topics such as XML Forms that should be of particular interest to Web developers, and it builds on all of the concepts presented through the book to build a complete Web site based on XML.

You can, of course, read the book from cover to cover. In fact, I recommend that you skim all of the chapters in order at least once. If you are new to XML, you will want to read Part 1 carefully before jumping to either Part 2 or Part 3. Chapter 1 is designed to orient you to XML by describing how XML came about and the reasons for its importance, and suggesting possible applications of the technology. The chapter also introduces technologies such as DTDs, XSL, and the DOM, and it describes XML's relationship with HTML and Cascading Style Sheets (CSS).

Chapter 2 introduces the structured document and provides a quick tour of XML markup to get you started. Note that Chapter 2 is not an intensive tutorial on XML—you can get that from one of the introductory books on the topic. Rather, this chapter is designed to get you up to speed quickly so you can begin real-world XML development as soon as possible.

A key chapter in this book, Chapter 3, introduces XSL and its associated transformation language, XSLT. XSLT is a primary means for accessing and processing XML elements. Many of the techniques presented throughout the rest of the book hinge on concepts presented in this chapter. Therefore, you will want to read this chapter carefully and refer back to it often.

Finally, Part 1 wraps up with Chapter 4, which discusses several XML vocabularies that are of particular interest to Web developers. This chapter presents vocabularies to handle time-based multimedia, vector graphics, speech, and a great deal more. In all likelihood, you will want to make use of one or more of these vocabularies in your own development efforts.

Kicking off Part 2, Chapter 5 examines another critical topic, the DOM as it is described in the DOM level 1 specification. This chapter is filled with reference information. So, again, you will want to refer back to it often.

If you are planning to do client-side development, then Chapter 6 is for you. This chapter examines the XML support built into Internet Explorer and describes how Microsoft extends the DOM API as it is described in the DOM specification. In this chapter, you'll learn how to write inline XML and create XML data islands within your HTML pages. You'll also learn how to create data source objects and populate tables from data stored in a database. In addition, this chapter examines the Channel Definition Format and the Open Software Description specification. Together, these two technologies will allow you to create push channels and offer software components over these channels.

Building on that, Chapter 7 presents several projects in Internet Explorer. These projects specifically take advantage of the DOM while offering real-world solutions to Web problems. For example, this chapter shows how to open an XML file, load a document into the DOM, and access its elements through API calls. The example applications include a Web site navigation system and a visual tool for documenting the structure of an XML document.

Chapter 8 builds on the concepts presented in Chapter 3 by showing effective techniques for presenting XML in the browser using XSL. This chapter shows how to determine browser support, select and load an XSL style sheet from a list of style sheets, create and filter result sets, and more.

Part 3 covers server-side development, starting with a roundup of the methods you can use to extend your Web server to send, receive, and process XML. In these chapters, you will learn about CGI and Perl solutions for delivering XML (Chapter 9), how to integrate Java-based XML processors and Java servlets (Chapter 10), and how to process XML from within Active Server Pages (Chapter 11).

Part 4 covers advanced topics such as XML Forms (Chapter 12) and the new XML Schema proposal (Chapter 13). Chapter 14 wraps up all of the concepts presented in the book by presenting a full-blown Web site based on XML. The example Web site uses Active Server Pages to process files marked up with XML. The site includes XML template files, style sheets, and server pages that you can use to create your own site for serving XML.

Concluding Thoughts

For me, writing this Preface marks the end of a wondrous journey. That journey has taken me through passages of XML, into the valleys of style, and up the heights of the DOM. It has been an exploration of the modules of CGI/Perl and a voyage across the seas of Java processors. Now, as I conclude my journey, I feel a bit like one of the early cartographers—mapping his way as he goes. And like many such mapmakers, I wish I had stayed in one place or another to explore just a little more. So I pass this map on to you in the hopes you will explore those places I have missed. For me, it is time for a new journey. But for you, the journey has already begun.

Part One

- Enabling Web Sites with XML
- XML, Web Style
- Transforming XML
- Web Vocabularies

XML, XSL, and Web Vocabularies

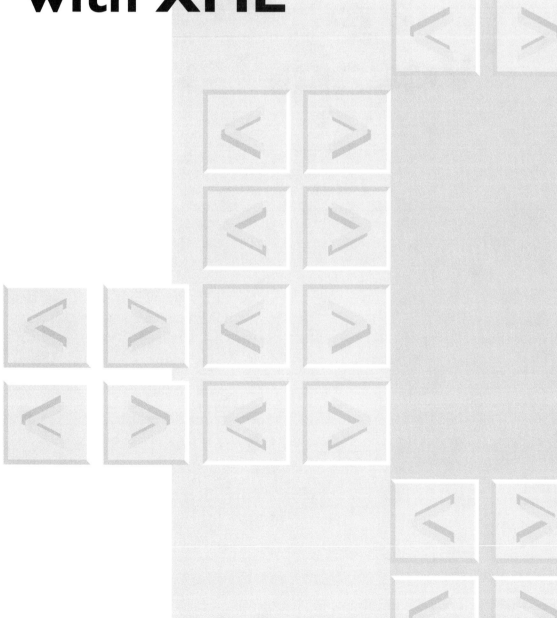

Enabling Web Sites with XML

A s I gaze at the XML landscape, I see a tremendous amount of hype over a relatively simple technology. After all, XML is in many ways nothing more than a standard method to describe data. Nevertheless, I see IS managers wandering the halls of XML conferences with mandates from the CEO to "just do it in XML." Now, these same managers are trying to figure out what impact their mandate will have, while all the time asking: "Why blow the budget on an emerging technology with fluctuating standards, unstable tools, and an immature market?"

Indeed, there is a tremendous amount of hype circulating through the hallways, and it seems that XML is infecting virtually every area of computing. But for all of the over promising, the hype serves one important purpose—it raises awareness.

Now it's time to separate the wheat from the chaff. This chapter looks at the factors that drove the World Wide Web Consortium (W3C) to recommend an "extensible" language for the Web, examines the benefits this new markup language brings to the table, and discusses the role XML will play over the next several years. In short,

3

this chapter addresses the fundamental question IS managers have been asking: "Why XML?"

1.1 | HTML and the Balkanization of the Web

When Tim Berners-Lee defined HTML, he envisioned a simple markup language that could be used to present scientific documents within a browser. Like the language, early browsers such as Cello and Lynx were primitive, even simplistic. In fact, it wasn't until the advent of the Mosaic browser that the Web started experiencing widespread use. Mosaic was a graphical browser that made it easy to display elements other than simple text elements. This allowed the display of graphic images, which greatly improved the user's experience. Then, a company by the name of Netscape began to commercialize the browser, and the Web browser market was born.

When Netscape went public, the company owned 85 percent of the browser market. To gain market share, rival companies, most notably Microsoft, began adding features and in the process extending the HTML language. Netscape countered with its own extensions. Soon, the two commercial browsers supported scripting languages, virtual reality, and Java applets. Of course, the HTML standard did not as yet support these features, so the W3C reacted by modifying the HTML standard to support the embedding of objects, new <SCRIPT> tags, and the like. Soon, however, it became apparent that browser vendors were enhancing browsers, and by extension HTML, faster than the consortium could react.

More importantly, browser manufacturers motivated by their own agendas were taking common features in different directions. Even now standard features like tables exhibited different behaviors in the two major browsers. Netscape had JavaScript; Microsoft had

JScript and VBScript. David Siegel may have summed it up best in the premiere issue of *Web Techniques* magazine when he wrote: "Netscape isn't overly concerned about standards or the information sector. Netscape is interested in dominating the other two sectors [exchange and entertainment], so it really doesn't care if the W3C finds acceptance among the information crowd." To this day, the major browsers support Cascading Style Sheets, the Document Object Model, and even HTML 4 to varying degrees, and include enhancements that won't run in a competitor's browser. The result is that Web developers are constantly challenged to support the latest features without having to create variant Web pages for each browser.

1.2 | Web Developer: Jack of All Trades

"Jack of all trades, master of none," as the old saying goes. While this may not be a fair characterization of Web developers, it does impart one important point. Web developers must contend with a plethora of technologies that include ActiveX, JavaBeans, applets and servlets, Active Server Pages and Java Server Pages, graphic images, CGI, and lot more. Often, Web developers are under the gun to get pages up quickly while ensuring that they are both usable and presentable. And these developers are painfully aware of the Balkanization problem. Consequently, Web developers often choose the "least common denominator" approach to Web development. That is, they select the smallest set of features that will run in 80 to 90 percent of the browsers visiting their sites. Typically, this means supporting a core set of HTML 3.0 tags, GIF images, and a very small subset of ECMAscript (the "officially" sanctioned version of JavaScript/ Jscript). Anything more elaborate means supporting browser-specific features or behaviors, and that means parsing HTTP requests to detect a browser's version and type, and maintaining slightly differing versions of a Web site.

The point is that despite advances in browser technology, Web developers are reluctant to employ more than a basic set of features. Anything more increases the complexity of the problem by several orders of magnitude.

1.3 | The Return to Spaghetti Code

Another problem plaguing Web pages is spaghetti code. Early programmers using procedural languages such as BASIC and Fortran referred to their programs as spaghetti code because they lacked structure, using GOTO statements to point virtually anywhere in a program. Adding to the spaghetti effect was the fact that these programs crammed as many characters as possible on a single line in order to conserve precious bytes. The result was not pretty.

Similarly, the HTML code for most Web pages today lacks any sort of structure. They embed formatting information directly in with data, include scripts to process forms, and embed controls within the page. Because browsers were designed to render a page at all costs, they permit code which is either poorly formed or syntactically incorrect. For example, you can get away with marking up a paragraph with an opening <P> tag and omit the closing tag. The browser assumes you meant to close the paragraph.

The W3C responded to the structure problem in part by introducing Cascading Style Sheets (CSS). The goal of CSS is to separate the presentation markup from the actual data. While CSS goes a long way to bringing order to HTML documents, it doesn't separate out the logic—scripts, applets, ActiveX components, and so on—that is increasingly being built into Web pages.

Also, the Balkanization of Web browsers continues to add fuel to the fire. Despite the fact that the CSS level 2 recommendation has been available since March 1998 (well over a year), neither of the two major browsers supports it at the time of this writing.

1.4 | The Evolution of XML

When Tim Berners-Lee created HTML, he created his hypertext publishing language using another markup language, SGML (Standard Generalized Markup Language). Already an international standard (ISO 8879), SGML was being used to publish very large documents, such as airplane maintenance manuals. Invented by Charles F. Goldfarb in 1974, SGML allows you to create custom elements and develop vocabularies that allow other applications to use these elements. In effect, SGML allows you to create your own markup language and that's just what Berners-Lee did.

In looking at the problems described earlier in this chapter, the W3C looked to SGML as a potential solution. SGML possessed two important properties that made it particularly attractive: it was extensible; and it separated presentation, data, and processing. However, SGML was designed to manage large document collections, some eclipsing the size of the Web itself. Consequently, SGML contains lots of features, many of which are only useful in these highly specialized applications.

From a Web-authoring perspective, SGML was too complex. After all, it was the simplicity of HTML that made it so popular in the first place. So, the XML Working Group looked at all of SGML's features and came up with their own tailored version. At the same time, the XML working group added restrictions to the language that made it more suitable for the Web. For example, in certain cases, SGML allows you to omit some markup, such as closing an element. In such cases, the SGML parser can infer the missing markup based on rules of the language.

By contrast, XML doesn't allow you to omit closing tags. Because XML is always well-formed, an application can scan an XML text stream to locate items without performing a complete parse.

 Note: *The process of scanning XML without parsing it is called "hacking."*

Another feature of XML allows a document to be processed even though parts of it are missing. For example, a document type definition may not be required in order to process a document. This ability to provide documents without requiring all of their components means that documents can be served in fewer bytes, thus enhancing performance. Of course, these optional pieces must be carefully described. We'll talk about this later in the book.

1.5 | What Is XML and What Can I Do with It?

So, what exactly is XML? Experts often have difficulty answering this question because it is used in so many different ways and has so many applications. In fact, they are confusing "what" with "how." So, let's take a stab at creating a working definition. Simply put, XML is a means for representing and describing data. The language allows you to define markup tags that can be wrapped around data in order to describe it at a finer granularity than current systems typically do. Because XML is used to describe data, its uses and applications vary widely, which in turn has led to confusion in describing it.

XML is simple yet extensible. That is, XML's concepts and syntax are easy to learn. Because it is text based, it is human readable and easy to process. However, don't let XML's simplicity lull you into a sense that its capabilities are simplistic. Quite the contrary. You can build very sophisticated applications from the simple building blocks XML provides. As you have likely heard, you can create your own tags. More accurately, you can create your own tagging language. That's exactly what Tim Berners-Lee did with SGML.

Some describe XML as just another data format. That is because you can take any text-based data and structure it as XML elements that you define. The data could be the text to a magazine article, or it might be records from a database. In fact, XML allows you to describe virtually any text-based data stream in any fashion you like. Any other XML application capable of parsing XML will then be able to understand the structure of your stream. If you want the application to deal with your elements more intelligently, then you can provide a document type definition containing a vocabulary and grammar that allows other applications to understand the semantics of your elements. All of this means you can share XML documents as you would using a common data file format.

When you think about it, this is what proprietary file formats do—they take data and embed information that allows the document to be processed in some way. But, consider that since XML is a text-oriented format based on the Unicode character set, it has no platform or language limitations—it is recognized equally well on a VAX/VMS or IBM mainframe as it is on a Macintosh. It can live on a Unix workstation, a Windows PC, or a Cray supercomputer.

XML can even be used as an intermediary when translating between two file formats. For example, Microsoft uses XML behind the scenes of its Office 2000 suite in order to translate between various file formats, including Rich Text Format (RTF) and HTML. This allows you to load a Microsoft Word document, save it out as HTML, edit the document using an HTML editor, then reload the document back into Word without losing the word processor's formatting information.

Of course, Microsoft couldn't pull off this feat without taking advantage of another feature of XML: Metadata. If you've ever used a

"<META>...<\META>"-tagged element in HTML, then you've already seen metadata on the Web. Like the <META> element, metadata allows you to embed information that describes your document, and for other applications to use this information to process your document in various ways. For example, Web developers use the <META> element to provide keywords that search engines use to help categorize your Web page.

Another example of the use of metadata is the Platform for Internet Content Selection (PICS). This standard defines a way for Web sites to rate the content of a single page, a section of your site, or the entire site. Most people describe PICS as a rating system similar to that used by the movie industry where Web pages can be rated based on the degree of violent content, nudity, profanity, and so on. Your Web browser could then be configured to filter out inappropriate material. However, PICS is more general purpose, allowing virtually any kind of labeling system to be implemented. For instance, a news-oriented Web site could create a system that labels different types of news stories. This would allow a reader to filter out stories in which they were not interested, and to receive more targeted content. Similarly, an online book seller could devise a labeling system that categorizes books. Another system could rate content based on cost in a pay-per-view model. In each case, the ratings or labels serve as information about the content, which can be used in one fashion or another.

1.6 | Schemas, Vocabularies, and DTDs

By far, the most commonly cited use of XML is the sharing of data. However, if you just hand someone your carefully crafted XML document, the most they can do with it is run it through a parser, and if it has an XSL style sheet, process it. On the other hand, if you want an application to "understand" your document, you must provide some sort of a schema. A schema is a conceptual framework that describes the underlying structure of your collection of elements.

Schemas serve several important purposes. First, they define the "vocabularies" of element types and attributes for a given class of documents and allow you to share those documents with other applications. For example, musicians could define a vocabulary that allows them to trade sheet music over the Web, or chemical engineers might define a vocabulary that makes it convenient to express notations for molecular structures.

Keep in mind that a document may not necessarily be the traditional document you normally think of. It may be a database document, a middleware message, or a Web page. For example, a database document might consist of live data assembled from multiple data sources. In effect, vocabularies provide a common framework for applications to "speak" to each other. At the enterprise level, element type collections from different departments will likely be stored in dictionaries as XML becomes more pervasive. An enterprise application could then look up a schema representing, say, the fields from a database table, and output it into a data structure that can be used in programming the database.

These schemas can be formally defined as document type definitions (DTDs). Once you have these formal rules, applications can use them to validate structures and objects to ensure they are receiving the correct information appropriately formatted. For example, HTML has an associated DTD that formally defines a vocabulary, which allows Web developers to render documents in a browser. Browsers refer to this DTD to ensure that your HTML documents have the proper structure, and that elements contain the correct attributes and subelements. Even when validation is not required, schemas can be used as a part of the documentation process.

Schemas also play an important role in information retrieval. For instance, metadata defined by an XML schema can provide information to software agents, or may be used as part of the discovery process. Information-retrieval applications gain a new level of precision and function using metadata.

1.7 | What About XSL?

One benefit of XML is that it separates semantics, presentation, and data. The semantics of a document refer to scripts, program logic, and other constructs that do something with your data.* An example might be a JavaScript that validates data contained within an element. The presentation portion refers to how your data is rendered or displayed on screen. When you separate these two components, you are left with just the elements that describe your data and, of course, the data itself.

The presentation portion is handled by a complementary language, XSL (Extensible Stylesheet Language). XSL is comprised of two components; a collection of formatting objects similar to those in CSS that allow you to apply formatting information to your XML elements. The other component, XSL Transformations (XSLT), allows you to control how your output document tree is created and to transform or convert XML elements into other things. For example, an element representing a database query could be transformed into an actual SQL query, or possibly a CGI script.

The XSL specification separates the transformation language out into its own specification, leaving just a description of the formatting objects that XSL processors must support. Both XSL and XSLT have extensive syntaxes. This book primarily uses XSLT to transform XML

---

*"Semantics" has two meanings in the XML world. Strictly speaking, "semantics" is the meaning of the data in a conceptual sense, and data modelers often use the term in that way. However, since processing is as close as computers get to understanding, programmers often refer to the "semantics of processing," which is the sense in which I use the term in this book.

into HTML. As part of the process, these transformations generate CSS style sheets to render HTML in the browser. This is how Web developers will actually employ XML on the Web until there is browser support for XSL formatting objects.

1.8 | XML and HTML: Peaceful Coexistence

Some of the architects of XML originally thought that it would someday replace HTML. The W3C went as far as to define the Document Object Model (DOM) in terms of XML: To be compliant with the core DOM specification, browsers must support XML. However, support for the HTML DOM is optional according to the specification.

Now, however, it is clear that HTML is not likely to go away anytime soon. The problem with replacing HTML has do with its success. The markup language is simple and easy to use, which has led to the development of millions of Web pages. HTML coders need a good reason to justify learning a new technology to publish Web pages. As you will see over the course of this book, there is plenty of justification. Still, there is a percentage of HTML coders, particularly individuals building personal Home pages, that will have no need to transition to the more powerful XML.

For the rest of us, there is the old legacy problem: Converting the millions of HTML pages on the Web to XML would not be practical. Further, grandfathering out HTML pages could take decades. Either way, HTML and its related style sheet language, CSS, are still good at what they do best—presenting Web pages. On the other hand, the work on improving HTML is more or less complete, and you are not likely to see extensive changes to the HTML language in the coming years.

So, where does XML fit in? Here's how XML on the Web is likely to play out. Most new browsers, as a matter of course, will natively support XML. This means that over time, you will be able to stream XML to the client and use scripting to process it. However, the degree to which these browsers support and possibly extend XML, may make client-side processing of XML a bit tricky. Remember the Balkanization problem? Web developers still jump through hoops to get many of HTML 4's features to behave consistently in the two major browsers. Therefore, client-side processing will likely make the most sense in an Intranet environment where the IS department mandates which browser is to be used and you, as a Web developer, have the luxury of writing code specific to that browser. As a further advantage of this approach, the XML will be available for client-side data processing such as updating a database or spreadsheet.

For Web developers in general, I believe the greatest benefits of XML will be realized using a server-side approach. The reason is that we can solve some of the thornier problems, such as the Balkanization of Web browsers, using a combination of XML and XSL Transformations (XSLT) on the server. Imagine a system that stores its documents in XML format, then uses XSLT to dynamically transform these documents into basic HTML. You can even define an XSL style sheet for each brand of browser you intend to support, and with a little browser detection serve HTML optimized for that specific browser. In fact, Part 3 of this book will show you how to do just that.*

1.9 | Conclusion

It has been said that we have passed from the industrial age to the information age. No one is more aware of this fact than the Web devel-

---

*On the other hand, if browsers implement XSL formatting objects, HTML and its problems could be avoided altogether.

oper. At the center of the information universe is data. XML allows us to describe that data in ways that give meaning, understanding, even intelligence to it. It is little wonder that XML commands so much attention. Wherever there is data, XML can be applied.

The reason XML is becoming such a vital skill in the Web developer's arsenal is because XML is being sewn into the very fabric of the Web infrastructure. That infrastructure includes all three tiers: Web servers, Web browsers, and back-end databases. On the Web server front, for example, the Apache group's Cocoon project already allows you to serve up XML documents using Java servlets. On the browser side, Internet Explorer 5 already supports XML, and the next release of Netscape Navigator is expected to include similar support.

Maybe the most amazing aspects of XML are the truly ingenious ways developers have applied it. One such example is the Real Name system developed by Centraal Corporation. The Real Name system provides an alternative to URLs by allowing users to type in a basic brand name to locate a company or product. Instead of typing in www.cocacola.com, for instance, you can just enter Coca Cola. XML is used to map the brand name to the appropriate Web page, as well as to attach properties to the address. The Real Name system initially gained momentum when Netscape expressed interest in the technology. The company has since cooled to the idea, so the future of the Real Name system is uncertain. Nevertheless, it demonstrates an innovative idea to which XML is being applied.

Ultimately, that's what this book is about: looking for new creative ways of applying XML and exploiting the opportunities. Now, all that is left is for you to turn the page and begin the journey.

1.10 | References

Siegel, David. "The Balkanization of the Web." *Web Techniques* No. 1 (April 1996).

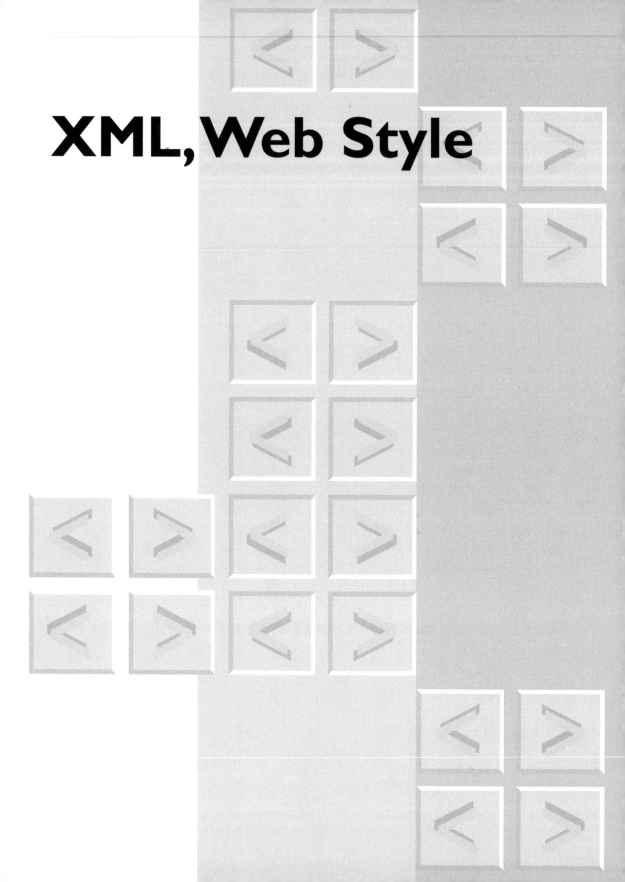

XML, Web Style

I t may seem a bit strange to title a chapter as I did this one. After all, XML was designed specifically for the Web. But XML has gained support in so many areas of computing that we sometimes forget that XML is a Web-based technology. Indeed, it is some of these other areas of computing, most notably database development, that have influenced the new directions that XML is taking.

There are many fine books on the market, including two in this book series,* that provide in-depth XML tutorials. Therefore, it is not the intention of this book to provide yet another tutorial in XML. Rather, this book focuses on using XML in practical situations. A brief tutorial on the fundamental concepts of XML documents is provided in Appendix A.

Fortunately, you as a Web developer already have some experience with markup. The primary difference is that in working with XML,

---

*The two in this series are *The XML Handbook,* by Charles F. Goldfarb and Paul Prescod, and *XML by Example,* by Sean McGrath.

you will be working with non-HTML markup elements of your own (or someone else's) creation.

2.1 | HTML and Structured Documents

In XML, we talk a great deal about structured documents. But what are they? Intuitively, we think of documents as a container of some kind of prose. A Microsoft Word file, a memo, an email message, even a Web page are generally considered documents. But, how would you classify a spreadsheet, a database record, or even a middleware message? In XML terms, these can all be considered documents, as well.

Especially when viewing static Web pages, it is easy to fall into the trap of only considering publishing-oriented documents. You may recall from Chapter 1, however, that the data of any application can be described using XML markup. We'll look at some examples momentarily, but it is important to keep in mind that publishing-oriented application data such as books, magazine articles, email messages, word processing documents, and even Web pages are but one class of data that XML can represent.

Nevertheless, asked what a Web document is, most Web developers will intuitively answer that it is an HTML page. Asked what a structured document is and those same developers will stare at you blankly. Every document has a structure, but in this book, when I say "structured document," I mean a document whose markup identifies the document's data elements at a useful level of granularity. An email message, for example, has a header containing sender and routing information, a subject field, a message body, a signature, and possibly some attachments. The message body can be further described as a series of paragraphs that are made up of individual sentences. Sentences also have structure: usually, a subject and a predicate. We expect to see these items and anticipate them in a certain order. We can even describe the structure of our email message in terms of a hierarchy. So far, this is a conceptualization, which could be depicted as shown in Figure 2–1.

One thing XML does is that it formalizes these conceptualizations. The value of this formalization is that we now have a predictable way of traversing through a document, selecting any discrete member, and processing it. As an XML author, your job will likely involve designing the logical structure of your documents. This can be done implicitly by the way you choose to order your elements, thus affecting the conceptual structure as depicted in Figure 2–1. On the other hand, XML provides a facility that allows you to formalize the structure using a specialized syntax (see Appendix C for details). Either way, a definition of the structure is called a schema and the rules that govern the use of elements in accordance with that schema are collectively referred to as a document type definition, or DTD.

XML developers often refer to formal DTDs as vocabularies, because in addition to providing the ability to validate a document, they give names to the element types you create and define when and how those elements should be used. This, in turn, is what allows documents to be shared. In some cases, that means you will be using someone else's vocabulary to mark up your documents. Chapter 4 looks at some typical vocabularies you may encounter in your XML travels.

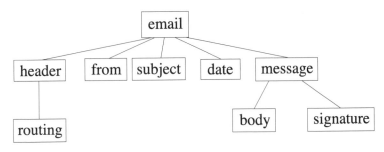

Figure 2-1   Conceptual structure of a typical email message.

The implication is that your job may not necessarily involve the creation of formal DTDs. Because XML does not require a DTD to process a document, there will also be times where you, as the author, decide how your elements should be ordered. The decisions you make can have a profound effect on the abilities of your application. The rest of this chapter will walk you through the process of designing the structure of your documents.

2.2 | Structuring Your Documents

In the following examples, we look at ways you can structure your documents and examine the ramifications of different approaches to your structures. In representing these structures, it would be convenient to use DTD syntax to specify things like order, what's allowed, items that are optional or required, and items that can be repeated in the structure. However, we have yet to describe the syntax for creating formal DTDs.

DTD syntax can appear daunting to the average Web developer, and the introduction of another syntax at this point may serve to obscure the point of these examples. In fact, many Web-based applications will likely omit any formal DTD. However, this points out another need for DTDs besides the validation of XML documents: DTDs can be extremely useful in documenting the structure of your element collections.

Therefore, this section takes a less formal approach to represent document structure by simply showing the elements to be used and using indentation to represent sub-levels within the tree. There are numerous drawbacks to this approach, because we can't indicate whether elements and attributes are allowed in particular places, and whether they are optional, required, or repeatable. Nevertheless, the following examples are simple enough that this method should suffice until we can look at DTD syntax in more detail, in Appendix B.

2.2.1   *Navigating Your Web Site*

One common feature of many Web sites is a navigation bar, which is usually displayed along the left-hand side of the browser window. The navigation bar itself is often a long laundry list of what's on the site. The problem with this approach is that you must hunt through this lengthy list to find what you're looking for. And because the navigation bar is contained within a table, it scrolls off the screen as you scroll through the document. If the list is long, you may find yourself scrolling back and forth to find what you're looking for.

To solve this, we can devise a structured way to navigate around the site using drop-down lists. Ultimately, we want to create a navigation bar containing menu items that represents the main sections of our Web site. When you click on a menu item, it drops down a list of the Web pages in the section of the site. We will assume that a script or some other program will present the navigation bar and handle the user interaction. Our job is to design an XML document to represent the contents of the site.

In creating a new structure, those new to XML may be eager to create large taxonomies that categorize every detail. However, consider what happens when you take this too far. For example, consider this first attempt at creating a structure:

```
<SiteNav>
  <MajorSection>
    <MinorSection>
      <WebDocument>
      </WebDocument>
    </MinorSection>
  </MajorSection>
</SiteNav>
```

The indentation indicates our structure. While this approach works, it's very rigid. That is, the structure requires that you have a major section that contains a minor section, which in turn contains the Web document the user is drilling down to. Of course, there's no formal DTD to enforce these rules. By not following them, however, the application will never know how to process all of the different cases and you completely lose the benefits structure offers.

A program can, however, process the same structure recursively. That is, we can use a single element to represent every entry in the list, and simply nest the elements as needed:

```
<SiteNav>
    <ItemEntry>
        <ItemEntry>
            <ItemEntry>
            </ItemEntry>
        </ItemEntry>
    </ItemEntry>
</SiteNav>
```

As you can see, our structure can be as complex as we desire, while the design of the element remains relatively simple.

Now, let's design the element that will contain entries in the list. We need a descriptive title which will be displayed in the menu. If you mouse-over the item, we would also like a longer description to pop up next to the item. Finally, when the user clicks on the item, we need to hyperlink to that section and display a set of subchoices. Here's how our element might look with data in it:

```
<ItemEntry>
    <href>dom/index.html</href>
    <Title>Object Model</Title>
    <Description>Home page for the DOM</Description>
</ItemEntry>
```

This meets all of our criteria. We have an ItemEntry element with three subelements: an href element to store the URL of the page to link to, a `Title` element to be displayed in the menu, and a `Description` element to maintain our longer description. This approach works fine, but let's consider the alternative of using attributes to describe our element:

```
<ItemEntry
  href="dom/index.html"
  Description="Home page for the DOM">
  Object Model
</ItemEntry>
```

Now, we have a single element. The `href` and `Description` have been recast as attributes which describe the element, and the data to be displayed is now the content of `<ItemEntry>`.

This example points out one of the common dilemmas you will typically face when structuring your documents. Should you use attributes or subelements? To answer this, consider what we have done to the structure. By using attributes, we have completely flattened the structure. In fact, attribute lists have no hierarchy. In so doing, however, we have neatly packaged information into an object. The element's content *is* the information, and the attributes serve to further describe our "information object."

Finally, our finished document looks something like this:

```
<!-- Copyright (c) Michael Floyd 1999 -->
<?XML version="1.0"?>

<SiteNav>
  <ItemEntry
    href="dom/index.html"
    Description="Home page for the DOM">
    Object Model
  </ItemEntry>

  <ItemEntry
    href="present/index.html"
    Description="DOM Overview">Overview
  </ItemEntry>
```

```
    <ItemEntry
    href="present/index.html"
    Description="Home page for Style Sheets">
    Presentation
</ItemEntry>


<ItemEntry
   href="markup/index.html"
   Description="Home page for Markup Languages">
   Markup
</ItemEntry>


<ItemEntry
   href="scripting/index.html"
   Description="Scripting Home page">Scripting
</ItemEntry>


<ItemEntry
    href="tools/index.html"
    Description="Get the tools">Tools
</ItemEntry>


<ItemEntry
   href="resources/index.html"
   Description="Books, articles, and other sites">
   Resources
</ItemEntry>


<ItemEntry
   href="bio.html"
   Description="Find out about BeyondHTML.com">
   About Us
</ItemEntry>
</SiteNav>
```

The vocabulary employs a general object called SiteNav, which contains the objects that describe the navigation entries. The only other object is ItemEntry. You describe all list entries using this single object. You can nest an ItemEntry within another to create subcategories and individual article entries.

I should point out there is yet another approach we could have taken, but this depends on the processing application and/or your skills as a programmer. The alternative method to represent your navigational structure is to view the tree from the document's perspective. This is the metacontent approach where a "self describing" document contains key information that can be used by the navigation bar. Each document can be scanned and an XML structure is then generated. The metacontent approach can also be used to represent a document's dependencies on other resources. This is a somewhat time consuming process and is probably better suited to site management applications, such as checking for broken links or missing resources.

2.2.2 *An XML Database Example: Creating a Product Directory*

In our next example, we plan to create a product directory of XML tools that users can search. When they select a record, we'd like to display the product along with pertinent information about the product and provide a link to the product's Home page so the user can get more information. Later in this book, we'll create such a database. For now, however, let's examine how we might structure an XML document to represent a record in the database.

```
<productDB>
  <product>
    <prodName></prodName>
    <company name="defaultValue"
        street1="defaultValue"
        street2="defaultValue"
        city="defaultValue"
        state="defaultValue"
        province="defaultValue"
        country="defaultValue"
        phone="defaultValue"
        fax ="defaultValue"
```

```
            href="defaultValue" />
        <version></version>
        <price></price>
        <sys-requirements></sys-requirements>
        <description></description>
        <prodURL href="defaultValue"/>
      </product>
      ...
    </productDB>
```

In this case, we have chosen to use subelements in most places rather than attributes, with the exception of the company and prod URL elements. The company element could have come from the same database table, or it could have come from a completely different data source. Nevertheless, we have a single, neatly packaged information object that represents a company.

Unfortunately, there is a flaw in this example. The difficulty with this approach has little to do with structure. After all, a company record such as this has little structure to speak of. The problem comes in the implementation when we wish to search for a company by name, or list all companies in a particular area code. We can, of course, search an attribute list for a particular value. However, the coding process becomes more tedious. In addition, searching a list is generally less efficient than traversing a tree. With that in mind, the following shows the alternative approach:

```
<company name="defaultValue">
    <address>
        <street1> </street1>
        <street2> </street2>
        <city> </city>
        <state> </state>
        <province></province>
        <country></country>
    </address>
    <phone></phone>
    <fax></fax>
    <website href="defaultValue/>
</company>
```

Finally, here is a complete XML document with the new structure. The document contains three records. As you will see in the next chapter, XSL provides a mechanism that allows you to iterate and process each of those records.

```xml
<?xml version="1.0"?>

<productDB>
    <product>
        <prodName>XML Toolbox</prodName>
        <company name="BeyondHTML">
            <address>
                <street1>123 West Fourth Street</street1>
                <street2>Suite 5</street2>
                <city>Anytown</city>
                <state>CA</state>
                <province/>
                <country>USA</country>
            </address>
            <phone>123-456-7890</phone>
            <fax>123-987-6543</fax>
            <website href="http://www.beyondhtml.com"/>
        </company>
        <version>1.0</version>
        <price>99.95</price>
        <sys-requirements>
            Any Java Platform
        </sys-requirements>
        <description>
            XML Toolbox is a collection of tools for creating
            and processing XML documents.
        </description>
        <prodURL
        href="http://www.beyondhtml.com/toolbox.html"/>
    </product>

    <product>
        <name>xml4j</name>
        <company record="IBM Record">IBM</company>
        <version>1.1.1.4</version>
        <price>Freely available</price>
        <sys-requirements>
            Any Java platform
        </sys-requirements>
```

```
<description>
    xml4j is an XML processor that is compliant with
    the XML 1.0 working draft specification
</description>
</product>

<product>
    <name>MSXML</name>
    <company>Microsoft/DataChannel</company>
    <version>N/A</version>
    <price>Freely available</price>
    <sys-requirements>
        Any Java platform
    </sys-requirements>
    <description>
        MSXML is an XML processor that is compliant with
        the XML 1.0 working draft specification
    </description>
</product>

</productDB>
```

2.3 | Conclusion

In terms of the syntax, marking up a document using XML elements is no more difficult than marking up HTML documents. The part of the process that requires more thought lies in how you structure your elements. The deeper you go in the structure tree, the more specialized your elements become. Specialization helps to describe your data in detailed ways, but it must be weighed against an element's ability to be reused. By keeping your elements somewhat general, they can be reused throughout your site.

Finally, even though the purpose of XML is to separate data, processing, and presentation, you must always keep these in mind when creating your elements. For example, you may want to create a collection of general purpose element types that help describe the presentation of text. You can do this by creating an <emphasis> element type.

This element type doesn't worry about the way a system will emphasize text, just that it should be treated specially. The actual way your emphasized text gets treated is specified by your style sheets. That's one of the subjects we will tackle in the next chapter as we learn to transform XML into HTML.

Transforming XML

When the W3C XSL Working Group originally conceived XSL, they designed several general-purpose features into the language, which they borrowed from an earlier style sheet language, DSSSL (sometimes pronounced "dissel"). One group of features was included specifically to give developers the ability to convert or "transform" XML source documents into other forms. For example, you can define an XSL style sheet that transforms XML into HTML. For Web developers, this is a very powerful feature because it allows you to define several style sheets, each of which transforms the same XML document into HTML optimized to display in a specific browser. With a little browser detection, you can render XML data in virtually any browser, even a browser without XML capabilities. I'll show you how to do just that later in this book.

There are, of course, many other transformations you might perform. For instance, you might want to create a transformation that

This chapter references XSL Transformations (XSLT) specification version 1.0 W3C Working Draft, 21 April 1999.

generates style sheets for presenting XML. You may want to translate a DTD into XML Schema syntax. Or, you may want to generate XML from XML, such as in creating messages in response to a request. In fact, transformations will be handy whenever you want to communicate between two or more software entities in an interactive fashion.

The group of features that support transformations is called XSL Transformations, or simply XSLT. Originally part of the Extensible Stylesheet Language (XSL) specification, the W3C has since separated XSLT into its own specification. XSLT can operate independently of XSL. That is to say, you will be able to create transformations without necessarily requiring XSL's formatting objects to render the output. However, much of the machinery under the XSLT hood is the same. You might say that while you can do without XSL's formatting capabilities to transform XML, you can't render XML without the facilities described in XSLT. Moreover, XSLT has itself been subdivided and relies on XPath (XML Path Language) spec to address components of a document.

The point is, this pivotal chapter is one that you will want to refer back to often. Later chapters discussing XSL refer to this chapter to describe the inner workings of XSL. Also, we will be making extensive use of XSLT and XPath in subsequent chapters to transform XML to HTML, a standard task for cutting-edge Web developers.

3.1 | The XPath Data Model

Before you begin writing your transformations, it's important to understand the XPath data model that underlies the processing of stylesheets. When you process an XML document, the XML processor parses your document into its constituent elements, attributes, comments, processing instructions, and so on. As the XML processor parses a document, it creates for each such constituent a "node" in a tree structure.

You may be familiar with tree structures. Every time you work with files in a directory, you reference the directory tree. Beginning with your root directory, every node in the tree is either another directory or is a file. Subdirectories are *branches* in the tree that take you along a specific path, and files represent the *leaves* in the tree.

In XML content terms, every node in the tree is either an element or data character, and the first element is called the "document element." Subsequent elements are called "subelements." As a first example, consider the following XML document, which contains a typical news story that you might see on one of the trade-magazine Web sites:

```
<?xml version="1.0"?>

<Article>
   <Footers>
      <RtPage>(c) 1999 BeyondHTML</RtPage>
      <LeftPage>Emerging Standards</LeftPage>
   </Footers>
   <RunHead>Scalable Vector Graphics</RunHead>
   <Table> ...</Table>
   <Listing>...</Listing>
   <Example> ...</Example>
   <Figure> ...</Figure>
   <Text>
      <Headline>New Web Graphics Standard Emerges</Headline>
      <Deck>Vector graphics allows images to be resized,
         cropped and printed at different resolutions
      </Deck>
      <Dateline>March 1, 1999</Dateline>
      <Byline Email="mfloyd@beyondhtml.com">Michael Floyd
      </Byline>

      <ArtText>
         <Head1>Introduction</Head1>
         While XML has primarily been used for text, the
World Wide Web Consortium (W3C) released the first public
working draft of the Scalable Vector Graphics (SVG)
format, which is defined in XML. SVG is intended...
      </ArtText>
   </Text>
</Article>
```

Figure 3-1 presents a conceptual view of how the resulting tree structure might look. Like directory trees, nodes may either branch to other points in the tree, or they may terminate the branch (leaf node).

Figure 3-1, of course, presents a very simplistic view. Real XML documents contain more than just elements: They contain comments, processing instructions, and the like. Also, the elements themselves will likely make use of attributes. So, XPath defines several types of nodes:

- Root nodes
- Element nodes
- Attribute nodes
- Text nodes
- Comment nodes
- Processing Instruction nodes
- Namespace nodes

The root node simply refers to the root of the tree and is the point where all processing begins. The root node has one descendant called the document element node. When your document is parsed, the value of the document element node is assigned to the root element. In Figure 3-1, the document element node is Article.

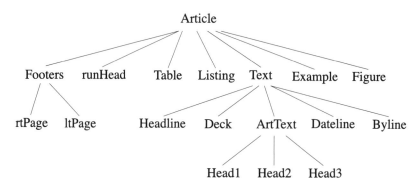

Figure 3–1 Conceptual view of the structure for an Article document.

Each node has an associated string value. Depending on the type of node, the string value may be part of the node, or it may be a computed value based on descendant nodes in the tree.

For every element in your document, there is a complementary element node in the tree. Your element may contain text-based content, comments, processing instructions or other elements. So, child elements may be of any of those node types. In addition, each element has an associated set of attribute nodes: For each attribute defined for your element, there is an attribute node for that element in the tree. The importance of this hierarchy will become obvious as we discuss patterns.

As you create your transformations, you select specific nodes in the tree and specify instructions, called "templates," for processing them. The XSL processor locates the node or nodes in the source tree, creates a new XSL element node according to the instructions in your template, and places that *result* element node in a second tree, called the "result tree."

3.2 | Template Rules

As a style-sheet developer, you can control how the result tree is created using template rules. A template rule consists of a pattern that is used to locate one or more nodes in the source tree, and a template containing instructions for creating part of the result tree.

Template rules are defined using `<xsl:template>` elements. Here's what a template rule looks like:

```
<xsl:template match = "Headline">
    <H1>
       <xsl:apply-templates/>
    </H1>
</xsl:template>
```

This template rule contains a match attribute with the value "Headline." This attribute value is called a pattern. The rest of the rule is the template that will form part of the result tree. When the processor finds a Headline element in the source tree, the template rule is applied to Headline's content. The <xsl:apply-templates> simply instructs the processor to process the current node and its descendant nodes.

To use your template rules, you'll have to create a style sheet using the <xsl:stylesheet> element. So, before we examine patterns and templates in detail, let's step back a moment and look at the <xsl:stylesheet> element.

3.3 | Creating a Style Sheet

XSL style sheets are actually XML documents. That is, XSL is defined in XML using a formal DTD. From the tree perspective, the <xsl:stylesheet> element is the root element of your style-sheet document. And from an authoring perspective, you can think of <xsl:stylesheet> as a container for the other elements (including your <xsl:template> elements) in your style sheet.

Using the <xsl:stylesheet> element is straightforward: The element has an opening tag that includes one required and two optional attributes, and a closing tag. XSL processors use namespaces, both to avoid possible naming collisions and to assist processors in identifying XSL elements. Thus, all XSL element type names are given an xsl: prefix. In order to be recognized, you must define the xsl: namespace within an attribute as:

```
xmlns:xsl = "http://www.w3.org/XSL/Transform/1.0"
```

From this point on, element type names carrying the xsl: prefix will be recognized in the style sheet (but not in the source document).

 Note: *XSL processors that follow the December 1998 working draft previously used the URI http://www.w3.org/TR/WD-xsl in the namespace definition.*

When generating the result tree, the XSL processor normally creates an XML representation of the tree. That's fine if you plan to output XML. However, there will be times when you want to output other formats. In general, XSL defines a result-namespace attribute, result-ns, for this purpose. The result-ns attribute takes a URI which points to a namespace. This namespace is a hint to the XSL processor that it should do something other than output XML. In many cases, the processor will not know the semantics of the output format. Typically, you will use the result-ns attribute to specify the XSL formatting objects namespace in order to output formatted XML. To do this, you will define the following namespace:

```
xmlns:fo = "http://www.w3.org/TR/WD-xsl/FO"
```

Throughout this book, we will be creating transformations that convert XML into HTML. The result namespace mechanism allows us to do just that. Let's take a look at an example:

```
<xsl:stylesheet
    xmlns:xsl = "http://www.w3.org/XSL/Transform/1.0"
    xmlns="http://www.w3.org/TR/REC-html40"
    result-ns = "">
```

In this example, we define the xsl namespace, which tells the processor that all element type names with the xsl: prefix are XSL element types. The second definition creates a namespace that points to the HTML 4.0 recommendation. This instructs the XSL processor to output its result in HTML according to the rules in our style sheet. Finally, we must define the result-ns attribute. If we didn't, the result tree would be output as XML.

As previously mentioned, you create a style sheet by placing template rules within a style-sheet element. The following example shows a simple, but complete, style sheet:

```
<xsl:stylesheet
    xmlns:xsl = "http://www.w3.org/XSL/Transform/1.0"
```

```
        result-ns = "">

        <xsl:template match = "Headline">
                <xsl:apply-templates/>
        </xsl:template>

        <xsl:template match = "Byline">
                <xsl:apply-templates/>
        </xsl:template>

    </xsl:stylesheet>
```

This style sheet contains two template rules: one that looks for Headline elements; and the other for Byline elements. When found, these elements are simply placed in the result tree.

The style sheet element type supports nearly a dozen subelement types, which are summarized in Table 3-1. Keep in mind that the XSL language is declarative, so the order for these elements is not generally important.

By far, the most common subelement used in this book is the template element. Before we can talk about templates, however, you'll need to know how to use patterns.

3.4 | Patterns

XSLT uses a syntax, defined in a separate W3C spec, called the XML Path Language, or XPath. XPath allows you to easily traverse a tree's structure and select one or more of its nodes. Remember these nodes represent individual elements, so once you have selected them, you can manipulate, reorder, or transform them in any way you desire. The mechanism that allows you to select tree nodes is a "pattern." A pattern is actually a restricted form of what XSLT calls location paths. We'll get to location paths in a moment.

Table 3-1   Elements that can be used in the style sheet element

Element	Description
import	Imports a style sheet and allows multiple style sheets to override each other.
include	Allows style sheets to be combined.
strip-space	Forces white space to be stripped from a text element.
preserve-space	Preserves white space for a given text element.
key	Takes a name and a value identifying a key and returns a set of nodes for a given document.
functions	Allows you to declare extended functions to the XSLT expression language.
locale	Declares a locale that controls formatting of numbers.
attribute-set	Allows you to create a set of named attributes.
variable	Binds a value to a variable name.
param-variable	Like variable, but allows an application to change the variable binding and pass values.
template	Defines the rules for processing an element.

The syntax for creating a pattern is straightforward. Do you recall the directory structure example earlier in this chapter? Pattern syntax resembles the command-line syntax you use to navigate the paths within directory structures. Just as with navigating directory paths, it is important to keep in mind that the patterns you specify are always in relation to your current position, called the "context node," in the tree. The simplest pattern is one that identifies an element type. For example:

```
match = "chapter"
```

is a pattern that matches any child element that's a chapter. Patterns are generally given as attributes of an element. For example, the following is used in a template element:

```
<xsl:template match = "chapter">
   ...
</xsl:template>
```

There are other places patterns can be used as you'll later see.

There are a number of operators that allow you to control how patterns are searched for within the tree. As I mentioned, pattern syntax resembles that for traversing directory structures. For instance, a period (.) represents the current node in the tree, just as it would represent the current directory in a directory structure. Likewise, two periods (..) point up a level in the tree by referring to the parent of the current node. The slash character allows you to select specific child patterns. For example:

```
"chapter/title/paragraph"
```

starts at the current node and looks for a `chapter` child, then a `title`, and ultimately matches with any `paragraph` descendants with that ancestry. Each pattern fragment between the slashes is referred to as a step. Again, this is very much like directory paths, so it should feel intuitive.

You can also use the wildcard character (*) to match all elements. For example:

```
*/subhead
```

selects all `subhead` grandchildren of the current node. On the other hand:

```
chapter/*
```

matches any element that has a `chapter` parent. Another operator, //, matches all descendants rather than just the immediate child nodes. For example:

```
chapter//subhead
```

matches all subhead elements with a chapter somewhere in their ancestry. Finally, you can specify either relative or absolute paths through the document tree. An absolute path always begins with a slash, and begins with the root node of the document.

Patterns also allow you to search alternative paths in the tree using the pipe character, |. For instance, you could select either a chapter or an appendix using:

```
chapter | appendix
```

In this case, the XSLT processor searches both paths and returns any nodes that match. You can also string longer patterns together. As you construct your patterns, however, keep in mind that / takes precedence over |. For example:

```
*/chapter/title | ../preface/title
```

will attempt to select the title nodes that are children of chapter grandchildren of the current node, and additionally look to the parent of the current node for all `preface/title` descendants. You may have also noticed that I've added some white space between the selectors on either side of the pipe character. White space is not significant between steps, so you can break patterns for better readability.

3.4.1 Other Node Types

So far, I've described the syntax for accessing element nodes within the source tree. To distinguish other node types you'll have to identify them for the XSL processor. For example, to select an attribute, you must prefix the attribute name with the @ symbol. The pattern syntax is pretty much the same, though. For example:

```
figure/@caption
```

selects the caption attributes of all figure elements that are children of the current node. The @* pattern selects all attributes.

To summarize, Table 3-2 gives a complete list of the most common characters you can use to construct patterns.

To select other node types, you can make use of the collection of Boolean functions listed in Table 3-3. They are called Boolean functions, because in addition to selecting nodes, they return a true or false value depending upon whether the specified node was found. Thus, they are also useful in testing a node's type and in comparison operations as noted in the following section.

To select a node using one of these functions, simply include a select pattern as an argument to the function. For instance, you can select comments in the source tree using the comment function. Using the `comment()` function without any arguments selects all comment nodes. Similarly, the `pi()` pattern matches all processing instruction nodes. In addition, you can specify an argument that indicates a target for the processing instruction, such as `pi("xml-stylesheet")`.

Table 3-2   Characters used to construct patterns

Character	Description
|	Expresses alternatives; for example, (emph|b)
.	Selects the current node.
/	Separates child steps.
//	Matches descendants instead of children.
..	Selects the parent of the current node.
*	Wildcard character; matches with all elements.
@	Selects an attribute.

3.4.2   *Comparing, Testing, and Other Refinements*

You can refine the result returned by a pattern using [ ] (square brackets) after the pattern. For example:

```
list[@type]
```

matches list elements with a `type` attribute. Likewise:

```
book[editor]
```

matches `book` elements that have at least one `editor` child element. You can also test the string values of nodes. For example:

```
list[@type="ordered"]
```

matches type attributes with a value of `ordered`, and:

```
figure[@caption="Figure1"]
```

looks for "Figure1" captions. Finally:

```
contact[name="Joe Butler"]
```

selects contact elements with a child name element node with the value "Joe Butler."

XSLT also allows you to test nodes to determine their type. The result of the test is a Boolean value indicating `True` if the test passes, or `False` if it does not. The side effect is that context node changes as a result of the operation. That means that Article becomes the context node as a result of the operation in the last example.

Likewise, you can use comment() to check for a comment node type, and pi() to test for a processing instruction. Table 3-3 presents the various tests you can perform.

XSLT also allows you to test for positions relative to the current node. That's covered later in this chapter.

Table 3-3   Functions to determine a node's type

Test	Description
comment()	Test whether the current node is a comment.
node()	Returns true for any node type.
pi()	Determines whether the current node is a processing instruction.
text()	Tests for a text node.

3.5 | Templates

Now we have enough background to look at the templates within a template rule. When a pattern matches a node from the source tree, that node becomes the current node and the rule's template is instantiated. At this point, the XSL processor applies the instructions in the rule's template and places the results in the result tree. The context is the current node in the source tree. So, when you call `<xsl:apply-templates>`, the source node is processed. You can place your call to `<xsl:apply-templates>` anywhere within the template, so you can perform XSL processing before and after the node or nodes are processed.

XSL templates are freeform and consist of a series of instructions that, in general, create new XSL nodes in the result tree. For example, consider the following template rule:

```
<xsl:template match=".">
    <xsl:text>
        This text was generated by the style sheet.
    </xsl:text>
    <xsl:apply-templates/>
</xsl:template>
```

This template rule uses a pattern to select the current source node, then creates a new text node by instantiating `<xsl:text>`. The content for the node is contained within the opening and closing tags. Next, the template calls `<xsl:apply-templates>` to process the source node and create the new fragment in the result tree. This portion of the template rule is called the template.

It turns out that XSL facilitates the creation of text elements by allowing you to omit the `<xsl:text>` markup altogether and simply enter the text strings in the template. For instance:

```
<xsl:template match=".">
    This text was generated by the style sheet.
    <xsl:apply-templates/>
</xsl:template>
```

Let's say the current node is a text node whose content is:

```
This text is contained in the source XML document.
```

As XSLT combines adjacent text nodes, the result would be a single text node with the string-value:

```
This text was generated by the style sheet.This text is
contained in the source XML document.
```

The XSL processor assumes any character data not contained within an element should be treated as a text node.

The following example assumes that the HTML result namespace has been declared:

```
<xsl:template match="./bold">
    <B>
       <xsl:apply-templates/>
    </B>
</xsl:template>
```

This template matches child "bold" element nodes of the current source node. The template portion of the rule recognizes the <B> tag as HTML and simply includes it with the result. Next, the template issues an apply-templates to process the current node, and adds another node in the result tree with the closing </B> tag. Assuming the content from the source document was the string "Hello, World!", the result would be:

```
<B>Hello, World!</B>
```

In fact, this is how we will transform XML into HTML in subsequent chapters.

As a more complete example, consider the following style sheet for the news-story document presented at the start of this chapter. Our goal is to transform the XML source document into a resulting HTML document.

```
<xsl:stylesheet
    xmlns:xsl="http://www.w3.org/XSL/Transform/1.0"
    xmlns="http://www.w3.org/TR/REC-html40"
    result-ns="">

  <!-- Root template -->
  <xsl:template match="/">
    <HTML>
     <HEAD>
       <META http-equiv="Content-Type"
        content="text/html; charset=iso-8859-1"/>
      <TITLE>
        <xsl:apply-templates
         select="Story/SectionTitle"/>
      </TITLE>

     </HEAD>
     <BODY>
         <A HREF="news.html">
           <H1>
              <xsl:apply-templates
               select="Story/SectionTitle"/>
           </H1></A><BR></BR>

           <H2>
              <xsl:apply-templates
                select="Story/Headline"/>
            </H2>

           <P><I>
              <xsl:apply-templates
```

```
                        select="Story/Deck"/>
              </I></P>
              <BR></BR><BR></BR>

              <P>
                  By
                  <xsl:apply-templates
                    select="Story/Byline"/>
              </P>
              <P>
                  <xsl:apply-templates
                     select="Story//BodyText"/>
              </P>

        </BODY>
     </HTML>
</xsl:template>

<xsl:template match="BodyText">
    <P>
        <xsl:apply-templates/>
    </P>
</xsl:template>

<xsl:template match="bold">
    <B>
        <xsl:apply-templates/>
    </B>
</xsl:template>

<xsl:template match="italic">
    <I>
        <xsl:apply-templates/>
    </I>
</xsl:template>
```

The first step is to create the appropriate namespaces in the opening style-sheet tag. Next, we create a template to process the root element of the document. Here the pattern simply specifies the slash character indicating the document's root element. The template continues by adding the preliminary HTML for our result document. For the <TITLE> element, we call apply-templates with a pattern that identifies the news story's title. Now, the HTML's document title matches that of the news story. The rest of the template processes the <BODY> of the document and adds the closing HTML tags. The following templates in this example match BodyText, bold, and italic elements, respectively. Their function should be apparent from the previous example.

There's one final point regarding text nodes: Eliminating the <xsl:text> markup may have a minor influence on the way the processor strips white space. I'll cover the effects of white space in later chapters.

3.5.1 *Creating Other Result Nodes*

XSL also allows you to directly create nodes other than text nodes, which are placed in the result tree. In particular, XSL provides markup that lets you generate nodes for comments, processing instructions, new elements and their associated attributes. For example, you can create new element nodes with <xsl:element>. The content of the instruction element is a template for the attributes and children of your result element node. You must include a name attribute to identify your element type name. However, the name may either be a computed name, or one that you specify. If you want to generate a name, simply use the xsl namespace followed by the pound sign (#) and a name expression to compute a qualified name.

A complementary instruction element <xsl:attribute> allows you to add attributes to result element nodes. These element nodes could either be instantiated from literal result elements in your style sheet or elements created with xsl:element. The name of the attribute to be created is specified with a name attribute, and an optional namespace attribute. Often, elements have several attributes and creating each attribute separately can be tedious work. So, XSLT also lets you create attribute sets, like this:

```
<xsl:attribute-set name="head-style">
   <xsl:attribute name="font-size">12pt</xsl:attribute>
   <xsl:attribute name="font-weight">bold</xsl:attribute>
</xsl:attribute-set>
```

```
<xsl:template match="Article/Headline">
   <xsl:element name="myElem">
      <xsl:use attribute-set="head-style"/>
      <xsl:apply-templates/>
   </xsl:element>
</xsl:template>
```

You can also add comments to your documents using <xsl:comment>. Usage is similar to <xsl:text>: Simply include your comment text within opening and closing tags. For example,

```
<xsl:comment>
   Copyright (c) 1999, Michael Floyd. All Rights Reserved
</xsl:comment>
```

The XSL processor will generate the appropriate comment delimiters. Keep in mind, however, that the content may contain only character data.

Finally, XML provides a facility called "processing instructions" that allows you to include information within a document that can be used by an application. The most recognizable processing instruction is the xml declaration found in the prolog of most XML documents. Processing instructions might also be useful in specifying a file format to a word processor, or in describing a properties file for a Java applet. So, XSL provides <xsl:pi> for this purpose. The <xsl:pi> element requires a name attribute to identify the processing instruction target, and sends the instantiated instruction node untouched to the result tree. The instruction must contain characters—anything other than characters generates an error.

3.6 | Expressions

Note: At this writing, XSLT and XPATH were not yet finalized by the W3C. The remainder of this chapter describes the version implemented in IE 5.0.

Location paths belong to a larger set of statements called expressions. When you select a node or set of nodes with a pattern, you are actually evaluating a location path expression, which returns a node-set.

More generally, when an expression is evaluated, you get back an object whose type is one of the following:

- Boolean

- number

- string

- node-set

A Boolean value represents either a True or False condition. The number type is represented as a floating-point real number. Thus, it can contain decimal notation, be negative or positive (including negative or positive zero), or NaN which represents Not a Number. A node set refers to nodes in the source or result tree.

3.6.1 *Location Paths*

The pattern syntax you've seen so far actually uses a restricted form of what XPath calls "location paths." Location paths are designed to allow greater control of your searches within the document's tree structure. So, the syntax is necessarily verbose. In many cases, you'll be able to get by with the abbreviated form described above. When you need to perform finer-grained searches, then you have the full power of location paths at your disposal.

A location path consists of an axis identifier, a node test, and zero or more predicates. The axis identifier selects a list of nodes, which is technically referred to as the axis. An axis is an ordered list that represents a fragment of the document tree. This is in contrast to the overall location path, which yields a "set" of nodes. In any case, the list of nodes, or axis, is then narrowed down using a node test to produce what XSLT calls the initial node-set. Then, the node-set can be further narrowed using a predicate. What does all of that mean? Let's look at an example:

```
from-children(headline)
```

In this example, children is the axis identifier, and headline is a test that returns true for headline nodes. The result is that this expression selects headline nodes that are children of the current node. You can also use the pattern syntax within the argument as described earlier in this chapter. For example, you can select all element children by using the wildcard character (*) in the argument in place of headline. The following example selects all nodes that are text-node descendants:

```
from-descendants(text())
```

Of course, you can string together location paths. The following example selects the immediate BodyText child nodes of the current node, then chooses all of their descendants that are italicized:

```
from-children(BodyText)/from-descendants(italic)
```

You can also select positions using the position() function. For example, the following selects the first paragraph child of the context node:

```
from-children(paragraph[position()=1])
```

As always, an initial / selects the document root. The following uses the position() expression (described in the following section) to select the second section of the fifth chapter of the doc document element:

```
/from-children(doc)/
from-children(chapter[position()=5])/
from-children(section[position()=2])
```

As you can see, location paths can quickly become complex. In most cases, you'll be able to get by just fine using the abbreviated location path syntax described earlier. If, however, you find it difficult to get the precise node-set, you can always resort to full location paths. Table 3-4 provides a complete list of location path axes in XSLT.

Table 3-4   Location path axes

Axis Identifier	Description
from-ancestor	Selects ancestor of the current node.
from-ancestors-or self	Creates an axis in reverse-document order starting with the current node containing ancestor nodes.
from-attributes	Selects the attributes of the current node.
from-children	Specifies child nodes.
from-descendants	Selects descendants of the current node.
from-descendants-or-self	Creates an axis with the current node and descendant nodes.
from-following	Specifies all nodes in the document following the current node.
from-following-siblings	Creates an axis with the siblings that follow the current node. The axis contains nodes in document order.
from-parent	Constructs an axis that includes the parent of the current node.
from-preceeding	Specifies nodes before the current node
from-preceeding-siblings	Creates an axis with the siblings that precede the current node. The axis contains nodes in reverse-document order.
from-self	Selects the current node.

3.6.2   *Node-Set Expressions*

When a node in the tree is selected, it becomes the context node. So, when an expression is evaluated it is within that context. The context consists of:

- ■ Context node
- ■ Context position and size

■ Variable binding set

■ Function library

■ Namespace declaration set

The XSLT specification adds functions and operators that allow you determine the number of nodes in a tree fragment, get the position of the current node, and so on. There are functions that support Boolean operations, and functions to manipulate strings and numbers. Of course, an expression can simply be a location path. In that case, the expression returns the set of nodes selected by the path. Table 3-5 summarizes these functions.

Table 3-5   Functions that operate on node sets

Expression	Description
last()	Returns the context size.
position()	Returns the context position.
count()	Returns the number of nodes in the argument node-set.
id()	Select element nodes by their unique ID.
key()	Returns node-set containing the specified key.
document()	Returns tree fragments of XML document other than the initial source document.
local-name()	Takes a node-set and returns a string with the local part of the name of the first node in the set.
namespace-uri()	Takes a node-set and returns a string containing the namespace of the first node in the set.
name()	Takes a node-set and returns a name as defined by XML Namespaces Recommendation representing the first node in the node-set.
generate-Id()	Generates a string that can be used as a unique identifier.

3.6.3 *String Expressions*

XSLT also supports a number of string-manipulation expressions. The basic function, `string()`, converts an object to a string. A number is converted to a string by returning a string in the form of a number. If the number is negative, a negative sign (-) precedes the string. Boolean values are converted to the strings, 'true' and 'false.' If the object is a node set, the first node (in document order) is selected and that value is converted to a string. An empty string is returned if the set is empty. A result tree fragment is converted to a string by treating it as a single document fragment node. In all cases, the argument defaults to the current node if it is omitted. Table 3-6 summarizes the XSLTs string expressions.

Table 3-6   String functions

Expression	*Description*
string()	Converts an object to a Unicode character string.
concat()	Concatenates two strings and returns the result.
contains()	Determines whether a substring is contained within a string.
starts-with()	Takes two string arguments: If the second string starts with the characters in the first string, this function returns with a value of true.
substring-before()	Returns the substring preceding a specified character.
substring-after()	Returns the substring following a specified character.
normalize()	Removes leading/trailing white space and reduces extra white space to a single space.
translate()	Translates a string of characters.
format-number()	Formats number strings.

The `concat()` function takes two strings and appends the second string to the first. Thus:

```
concat("String 1 ", "String 2")
```

yields:

```
String 1 String 2
```

The `contains()` function checks to see if a substring is contained within a string of characters. For example:

```
contains("ML", "HTML")
```

returns a value of `True`. At the time of this writing, it was not known whether case-sensitive comparisons would be allowed. A case-sensitive comparison would mean, for example that the following would return `False`:

```
contains("ml", "HTML")
```

The same is true for other string comparisons including `starts-with()`, `substring-before()`, and `substring-after()`. The `starts-with()` functions checks whether the second string in its argument list starts with the first argument string, returning true if it does. The `substring-before()` function allows you to specify a character within a string and returns the preceding portion of the string. For example:

```
substring-before("Mickey Mouse", "e")
```

returns the string "Mick." Note that there are two e's in this string. In this case, the processor uses the first character or substring encountered. The `substring-after()` function operates similarly, returning the substring following the specified characters.

The `normalize()` function returns the argument string with white space normalized by stripping leading and trailing white space and replacing sequences of white-space characters by a single space.

3.6.4 *Numbers*

The `number()` function takes a string representing a number and converts it to that value. The string may contain white space. The Boolean value `True` is converted to 1, and `False` is converted to 0. If the string does not represent a number, then the function returns a value of 0. If the argument contains a node-set or a result tree fragment, then it is converted to a string and then evaluated as just described. Finally, if you omit the argument altogether, the current node is used.

The `div` operator divides two numbers and returns a floating-point number as specified by the IEEE 754 specification. The `quo` operator also divides two numbers, but truncates the result and returns an integer. The `mod()` function similarly divides two numbers, but returns the remainder as an integer. For example:

```
10 quo 3
```

Table 3-7   Floating-point functions and operators

Expression	Description
div	Operator that divides to numbers and returns a floating-point value.
quo	Divides two numbers and returns an integer.
mod	Returns the remainder of a floating-point division operation.
number()	Function that converts the value specified in its argument to a number.
sum()	Returns the sum of the values of the nodes in the argument node-set.
round()	Returns the round of a number as an integer.
floor()	Returns the largest integer not greater than the argument.
ceiling()	Returns the smallest integer not smaller than the argument.

returns the value 3.

```
10 mod 3
```

returns the value 1.

The `sum()` function takes a node-set and returns the sum of the values of the nodes in the set. `round()` returns an integer after the value has been rounded off. The `floor()` function returns an integer representing the largest number not greater than the argument value. And `ceiling()` function returns the smallest integer that is not less than the argument value. Table 3-7 summarizes these functions.

3.6.5   *Booleans*

Booleans are objects that can have one of two values: They are either 'True' or 'False.' Booleans are particularly useful when comparing two values. If the test is successful, the value returned is `True`, otherwise it is `False`. XSLT provides five functions (as described in Table 3-8) that

Table 3-8   Boolean functions and operators

Expression	*Description*
boolean()	Evaluates its argument value and returns a Boolean value.
=,<,>,<=, >=	Converts each operand to a number and compares the two numbers.
or	Returns true if either operand is true.
and	Returns true only when both operands are true.
not()	Returns the opposite Boolean value.
true()	Returns a value of true.
false()	Returns a value of false.
lang()	Compares the language of the context node.

allow to you make these comparisons. There are also five operators that can return a Boolean value.

The first function in Table 3-8, `boolean()`, simply converts its argument to a Boolean. The argument can be a number, node list, result tree fragment, or a string. If you are testing for a number, `boolean()` returns `True` if it is neither zero (positive or negative) nor NaN (Not a Number). If the argument is a node-list or a result fragment, `boolean()` returns a value of `True` so long as the list is not empty. If you omit the argument, `boolean()` defaults to whatever is in the current node.

The `not()` function negates whatever Boolean value the argument would normally return. Thus, `not()` returns a value of `True` when its argument is `False`. The `true()` function always returns a `True` value, and likewise, `false()` always returns `False`.

The other items listed in Table 3-8 are Boolean operators that directly test the values on either side of the operand. For <, >, <= or >=, each operand is converted to a number and then the two numbers are compared. For example, 1 < 2 returns a value of `True` and 2 <= 1 returns `False`. The = operator is treated differently depending on the argument type. Number types are treated as just described for the other operands. However, if the argument is not of type number, the operands are converted to strings and the string values are compared.

The `or` operator evaluates each operand and converts it to a Boolean, then compares the two Boolean values. The result of the operation is true if either value is true. The and operator is converted similarly. However, both operands must be true for the result to return true.

XML allows you to specify the language for elements using an xml:lang attribute. The `lang()` function examines this value for the current node and compares it to the language specified in its argument. If the `xml:lang` attribute was not specified for the current node, the `lang()` function looks up the tree for ancestors that have specified the xml:lang attribute and uses that value. If no

attribute was specified, the lookup fails and the lang() function returns false.

3.6.6 *Extension Functions*

While the expression language contains features found in a programming language, it is not intended as one. Instead, XSLT provides an
extension mechanism that allows you to access languages such as
JavaScript, VBScript, and Java. The specification does not require
that an XSLT processor support extensions for any particular language, so you will want to check the documentation for your specific
processor to see if it has this support.

3.7 | Additional Features

XSLT provides a number of additional features that will make it easier
to process elements. For example, XSLT provides a `for-each` element
that instructs the processor to perform iterative processing on every
found node meeting your criteria. This is particularly useful when you
need to process a large number of element nodes that have the same
structure. A typical example is when you have a collection of element
nodes that represent records in a database. Consider the following
XML document, which represents the listings in a product directory.

```
<?xml version="1.0"?>

<productDB>

   <product>
      <name>XML Toolbox</name>
      <company>BeyondHTML</company>
      <version>1.0</version>
```

```
        <price>99.95</price>
        <sys-requirements>Any Java Platform</sys-requirements>
        <description>
            XML Toolbox is a collection of tools for creating
and processing XML documents
        </description>
    </product>


    <product>
        <name>xml4j</name>
        <company>IBM</company>
        <version>1.1.1.4</version>
        <price>Freely available</price>
        <sys-requirements>Any Java platform</sys-requirements>
        <description>
            xml4j is an XML processor that is compliant with the
XML 1.0 working draft specification
        </description>
    </product>

    <product>
        <name>MSXML</name>
        <company>Microsoft/DataChannel</company>
        <version>N/A</version>
        <price>Freely available</price>
        <sys-requirements>Any Java platform</sys-requirements>
        <description>
            MSXML is an XML processor that is compliant with the
XML 1.0 working draft specification
        </description>
    </product>

</productDB>
```

This XML document contains a set of database records from a product directory. Each record is represented by a product element, which contains a name, company, version, price, sys-requirements, and description field. The records could have been generated dynamically as part of a database search, for example.

The following style sheet uses <xsl:for-each> to iterate through and process each record.

```
<?xml version="1.0"?>

<xsl:stylesheet xmlns:xsl="http://www.w3.org/
TR/WD-xsl">

  <xsl:template match="/productDB">
   <HTML>
   <HEAD>
      <TITLE>
         XML Tools Database Search
      </TITLE>
   </HEAD>
   <BODY>
   <H1>XML Tools Database Search Results</H1>

   <TABLE Border="1" width="100%">
      <TR>
         <TD>Product Name</TD>
         <TD>Product Version</TD>
         <TD>Product Price</TD>
      </TR>
       <TR style="color:green">

        <xsl:for-each select="name">
           <TD>
           <xsl:apply-templates/>
           </TD>

           <xsl:for-each select="../version">
             <TD><xsl:apply-templates/></TD>
           </xsl:for-each>

           <xsl:for-each select="../price">
             <TD>
             <xsl:apply-templates/></TD>
           </xsl:for-each>
         </xsl:for-each>

       </TR>
      </xsl:for-each>
      </TABLE>
   </BODY>
   </HTML>
  </xsl:template>

</xsl:stylesheet>
```

This example creates a summary report by transforming the name, version, and price field elements and placing them into an HTML table. The template rule uses a pattern to select the document element, `productDB`. Next, the template generates some preliminary HTML elements including the page `<TITLE>`, appropriate labels, and the start of the HTML table. The first row of the table contains the headings for each column.

To iterate through the fields, we specify a select attribute for each field node to be processed. All that is left to do is to create each table column and call apply-templates to process the nodes.

3.7.1 *Conditional Processing*

XSLT also supports conditional processing. That is, you can process an element if it meets a condition that you specify. The first element, `<xsl:if>` operates like an if..then construct found in many programming languages. You specify the condition using an attribute. The condition results in a Boolean expression which returns either True or False. If the condition is True, the processing is carried out. Let's look at a short example.

The following test converts the price string in the database to a number. If the conversion is successful, the value is a valid number, so we add a dollar sign in front of it.

```
<xsl:template match="product/price">
  <xsl:if test="number()">
     $
  </xsl:if>
  <xsl:apply-templates/>
</xsl:template>
```

The other element, `<xsl:choose>`, allows you to select from a set of choices. You set up the choices using a sequence of `<xsl:when>` elements. Each case represents a choice. The last case uses `<xsl:otherwise>` and serves as a catchall for the other cases. Here is an example:

```
<xsl:choose>
    <xsl:when test='../../doc'>
            is doc/*
    </xsl:when>
    <xsl:when test='ancestor(doc/a/a)'>
            is doc/a/a/*
    </xsl:when>
    <xsl:when test='ancestor(doc/b/b)'>
            is doc/b/b/*
    </xsl:when>
    <xsl:otherwise>
            in otherwise clause
    </xsl:otherwise>
</xsl:choose>
```

This sample evaluates the contents of a variable called `test`, and if a when case evaluates to True, it sets the context to the prescribed location in `test`. If no case evaluates to True, then the otherwise choice is used.

3.7.2 *Sorting*

Another useful feature is the ability to sort. XSLT supplies `<xsl:sort>` for just that purpose. You can use this element within either `<xsl:apply-templates>` or `<xsl:for-each>`. You specify a sort key using a select attribute. The sort element takes some additional attributes including order, which specifies the sort order as ascending or descending. By default, the sort order is ascending. The lang attribute identifies the language of the sort keys, and data-type determines the data type of the element nodes. The data type defaults to text when it is not specified. Finally, a number attribute is also useful in that it converts the sort keys to numbers and then sorts according to their numeric values.

Borrowing from our previous database example, the following sorts the database records from the product directory using the name field as the sort key:

```
<xsl:template match="/productDB">
   <HTML>
   <HEAD>
     <TITLE>
        XML Tools Database Search
     </TITLE>
   </HEAD>
   <BODY>
   <H1>XML Tools Database Search Results</H1>

   <TABLE Border="1" width="100%">
     <xsl:for-each select="product">
              <xsl:sort select="name"/>
       <TR>
         <TD>Product Name</TD>
         <TD>Product Version</TD>
         <TD>Product Price</TD>
       </TR>
        <TR style="color:green">
          <xsl:for-each select="name">
            <TD>
            <xsl:apply-templates/>
            </TD>
...
   </xsl:template>
```

There is one last attribute, case-order, that allows you to specify whether upper or lower case letters take precedence in the sort. If you specify the value upper-first, then upper case letters take precedence. For example, assuming the sort order is ascending, Aardvark would be placed before aardvark in the output list. If lower-first were instead specified, then aardvark would take the pole position.

3.8 | Conclusion

As you can see, XSLT and XPath include extensive features for processing, formatting and transforming XML documents. We've covered many of their features including tree processing, template rules, patterns, and salient points of the expression language. However, there's a great deal more to XSLT. For example, XSLT supports variables. Rather than overwhelm you, this book will introduce these topics as we use them in later chapters.

Web Vocabularies

I n creating new XML instances for your Web applications, you implicitly define an order, structure, and context in which your elements can be used. For example, let's say you are creating a contact database containing a list of people and their contact information. When you place a `<name>` element inside of `<contact>` element, you imply that a name element can contain at least one `<contact>`. In terms of structure, that is useful information. However, it doesn't tell the whole story. For example, should more than one `<name>` element be allowed within a `<contact>` element? Intuitively, your first response might be "no." However, what if you wanted to include the name of a spouse? In that case, you might want to allow another name to be included. In fact, you may even want to allow a contact to be nested within the first contact. Other questions arise: Should you use an attribute or define another element to distinguish the spouse from the original contact? Ultimately, a robust long-term solution requires that you decide how elements are used, how they should be structured, what attributes they can contain, and so on.

Now, what happens when you want to share your document with someone else? An XML-aware application can scan your document, infer certain rules, and even make individual components of your document accessible through scripting or programming. That is quite a lot. Beyond surface viewing, however, the application can't communicate with your document nor interact with its logic. In other words, the application still doesn't "understand" your document. What you need is a way to promote communication between the two entities, so that they may, in effect, "speak" the same language. They need a common vocabulary.

According to Webster's Dictionary, a vocabulary is "the stock of words used by or known to a people or group of persons; a list or collection of the words or phrases of a language, technical field, etc., usually arranged in alphabetical order and defined."

In XML, a vocabulary is the set of definitions and rules that tell your application how your elements can be used and describe how they should be interpreted. In this sense, we use the term "vocabulary" and "Document Type Definition" interchangeably, although strictly speaking a DTD includes a grammar as well as a vocabulary. Vocabularies enable applications, documents, and other entities to speak the same language. Sometimes, applications must query, manipulate, output, or otherwise process a document. Other times, the document acts as an intermediary between two applications. In fact, this is the mechanism that allows two applications to share data. Even applications with different representations can share information.

You can define your own vocabularies, but more often you will be using domain-specific vocabularies designed by standards bodies, large companies, and others with common interests. Indeed, many believe that the collection of vocabularies will grow exponentially as the use of XML grows. This chapter introduces some of the vocabularies currently available that are of particular interest to Web developers.

4.1 | Scalable Vector Graphics

Until now, the Web has relied on three bitmap graphics formats to render images: Graphics Interchange Format (GIF), Joint Photographic Experts Group (JPEG), and Portable Network Graphics

(PNG). These formats have been popular in network environments because they are stored using efficient compression techniques, making them smaller in size. In addition, these formats can be streamed, meaning that because the data is serialized it can be rendered incrementally as soon as it arrives, rather than waiting for the complete data set before rendering the image. Bitmap graphics belong to a class of computer graphics called raster graphics where an image is rendered by filling in a matrix (or raster) of dots or pixels.

Another class of graphics, vector graphics (sometimes called stroke graphics), use short line segments (called vectors) to draw images. Web developers may not be as familiar with this type of graphics because until now, there has been no standard method built into browsers to efficiently store and stream the images.

The Scalable Vector Graphics (SVG) standard solves this problem by allowing authors to describe vector-based images using XML syntax. With nearly a half-dozen proposals made to the W3C, there has been some debate over how to bring vector graphics to the Web. With the consensus of an unusually large working group, the W3C has now settled on SVG, a vocabulary that allows you to describe 2-D graphics using XML syntax.

Because the syntax is text-based and only describes things like coordinates, size, fill colors and the like, the data set is relatively small. It is up to the viewer software to interpret these descriptions and render the image. Because the image isn't rendered until it reaches the client, it can be easily resized without distorting the image. This can't be said for bitmap images.

SVG can be used in two different ways. The first method creates SVG elements in a separate standalone file, which is then referenced either by a processing application or possibly included into a parent document, such as an XML Web page. Alternatively, fragments of SVG markup can be included directly into a Web page.

SVG defines three types of graphic objects: image, text, and vector graphic objects. The vector objects include line, polyline, polygon, and circle. You can group objects, style them, and transform them. They can also be composited with previously rendered objects. The feature set includes nested transformations, clipping paths, alpha masks, filter effects, and template objects.

More than just a vocabulary, SVG defines a Document Object Model that allows programmers to access vector graphic objects in order to do things like animation. We'll talk about DOMs in the next chapter. For now, it is only important to know that the SVG DOM defines a rich set of event handlers, such as `onmouseover`, that can be assigned to any SVG object. Best of all, you can script HTML and SVG elements at the same time and within the same Web page.

The following example presents an SVG document that describes how four rectangles are to be drawn.

```
<?xml version="1.0" standalone="no"?>
<!DOCTYPE svg PUBLIC "-//W3C//DTD SVG April 1999//EN"
   "http://www.w3.org/Graphics/SVG/svg-19990412.dtd">

<svg width="4in" height="3in">

   <desc>A Scalable Vector Graphics example that draws three
rectangles </desc>

     <rect width="20" height="50"/>
     <rect width="30" height="40"/>
     <rect width="45" height="45"/>
</svg>
```

The example starts with an `<?xml... >` processing instruction, which informs the processor that this document requires a DTD. The `<!DOCTYPE>` declaration gives the URL for the required DTD. Next, the `<svg>` element uses two attributes to set the overall size of the object to be drawn. Finally, the `<rect>` element describes each rectangle to be drawn.

The next example, created by Carmen Delessio, renders a tiger in an SVG viewer. Due to its length, only a portion of the example is presented. However, the listing should give you an idea of how SVG can be used.

```
<?xml version = "1.0" standalone = "yes"?>
<!DOCTYPE svg PUBLIC "-//W3C//DTD SVG April 1999//EN"
```

```
    "http://www.w3.org/Graphics/SVG/svg-19990412.dtd">

<svg width = "242px" height="383px">
<g style = "stroke: #000000" >
</g>
<g style = "fill: #f2cc99" >
    <polyline verts = " 69,18 82,8 99,3 118,5 135,12 149,21
156,13 165,9 177,13 183,28 180,50 164,91 155,107 154,114
151,121 141,127 139,136 155,206 157,251 126,342 133,357
128,376 83,376 75,368 67,350 61,350 53,369 4,369 2,361
5,354 12,342 16,321 4,257 4,244 7,218 9,179 26,127 43,93
32,77 30,70 24,67 16,49 17,35 18,23 30,12 40,7 53,7 62,12
69,18 69,18 69,18"/>
</g>
<g style = "fill: #e5b27f" >
    <polyline verts = " 142,79 136,74 138,82 133,78 133,84
127,78 128,85 124,80 125,87 119,82 119,90 125,99 125,96
128,100 128,94 131,98 132,93 135,97 136,93 138,97 139,94
141,98 143,94 144,85 142,79 142,79 142,79"/>
</g>
<g style = "fill: #eb8080" >
    <polyline verts = " 127,101 132,100 137,99 144,101
143,105 135,110 127,101 127,101 127,101"/>
</g>
<g style = "fill: #f2cc99" >
    <polyline verts = " 178,229 157,248 139,296 126,349
137,356 158,357 183,342 212,332 235,288 235,261 228,252
212,250 188,251 178,229 178,229 178,229"/>
</g>
<g style = "fill: #9c826b" >
    <polyline verts = " 56,229 48,241 48,250 57,281 63,325
71,338 81,315 76,321 79,311 83,301 75,308 80,298 73,303
76,296 71,298 74,292 69,293 74,284 78,278 71,278 74,274
68,273 70,268 66,267 68,261 60,266 62,259 65,253 57,258
59,251 55,254 55,248 60,237 54,240 58,234 54,236 56,229
56,229 56,229"/>
    <polyline verts = " 74,363 79,368 81,368 85,362 89,363
92,370 96,373 101,372 108,361 110,371 113,373 116,371
120,358 122,363 123,371 126,371 129,367 132,357 135,361
130,376 127,377 94,378 84,376 76,371 74,363 74,363
74,363"/>
    <polyline verts = " 212,250 219,251 228,258 236,270
235,287 225,304 205,332 177,343 171,352 158,357 166,352
168,346 168,339 165,333 155,327 155,323 161,320 165,316
169,316 167,312 171,313 168,308 173,309 170,306 177,306
175,308 177,311 174,311 176,316 171,315 174,319 168,320
```

```
168,323 175,327 179,332 183,326 184,332 189,323 190,328
194,320 194,325 199,316 201,320 204,313 206,316 208,310
211,305 219,298 226,288 229,279 228,266 224,259 217,253
212,250 212,250 212,250"/>
    <polyline verts = " 151,205 151,238 149,252 141,268
128,282 121,301 130,300 126,313 118,324 116,337 120,346
133,352 133,340 137,333 145,329 156,327 153,319 153,291
157,271 170,259 178,277 193,250 174,216 151,205 151,205
151,205"/>
    <polyline verts = " 78,127 90,142 95,155 108,164 125,167
139,175 150,206 152,191 141,140 121,148 100,136 78,127
78,127 78,127"/>
    <polyline verts = " 21,58 35,63 38,68 32,69 42,74 40,79
47,80 54,83 45,94 34,81 32,73 24,66 21,58 21,58 21,58"/>
    <polyline verts = " 71,34 67,34 66,27 59,24 54,17 48,17
39,22 30,26 28,31 31,39 38,46 29,45 36,54 41,61 41,70 50,69
54,71 55,58 67,52 76,43 76,39 68,44 71,34 71,34 71,34"/>
    <polyline verts = " 139,74 141,83 143,89 144,104 148,104
155,106 154,86 157,77 155,72 150,77 144,77 139,74 139,74
139,74"/>
    <polyline verts = " 105,44 102,53 108,58 111,62 112,55
105,44 105,44 105,44"/>
    <polyline verts = " 141,48 141,54 144,58 139,62 137,66
136,59 137,52 141,48 141,48 141,48"/>
    <polyline verts = " 98,135 104,130 105,134 108,132
108,135 112,134 113,137 116,136 116,139 119,139 124,141
128,140 133,138 140,133 139,140 126,146 104,144 98,135
98,135 98,135"/>
    <polyline verts = " 97,116 103,119 103,116 111,118
116,117 122,114 127,107 135,111 142,107 141,114 145,118
149,121 145,125 140,124 127,121 113,125 100,124 97,116
97,116 97,116"/>
<!- Due to its length, the remainder of this example has been
omitted. Please refer to the online example referenced in the
Reference section at the end of this chapter. ->


</svg>
```

The resulting image is shown in Figure 4-1. The image was displayed in a viewer, also written by Carmen. The viewer is written in Java and is freely available from his Web site (See Resources at the end of this chapter). You can see the advantage of having each line stored as a separate element. You can alter a single line or fill, and you can write code to act on the image and process the image in real time. With raster images, the most that is practical in real time is applying a filter to the entire image.

4.2 | Synchronized Multimedia Integration Language

SMIL, or Synchronized Multimedia Integration Language, is an XML-based language for assembling time-based, streaming multimedia presentations on the Web. SMIL defines element types that allow you to combine audio, video, animation, images, and text to create a complete multimedia presentation. You create these elements using your favorite multimedia authoring tool. Once you have the components to your presentation, you use SMIL to orchestrate the presentation. The elements give you control over where components are placed, and whether they should play sequentially or in parallel (simultaneously). In order to use SMIL, you will need an SMIL player. Fortunately, several have appeared on the market including RealNetworks' G2 player (see Resources at the end of this chapter for details).

The following example shows the basic structure for SMIL elements:

```
<smil>
  <head>
    <switch>
    <layout type="text/css">
       [region="PlayMedia"] { top: 76px; left: 100px }
    </layout>
    <layout>
      <region id="PlayMedia" top="76" left="100" />
    </layout>
    </switch>
    </head>
    <body>
      <seq>
        <img region="PlayMedia"
```

```
                        src="textfile" dur="10s" />
        </seq>
      </body>
    </smil>
```

The `<smil>` element is the root element. Within that element, you create a `<head>` and a `<body>`, just like in HTML. The `<head>` contains a series of layout elements that control how the various multimedia components are laid out in the browser window. In this short example, the region attribute controls the positioning of an `<img>` element. The `<switch>` element provides alternatives to the layout of your multimedia components. Here, we offer the alternative of using either CSS2 or SMIL to lay out our img element.

The `<body>` contains a single element, `<seq>` that tells the SMIL player to play this img in sequence. If we had provided a second multimedia object, say a sound clip, we could have used the `<par>` to play both elements in parallel.

This next example plays a video with two separate text streams. The example was generated using RealNetworks' SMIL Presentation wizard, and this document is designed to work with its G2 player.

```
<smil>
  <head>
    <meta name="bitmap" content="headnews.bmp" />
    <meta name="imgmap" content="headnews.map" />
    <meta name="height" content="174" />
    <meta name="width" content="352" />
    <layout type="text/smil-basic-layout">
      <region id="VideoChannel" left="0" top="0"
              height="144" width="176" />
      <region id="TextChannel1" left="176" top="0"
              height="144" width="176" />
      <region id="TextChannel2" left="0" top="144"
              height="30" width="352" />
    </layout>
  </head>
  <body>
    <par>
      <video src="RealVideo" id="Video"
```

Figure 4–1   Image of a tiger generated by Carmen Delessio's SVG Viewer.

```
                region="VideoChannel"/>
        <text   src="RealText" id="Headline Text"
                region="TextChannel1"/>
        <text   src="RealText" id="Ticker"
                region="TextChannel2"/>
    </par>
  </body>
</smil>
```

The example creates a "viewport" for a video feed and two separate text "viewports": one that gets a feed of news headlines and another that gets a feed of running ticker information, perhaps from advertisers.

4.3 | XHTML

As stated in Chapter 1, it has become increasingly clear that HTML is not going away anytime soon. In fact, some are now predicting a boom for a whole new class of applications that might include embedded devices, set-top boxes, Internet appliances, and the like. These applications will need to read Web documents, and will additionally require the simplicity of HTML. To support its case, a new draft specification for a vocabulary, XHTML, states:

> "Some estimates indicate that by the year 2002, 75% of Internet document viewing will be carried out on these alternate platforms. In most cases, these platforms will not have the computing power of a desktop platform, and will not be designed to accommodate ill-formed HTML as current user agents tend to do. Indeed, if these user agents do not receive well-formed XHTML, they may simply not display the document."

Here is a short example that points out the change you'll have to make to your HTML documents to allow XHTML viewers to read them.

```
<!DOCTYPE html PUBLIC "-//W3C//DTD XHTML 1.0 Strict//EN"
    "http://www.w3.org/TR/xhtml1/DTD/strict.dtd">
<html xmlns="http://www.w3.org/TR/xhtml1">
  <head>
    <title>BeyondHTML.com Home page</title>
  </head>
  <body>
    <P><IMG SRC="gifs/logo.gif"
      ALT="Jump to BeyondHTML Home Page" width="426"
      height="112">
    </P>
    <P>Welcome to BeyondHTML.com</P>
  </body>
</html>
```

There are few real differences between HTML 4.0 and XHTML at this point. In this case, the DOCTYPE declaration points to the strict XHTML DTD, and XML namespace has been declared. The only other difference is that this is an XML document and your markup must now be well formed. That means you must include end tags for all of your elements, as shown with the <P> element above. The tags are case-sensitive as well.

4.4 | WDDX

WDDX is an XML vocabulary for representing data structures. The vocabulary was proposed by Allaire (makers of Cold Fusion) to allow programs to exchange application-level data. For example, you may want to take a date/time field from a database, pass it to a programming script, calculate the time for another time zone, and return the new calculated field to the database application. This kind of interaction requires that both applications understand what a date/time field is, how it is formatted, and so on.

The vocabulary operates much the same way a modem operates: it takes a unit of data, packages it up into a packet of data, serializes it with other data packets and sends the packets to a receiving application. At the other end, the receiving application unpackages the packets, grabs the data and is off and running. Following is an example of a WDDX document:

```
<?xml version='1.0'?>
<!DOCTYPE wddxPacket SYSTEM 'wddx_0090.dtd'>

<wddxPacket version='0.9'>
    <header/>
    <data>
        <struct>
```

```
                    <var name='myString'>
                        <string>This is a sample string</string>
                    </var>

                    <var name='pi'>
                        <number>3.14</number>
                    </var>

                    <var name='bool'>
                        <boolean value='true'/>
                    </var>

                    <var name='contact'>
                        <recordset
                          rowCount='2'
                          fieldNames='NAME,PHONE'>
                           <field name='NAME'>
                                <string>Joe Butler</string>
                                <string>Kristin Butler</string>
                           </field>
                           <field name='PHONE'>
                                <number>123-456-7890</number>
                                <number>987-654-3210</number>
                           </field>
                        </recordset>
                    </var>
                </struct>
            </data>
        </wddxPacket>
```

The WDDX packet element uses two elements, a header which is empty in this case, and a data element containing one or more data structures. The example shows how you can represent any one of several data types: a string, number, date-time value, Boolean value, array, recordset, or an object. Numbers are represented as floating-point values, but the range of numbers is restricted to that of an 8-bit floating-point value. Date-time values are encoded according to the ISO 8601 standard (for example, 1999-6-29T08:06:22+4:0). Strings can be of arbitrary length, but are not allowed to contain a null character.

Arrays are indexed collections and may contain any other data type. The index value is an integer. Similarly, structures (sometimes called associative arrays) are string-indexed collections. Finally, recordsets are tabular data encapsulations: a set of named fields with the same number of rows of data. Only simple data types can be stored in recordsets.

4.5 | Channel Definition Format

The Channel Definition Format (CDF) is an XML vocabulary that lets you describe "push" channels for your Web site. The CDF was introduced by Microsoft and proposed as an open standard to the W3C in March 1997. Although never officially adopted, the standard is supported in Internet Explorer and on the Active Desktop in Windows 98 and Windows 2000.

The vocabulary allows you to create channels to which your visitors can subscribe. Subscribers can automatically receive notifications, updates, and navigational information from your Web site on a regularly scheduled basis. The benefit to you as a Web publisher is that you don't have to hope your visitors remember to visit your site. More importantly, you can create a loyal readership or community that follows your site on a regular basis. We will be looking at the CDF in detail in a later chapter, so I will defer a complete discussion until then.

4.6 | Java Speech Markup Language

The Java Speech Markup Language (JSML) is part of Sun's Java Speech API and can be used to annotate text for input to speech synthesizers. JSML provides elements that allow you to define the structure of a document, describe pronunciations of words and phrases, and place markers in the text. JSML also provides elements that allow you to control emphasis and pitch, phrasing, and speaking rate. JSML is fun to work with because it gives instant feedback: As you add additional markup, the quality and naturalness of the synthesized voice improves. JSML uses the Unicode character set, so JSML can be used to mark up text in most languages of the world. For more information, check the JSML Web site (see "Resources" for details).

4.7 | MusicML

Created by the Connection Factory, this DTD defines a vocabulary specifically for sheet music. The Connection Factory has also written a browser in Java to view a MusicML document. The browser is freely available from the company's Home page; see Resources at the end of this chapter for details. The vocabulary defines a root `<sheetmusic>` element and follows the basic structure shown below:

```
<sheetmusic>
    <musicrow size="two">
        <entrysegment>
          <entrypart></entrypart>
          <entrypart></entrypart>
        </entrysegment>
        <segment></segment>
        <segment></segment>
    </musicrow>
    <musicrow size="two"> </musicrow>
</sheetmusic>
```

Each line of music is defined in terms of a row, and each row has a double staff. Further, a `<musicrow>` is divided into logical pieces called segments, which can contain notes, and chords grouped together between two vertical bars. Within a segment there are subsegments for every staff.

At the beginning of every `<musicrow>` there are several special elements like the Clef which are defined for the entire `<musicrow>`. These special elements are grouped together in an `<entrysegment>`. You can find out more about MusicML by visiting the Connection Factory's Web site, listed at the end of this chapter.

4.8 | Other Vocabularies

There are a wide variety of DTDs, schemas, and other vocabularies emerging. However, it is unclear how browsers will support vocabularies as they come into widespread use. In some cases, vocabulary developers will provide scripts or Java applets to direct the browser. On the server side, software vendors will likely offer specialized software to complement their specific vocabulary. In the meantime, the trend seems to be toward writing specialized viewers in Java. In any case, there are a few additional vocabularies that deserve mention.

For example, the Structured Graph Format (SGF) is a vocabulary and software that allows site visitors to view your Web sites as Structured Graphs. Originally designed for project management and software engineering tasks, Structured Graphs can be used to support scalable editing and browsing of very large graphs.

The Tutorial Markup Language (TML) is another interesting vocabulary that allows Web developers to present online tutorials through their Web sites. The premise behind TML is that it allows you to separate the semantic content of a question from its presentation. Thus, questions (and answers) could be stored in a knowledge base. Different types of questions are supported within the same content model. TML is a superset of HTML, with new elements added to describe question information. A Unix version is freely available at the URL listed in the Resources section of this chapter. A commercial port to Windows NT is also available.

Finally, the UML eXchange Format, or UXF, proposes an application-neutral format that describes how Unified Modeling Language (UML) models can be interchanged. UXF is designed to express, publish, access, and exchange UML models.

UXF is a vocabulary that allows software developers to exchange UML models. It is designed to simplify the circulation of these models by providing a human-readable and intuitive format. This will allow UML models to be generalized to a greater extent, thus promoting reusability. Best of all, most existing Web applications can be used for handling UXF encoded information with relatively minor modifications. See the "Resources" section at the end of this chapter for additional information on all of these vocabularies.

4.8.1 *Resource Description Framework*

As we saw in Chapter 1, XML describes data. One of the key areas of data description is called metadata. That is, data about data. Metadata is particularly useful in allowing a Web document to describe features it contains. The ability for a document to describe itself to outside applications means the applications can process the document more intelligently. We have already discussed the use of HTML's <META> element to provide descriptions, keywords, and so on, to search engines. With the introduction of another standard called the Resource Description Framework (RDF), the next generation of search engine will discover a page's resources in order to provide better search engine capabilities.

RDF actually incorporates a number of technologies and solves several classes of problems. The aim is to manage the untold terabytes of data on the Web. Of course, we use software applications to manage, manipulate, and present all of this data, but there has been no general way for automating these processes.

In general, RDF is used to describe the content of your Web site and the resources and relationships that your documents rely upon. There are facilities in RDF that let you describe intellectual property rights of Web pages, improve the information collected by search engines, and create sitemaps that can be interpreted and used by software agents. Other areas RDF are being applied to include the PICS content rating system, push channels, digital library collections, and distributed authoring.

4.9 | Conclusion

The vocabularies presented in this chapter represent the tip of the iceberg. New vocabularies are surfacing daily to allow communication between real estate agents and their board of realtors, trucking companies and their clients, even between molecular biologists. With the proliferation of so many vocabularies, one looming question is: How can you locate these emerging vocabularies, before you set about writing your own?

The Organization for the Advancement of Structured Information Standards (OASIS), a non-profit consortium of users and vendors, founded XML.ORG. The purpose of this new portal site is to provide a registry and repository for the access and management of XML schemas, DTDs, namespaces, style sheets, and other resources. The idea is that industry groups will be able to register their XML data exchange specifications, and you will be able to search for specifications in your area of interest. More importantly, applications will be able to access XML resources directly from the repository when processing an XML document. In this way, XML.ORG will serve as a central clear-inghouse for access to XML-related specifications.

4.10 | Resources

Java Speech Markup Language.
http://java.sun.com/products/java-media/speech/forDevelopers/JSML/

Channel Definition Format Specification
http://www.w3.org/TR/NOTE-CDFsubmit.html

Synchronized Multimedia Integration Language Specification
http://www.w3.org/TR/REC-smil

Just SMIL Web site
http://smw.internet.com/smil/

Scalable Vector Graphics Specification
http://www.w3.org/TR/WD-SVG/

MusicML
http://www.tcf.nl/

Structured Graph Format
http://www.isl.hiroshima-u.ac.jp/projects/SGF/index.html

Tutorial Markup Language
http://www.ilrt.bris.ac.uk/netquest/

UML Exchange Format
http://www.yy.cs.keio.ac.jp/~suzuki/project/uxf/

Organization for the Advancement of Structured Information Standards (OASIS)
http://www.oasis-open.org

XML.ORG
http://www.xml.org

Carmen Delessio's wmf2svg utility with examples
http://www.blackdirt.com/graphics/svg/

4.11 | References

Scalable Vector Graphics (SVG) Specification, World Wide Web Consortium, April 12, 1999.

Synchronized Multimedia Integration Language (SMIL) 1.0 Specification, World Wide Web Consortium, June 15, 1998.

Webster's Encyclopedic Unabridged Dictionary of the English Language, Gramercy Books. New York. 1996.

Part Two

- The Document Object Model
- XML and Internet Explorer
- Projects for Internet Explorer
- Presenting XML in the Client

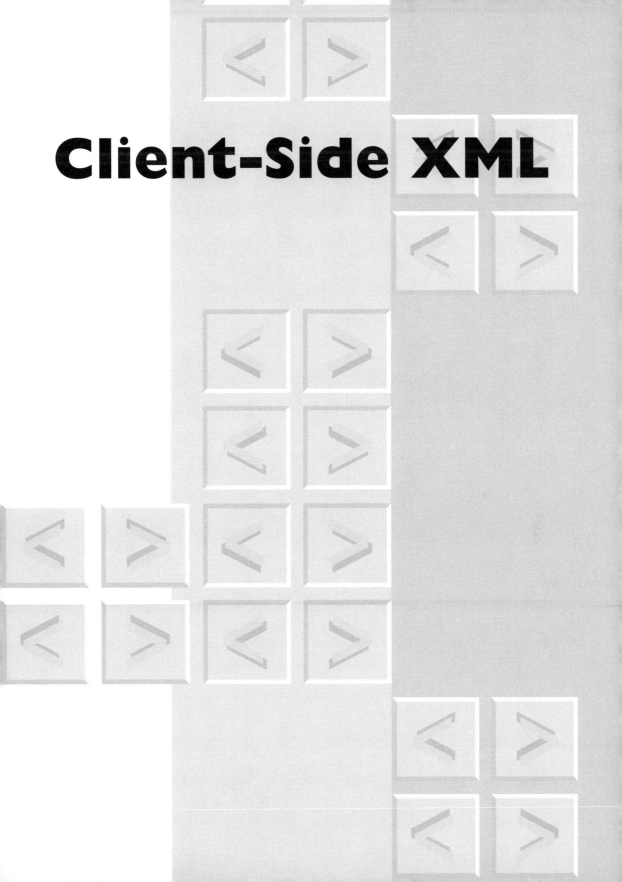

Client-Side XML

Document Object Model

Chapter
5

One of the more powerful features related to structured documents is the ability to access discrete members of the document tree. We have already seen this in the previous chapter when transforming specific XML elements into HTML for presentation. Most XML processors also allow you to access nodes in the document tree through a set of function calls, usually referred to as an Application Program Interface (API). The W3C has standardized these interfaces into the Document Object Model (DOM).

From the tool developer's perspective, the DOM determines which interfaces must be supported. However, it does not enforce any particular internal representation. This means that while tool vendors must provide application developers with a standard way to access document structures, they are free to represent these structures under the hood in any manner they wish.

In this chapter, we'll examine the essential features of the XML DOM. Depending on the XML processor you use, you can access and process members of the document tree using Java, C/C++, Python, JavaScript, and VBScript. This chapter focuses on JavaScript and Java.

5.1 | Introduction to the DOM

Technically speaking, the DOM covers both XML and HTML. The DOM specification differentiates between the Core DOM, which defines a set of XML object interfaces, and DOM HTML, which builds on the Core DOM interfaces. Our interest is primarily focused on XML, so the following discussions reference the Core DOM. Keep in mind, though, that the HTML DOM allows you to access HTML structures in a similar fashion.

The Core DOM defines two sets of interfaces. The first takes an object-oriented approach, presenting API calls through a hierarchy of classes that inherit features from ancestor classes. The other approach provides access to all of the methods and property values through a single Node interface. This creates a sort of "flattened" view of the API services. The approach you will take depends solely upon the tools you are using. In general, programming languages such as Java and C++ will offer this single interface, while higher-level languages like JavaScript and VBScript will allow direct access to the individual object types, making the programming chores much easier.

Whether you take the road to inheritance or use the flat API approach, it is useful to view the API in object-oriented terms. In that view, all objects in the hierarchy are node objects. The base objects implemented by the DOM are:

- Document

- Node

- NodeList

- NamedNodeMap

Each of these objects exposes attributes (properties) and functions (methods) that allow you to get information about an element, navigate the node tree, modify values and structures of objects, and so on.

Another useful way of looking at the DOM is by viewing its structure model. Again, child nodes are indented. Nodes without child nodes are listed on a single line.

```
Document
    Element (only one allowed), ProcessingInstruction,
    Comment, DocumentType
DocumentFragment
    Element, ProcessingInstruction, Comment, Text,
    CDATASection, EntityReference
DocumentType
EntityReference
    Element, ProcessingInstruction, Comment, Text,
    CDATASection, EntityReference
Element
    Element, Text, Comment, ProcessingInstruction,
    CDATASection, EntityReference
Attr
    Text, EntityReference
ProcessingInstruction
Comment
Text
CDATASection
Entity
    Element, ProcessingInstruction, Comment, Text
    CDATASection, EntityReference
Notation
```

The first node represents the top-level Document object. In other words, it designates the entire HTML or XML document. The Document node can contain one, and only one, element. The Document object may also contain a Processing Instruction (PI), comment, and a reference to its document type. The next node type, Document-Fragment, is a special case of the document object that allows you to temporarily save portions of the document tree. You might find this useful when performing a cut-and-paste, for example.

As you may recall, XML entity declarations allow you to associate a name with a content fragment in the document. The fragment can either be text within the document, part of a document type declaration, or a reference to an external file. Entities, which are represented by the Entity object in the Core DOM, are often used to break up larger documents into workable chunks. Note that Entity does not model the entity's declaration; it represents the entity itself. However, you can use the DocumentType object to access a list of entities within that document. When you want to, say, insert an entity within a document, you can access a reference to it using EntityReference.

Elements, the building blocks of XML, are supported by the Element object. Elements may contain another element, text, a comment, processing instruction, an entity reference, and CDATA. Attributes are supported by the Attr object and may contain either text or an entity reference. Comments and text, which are both leaf nodes, are supported by their respective objects. Processing instructions, which are used to supply applications with data, are supported by the Processing-Instruction object. Finally, the Notation object allows you to access notations, which are used to identify external binary data.

5.1.1   *The Document Interface*

The first object, Document, represents your XML document. Since it is the root of the document tree, Document is the primary means for accessing your source document. The Document object contains three attributes: `doctype`, `documentElement`, and `implementation`. The `doctype` attribute returns the document type declaration (`<!DOCTYPE>`) from your document. If no `<!DOCTYPE>` declaration is given, this value returns null. Also, `doctype` is a read-only value, so you can't use it to edit the document type declaration. The `documentElement` attribute allows you to access the root element of your document, which is the same element that was specified in the DOCTYPE declaration. Finally, the implementation attribute returns the `DOMImplementation` object that handles this document.

Strangely, the DOM does not define a standard method for loading an existing document object, nor does it provide a method for creating a new document object. Therefore, the first step in accessing the DOM will depend on the tool you are using. For example, DOM support is built into the MSXML parser found in Internet Explorer 5. To create a new Document object for IE5, you would write:

```
var docObject = CreateObject("Microsoft.XMLDOM");
```

Internet Explorer 4 provides some support for XML and the DOM. However, due to its early support prior to the finalization of XML and DOM standards, the syntax and behavior differ from IE5. (The examples presented here illustrate the new IE5 syntax.) In its latest incarnation in IE5, MSXML also provides several parameters that allow you to control multithreading. We will examine those features in the next chapter.

Microsoft provides two means for loading an existing document: `loadXML` and `load`. The `loadXML` method allows you to load an XML stream as a single string. This would be useful when the stream is dynamically generated and assigned to a variable:

```
docObject.loadXML("<customer>
    <first_name>Joe</first_name>
    <last_name>Smith</last_name></customer>")
```

Alternatively, you can load an existing document from a URL using the `load` method as follows:

```
docObject.load("http://xmlfiles/reports.xml");
```

Of course, this code is specific to MSXML. The means for accessing a Document object using other implementations will vary.

No matter which processor you use, once you have loaded the document, you should be able to access its root by querying the `documentElement` property. After you have a reference to that root object, you can begin creating any other objects you wish. You do this using any of the DOM methods, called factory methods, listed in Table 5-1. Specifically, these methods allow you to create new elements, text nodes, comments, processing instructions, CDATA sections, and entity references.

Table 5-1   Factory methods for the Document object

Method	Description
createElement	Takes the name of the element you want to create and returns a new element of the type specified. An exception is raised if the specified name contains an invalid character.
createAttribute	Takes the name of an attribute and returns an attribute object. An element can use the attribute instance by calling the setAttribute method. An exception is raised if the specified name contains an invalid character.
createDocumentFragment	Creates an empty DocumentFragment object.
createTextNode	Takes a string and creates a text node.
createComment	Takes a comment string and returns a comment node.
createCDATASection	Takes a string of data to be used in a CDATA section and returns a CDATA object. An exception is raised if the document is an HTML document and not an XML document.
createProcessingInstruction	Takes a string representing the target portion of a processing instruction and returns a ProcessingInstruction object. An exception occurs if an invalid character is given, or the source document is an HTML document.
createEntityReference	Takes a name and returns an entity reference object. An exception is raised if the name contains an invalid character, or if the source document is an HTML document.
getElementsByTagName	Takes a string that can be used to match elements and returns a NodeList of those elements. The wildcard character ("*") can be used to match all elements.

In practice, using these methods is straightforward. As a first example, lets assume you have loaded an XML document and you have the Document element. Note that the DOM makes no provision for creating a new XML document. To create a new element, you would write:

```
tagName = myElementTypeName;
myElement = Document.createElement(tagName);
```

Now, even though you have created the element, it is not automatically placed in the node tree. To do this, you will have to call one of the Node interface methods, `insertBefore`, `replaceChild`, or `appendChild`. These are listed with the other Node interface methods in Table 5-3. Once the new element has been placed in the tree, you can get its name by retrieving its `nodeName` property, accessing the name of its owner document, and so on. Table 5-2 presents all of the properties you can access for this element.

5.1.2 *Node Interface*

In accessing the document tree, the basic data type is a node type. Whether it is an element, a comment, or a text node, everything inherits properties and methods from this basic type. Thus, the node interface defines attributes that are designed to get and set information about nodes. For example, the `nodeName` attribute allows you to query a node and return its name. `nodeValue` allows you to return its value, and `attributes` provides access to the node's attribute list. You can even query the property of the current node to determine the name of the Document object associated with this node. Table 5-2 summarizes these properties.

Likewise, the methods for the node interface are designed to access and manipulate nodes.

The DOM also specifies two other interfaces, `NodeList` to handle ordered lists of Nodes and `NamedNodeMap` to handle unordered

Table 5-2 Properties accessible through the Node interface

Attribute	Description
nodeName	Returns the name for current node. This value is read only and cannot be set.
nodeValue	Returns the value for current node. This value is read only and cannot be set.
nodeType	Returns an integer value representing the node's type. The integer is assigned to a constant according to the following:

ELEMENT_NODE	= 1
ATTRIBUTE_NODE	= 2
TEXT_NODE	= 3
CDATA_SECTION_NODE	= 4
ENTITY_REFERENCE_NODE	= 5
ENTITY_NODE	= 6
PROCESSING_INSTRUCTION_NODE	= 7
COMMENT_NODE	= 8
DOCUMENT_NODE	= 9
DOCUMENT_TYPE_NODE	= 10
DOCUMENT_FRAGMENT_NODE	= 11
NOTATION_NODE	= 12

Attribute	Description
parentNode	Returns the parent of the current node. All nodes, except Document, DocumentFragment, and Attr, may have a parent. However, if a node has just been created and not yet added to the tree, or if it has been removed from the tree, this is null.
childNodes	Returns a NodeList containing all children of the current node. If there are no children, this is a NodeList containing no nodes. The content of the returned NodeList is "live" in the sense that, for instance, changes to the children of the node object that it was created from are immediately reflected in the nodes returned by NodeList; it is not a static snapshot of the content of the node. This is true for every NodeList, including the ones returned by the getElementsByTagName method.

Table 5-2 Continued

Attribute	Description
firstChild	Returns the first child of the current node. A null is returned if there is no child node.
lastChild	Returns the last child of the current node. A null is returned if there is no child node.
previousSibling	Returns the node immediately preceding the current node, or null if none exists.
nextSibling	Returns the node immediately following the current node, or null if none exists.
attributes	Returns a NamedNodeMap containing the attributes of the current node.
ownerDocument	Returns the Document object associated with the current node.

sets of nodes based on their name attribute. The `NodeList` interface describes an indexed array whose elements contain node objects. `NodeList` has just one property, `length`, which returns the length of the array. `NodeList` is a zero-based array, meaning that the index values begin at 0 and the last index value is the number of nodes minus 1. The only method `NodeList` supports is `item`, which takes an index value pointing to an element in the list and returns that element.

The other interface, `NamedNodeMap`, acts like an associative array, or a C `struct`. `NamedNodeMap` includes the `item` method that returns the node at a specified position. This method also contains a length attribute that indicates the number of nodes in the collection. `NamedNodeMap`'s four methods are shown in Table 5-4.

An interesting feature of the DOM is that `NodeLists` and `NamedNodeMaps` are defined to be "live." This means that whenever you change the structure of your document, the changes will be

Table 5-3   Methods for the Node object

Method	*Description*
insertBefore	Takes the name of a new node and a reference to an existing child node in the document tree and inserts the new node. If the reference is excluded, the new node is added to the end of the Node list.
	If the new child is a DocumentFragment object, all of its children are inserted in the same order before the reference. If the new child is already in the tree, it is first removed.
replaceChild	Takes the name of an existing child and replaces it with the newly specified child node. If the new child is already in the tree, it is first removed. The value returned is the node that was replaced.
removeChild	Takes the name of a child node and removes it from the Node list. Returns the name of the node to be removed.
appendChild	Takes the name of a new child node and adds it to the end of the node's list of child nodes. The new child is removed from its previous position if it was already in the tree. If the operation was successful, the new node is returned.
hasChildNodes	Checks the current node for the existence of child nodes and returns a Boolean value depending on whether the operation succeeded (True) or failed (False). This interface takes no parameters.
cloneNode	Clones (or copies) the current node and returns the copy. cloneNode takes a single Boolean value as a parameter: If set to True, it clones the entire subtree; otherwise, just the current Node is returned. Cloning an element copies all attributes and their values. However, text is not copied since it is stored as a child text node. Other Node types are simply returned.

Table 5-4   Methods for the NamedNodeMap object

Method	*Description*
getNamedItem	Takes a string identifying a node name and returns that node.
setNamedItem	Takes the name of a node and adds it to the node collection. If the node name already exists, it is replaced, thus overwriting the node. In this case, the replaced node is returned. Otherwise, a null value is returned. Also, if the node is an attribute that already exists, an exception is raised.
removeNamedItem	Takes the name of a node and removes it from the collection. If successful, the node is returned.
item	Takes an index value and returns the node at that position.

automatically reflected in your `NodeLists` and `NamedNodeMaps`. If this weren't the case, you would have to "refresh" these each time a change was made.

5.2 | Direct Interfaces

The object-oriented hierarchy presented above will be of primary interest to Web developers, particularly those working in scripting languages such as JavaScript (ECMAScript), or VBScript. However, the Core DOM also defines an alternative set of interfaces that can be accessed directly as a Node. In other words, you do not have to work through an object-oriented hierarchy. This approach will be of more interest to Web application developers and software developers working in third-generation programming languages like Java and C++.

Thus, if you are a script developer, you can skip ahead to the next chapter. If you are a Java or C++ developer, read on.

Why maintain two sets of interfaces? The reason is that while the object-oriented model is easy to work with and intuitive to understand, it can be costly to implement in terms of performance. So, the DOM provides this alternative set of direct interfaces that allows the performance-conscious C++ or Java programmer to work with an API that doesn't require expensive casting operations, or garbage-collection schemes.

The interfaces are separated into two categories: fundamental and extended. To be considered compliant, browsers must fully implement the fundamental interfaces including those that claim to support just the HTML DOM. The extended interfaces are not required by HTML DOM applications since these interfaces are specific to XML documents.

5.2.1 *Element Interface*

Of all the interfaces, the one you are likely to use most will be the Element interface. Like the other direct interfaces, the Element interface extends the Node interface described above. Most of the methods for this interface allow you to create and remove an element's attributes. This interface includes one property, `tagName`, which represents the element type name of the current element node. For example, consider the following XML structure:

```
<contact recordNum="2345">
    <name>Joe Butler</name>
    <address> ... </address>
    ...
</contact>
```

Assuming the `<contact>` element has been instantiated, the `tagName` property holds the value "`contact`." From there, you can use the methods in Table 5-5 to access the element's attributes.

Table 5-5   Methods for the Element interface

Method	Description
getAttribute	Takes a string identifying an attribute and returns its value.
setAttribute	Takes an attribute name and string containing its value and sets the attribute.
removeAttribute	Removes the specified attribute.
getAttributeNode	Retrieves the specified attribute node.
setAttributeNode	Takes an attribute node as a parameter and adds the node to the attribute list. If the new attribute replaces an existing one, the replaced attribute is returned. Otherwise, a null is returned.
removeAttributeNode	Removes the specified attribute node.
getElementsByTagName	Takes the element type name of an element and returns a NodeList of that element's subtree.
normalize	Strips leading and trailing white space for all text nodes in the DOM tree.

5.2.2   *The Attr Interface*

From the DOM's perspective, attributes are properties of elements. Thus, they are only allowed to be descendants of element nodes. And because attributes have no hierarchy, you cannot use Node attributes such as `parentNode`, `previousSibling`, and `nextSibling`. This means that from the application developer's perspective, the interface is quite simple. The `Attr` interface contains just two properties.

The first property, `name`, contains the current attribute's name.

A second property, `specified`, is a read-only property that contains a Boolean value. This property is true if a value was assigned in the source document. However, if the attribute was not assigned in the document this attribute is false, even when there is a default value declared in the DTD. Further, if the value is #IMPLIED in the DTD, the attribute does not appear in the structure model of the document.

The possible values for the attribute are usually defined in the DTD. The actual value is determined based on a set of rules. First, if the attribute has been assigned a value (such as in the source document), that value is the attribute's effective value. If no assignment has been made, then the DTD is checked for a default value. If no default value was declared in the DTD (or there is no DTD), then the attribute does not exist and must first be created.

5.2.3   The CharacterData Interface

This interface provides properties and methods that let you access and process character data. `CharacterData` provides two properties: The `data` property which stores the character data for the current node, and `length`, which returns the number of characters in the `data` property. Table 5-6 introduces methods for this interface.

Finally, none of the objects in object-oriented interface correspond exactly to this interface. However, some of the objects inherit properties and methods from `CharacterData`.

5.2.4   Text Interface

The Text interface provides access to the character data content of an element or an attribute value. The only method for this interface is `splitText`, which allows you to split a Text node into two separate nodes. The `splitText` method is summarized in Table 5-7.

Table 5-6   Methods for the CharacterData interface

Method	*Description*
substringData	Takes two parameters and returns a substring. The parameters are: offset—defines where to start in the string starting from 0. count—the number of characters to extract.
appendData	Takes a string parameter and appends it to the string in the data property. There is no return value.
insertData	Takes a string and an offset as arguments and inserts the string into the data property at that point.
deleteData	Using the string in the data property, this method goes to the specified offset in the string and removes the specified number of characters.
replaceData	Using the string in the data property, replaces the characters at the specified offset with a new string. Takes three arguments: offset—defines the starting position in the string. count—number of characters to replace. arg—the replacement string.

Table 5-7   Methods for the Text interface

Method	*Description*
splitText	Takes an offset value defining a position in the text of the current node and moves everything following the offset position into a sibling node. The newly created text node is returned.

5.2.5   *Extended Interfaces*

The previous interfaces, called fundamental interfaces, are common to both HTML and XML. However, HTML knows nothing of CDATA sections, entities and entity references. Therefore, the following extended interfaces are specific to XML.

5.2.5.1   The CDATASection Interface

The CDATASection interface inherits the CharacterData interface by way of the Text interface. You can access the content of the CDATA section through the DOMString attribute of the Text node. Working with CDATA sections can prove to be quite tricky, because DOMString may contain characters that need to be escaped outside of the CDATA sections. In some cases, it may not be possible to write out certain characters (for example, Kanji) as part of a CDATA section.

5.2.5.2   The DocumentType Interface

Currently, the DocumentType interface uses information provided in the DOCTYPE declaration of the source document and the associated DTD to provide an interface to the entities and notations defined for that document. DocumentType has three properties. The name property is the name of the DTD as specified in the DOCTYPE declaration of the source document. If there is no DOCTYPE declaration or DTD, the name property is set to a null value. The entities property is a NamedNodeMap containing all general entities as defined in the DTD, and the notations attribute is another NamedNodeMap containing the notations as declared in the DTD. The DOM does not allow the editing of entities or notations, so these are read-only values.

5.2.5.3   The Notation Interface

Notations are used to declare the format for unparsed entities and processing instruction targets. The Notation interface provides two properties that allow you to get the system (systemID) and public (publicID) identifiers of a notation. These are read-only properties. In addition, there is also a `nodeName` property, inherited from Node, that contains the declared name of the notation.

5.2.5.4   The Entity and EntityReference Interface

The Entity interface models a parsed or unparsed entity. Like the notation interface, it inherits the `nodeName` property from the Node interface and contains the name of the entity. The interface currently supports three properties: `publicId`, `systemId`, and `notationName`. Depending on your XML processor, entities may or may not be expanded as they are passed to the DOM. Whether or not your processor completely expands external entity references, character references and references to predefined entities are always expanded by the processor. If you plan to use references to external entities, you will need to consult the documentation to your specific processor for details.

5.2.5.5   The ProcessingInstruction Interface

In general, processing instructions are used to maintain processor-specific information in the text of the document. Examples of processing instructions include the `<?xml …?>` declaration at the top of most XML documents, and the `<?xml-stylesheet … ?>` instruction that informs the processor of external style sheets. This final interface, ProcessingInstruction allows you to access these processing instruction nodes. This interface contains just two attributes, `target` and `data`. The target attribute relates to the processing instruction's target. According to the XML specification, this is the first token following the processing instruction's opening delimiter. The `data` attribute refers to the content of the processing instruction.

5.3 | Conclusion

While HTML 4.0 allows you to embed scripts in a document, it does not define how scripts should manipulate the document's content, structure, and style. The DOM provides a standard API that allows you to write programs that work across modern browser and development platforms. More importantly, the DOM allows you to write scripts and applications to process customized document types in a language-neutral and platform-independent manner. Indeed, much of XML's power is directly related to the DOM.

In the following chapters, we will learn how to exploit the DOM to access XML elements and document structure in order to create some rather interesting applications. As your read on, you will want to refer back to this chapter frequently. To that end I say, "See you again!"

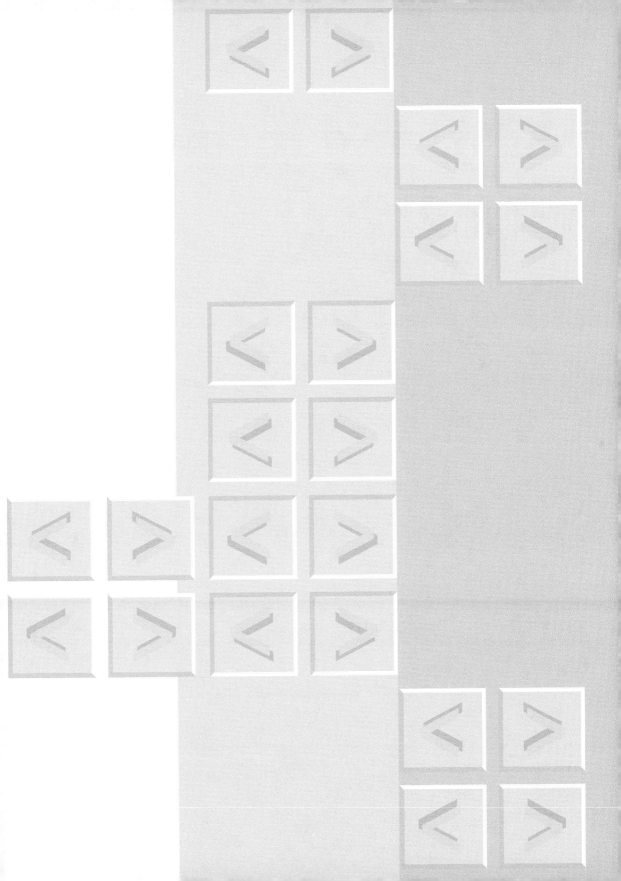

XML and Internet Explorer

A s XML technology matures, there are two approaches that are proving key to its deployment. The first approach processes XML on the server. In this scenario, XML data can be stored in a backend repository or database and processed completely on the server. At this point, XSLT can be applied to the XML data set, which transforms the XML to HTML for delivery on the client.

The second approach is similar in that it starts with XML data stored in a back-end repository. However, rather than processing the XML data on the server, it is delivered via HTTP as an XML stream. Once delivered to the client's desktop, an XML-enabled browser can take that stream and manipulate it using the Document Object Model (DOM). Agents will also support the ability to generate XML updates, which can be sent in both directions to inform clients of changes made to data on the middle tier or database server and vice versa. Consequently, the agents will be able to receive updates from the client and send them to a storage server. This second approach has the advantage that it offloads processing to the client.

This chapter focuses on how XML can be processed once it reaches the client browser. Because it is the first commercial browser to truly support XML and its related standards, we focus on Internet Explorer. However, keep in mind Netscape's Navigator is expected to support XML and related technologies in the near future.

6.1 | XML in Internet Explorer

Microsoft has been a long time proponent of XML. Indeed, Microsoft's Jean Paoli is one of the editors of the XML 1.0 specification and is reported to be the evangelizing force behind the scenes at the Redmond-based company. Thus, it is of little surprise that Internet Explorer 5 includes a fully validating XML parser, full DOM support, and a built-in XSL engine. This, combined with its many other features, means that you can begin experimenting with XML immediately.

Under the hood, Internet Explorer implements an XML-based storage methodology to save user data. This "UserData" can be used as a replacement for cookies, which means you can now overcome the 4K limit that cookies impose. Internet Explorer 5 also sports numerous other features including a new event model, dynamic properties, CSS behaviors, fast table layout, a new file extension (.hta) for HTML applications, and much more.

For Web developers, Internet Explorer 5 allows you to include XML directly in your HTML documents. Internet Explorer also supports direct browsing of native XML. This means that users can view XML within a document using style sheets. Currently, the only style sheet language supported for presentation is Cascading Style Sheets (CSS). While Microsoft claims support of XSL, the browser only supports a subset of XSL Transforms as described the XSL Working Draft, dated December 18, 1998. Namely, IE5 supports template rules and the pattern syntax described in Chapter 3 of this book.

Of course, Internet Explorer supports the Document Object Model and XML namespaces. The browser also supports other proposed standards supported by Microsoft, but not yet adopted. These include XML Schema, which proposes an XML syntax for DTDs and the addition of data types to the language.

Another feature Microsoft adds is an XML Data Source Object (DSO). In general, DSO's are ActiveX controls that link an object to a data source, usually providing a live connection. For the XML DSO, that means your Web pages can update themselves as new XML data streams arrive.

In addition, the browser includes support for Microsoft's Channel Definition Format (CDF), an XML vocabulary that allows you to describe push channels for your Web site. However, the browser doesn't stop there. You can combine CDF features with Open Software Description (OSD) to describe software components that your users can automatically download and install on the fly. In fact, Internet Explorer provides tremendous XML support, both under the hood and to the developer. So, without further ado, let's take a look.

6.1.1 *Inline XML*

A very simple way to get started with XML in IE5 is to include XML markup directly in your HTML documents. Microsoft calls this "inline XML." You can add inline XML to your HTML documents in one of two ways. The first approach defines a `script` element and makes use of the language attribute:

```
<script language=XML>
  <?xml version="1.0" ?>

  <!-- A typical record from a contact database -->
  <contact name="Joe Butler">
    <phone>123-456-7890</phone>
    <email>joe@somedomain.com</email>
  </contact>
</script>
```

One potential problem with this approach is that some users turn off scripting for security reasons. Thus, Internet Explorer defines an <XML> element that allows you to get around this problem. Using the <XML> element, the preceding example could be rewritten as follows:

```
<XML>
    <?xml version="1.0" ?>

    <!-- A typical record from a contact database -->
    <contact name="Joe Butler">
        <phone>123-456-7890</phone>
        <email>joe@somedomain.com</email>
    </contact>
</XML>
```

Microsoft calls these inline sections in your HTML code "XML data islands." Defining a data island by either method exposes your XML to the Document Object Model, meaning that you can then access elements programmatically.

Setting the Record Straight on Terminology

The term "inline" is a carryover from programming languages where you can insert or embed code written in one programming language (typically, assembly language) into a program written in another language (most often, C or C++).

Microsoft uses the term "data island" to refer to XML that is embedded in an HTML document. Since the <XML> element allows you to read in XML from an external source (such as a file), a data island may or may not consist of inline XML.

The XML element also accepts an ID attribute, which allows you to assign a name to your data island and access it through scripting. For example, to assign the name contactDB to our previous example, we could write:

```
<XML ID=contactDB>
```

Note that the ID attribute does not require quotes for the attribute value because the tag is HTML, not XML.

You can also read XML from an external file using the SRC attribute. The file can either be a path to a local file or a URL pointing to an external server. In that case, the XML could be a static document, or it could be generated dynamically and streamed down to the browser. Either way, here is how you would include it:

```
<XML ID=contactDB
SRC="http://www.beyondhtml.com/contact.cgi?search=B">
```

6.1.2   *XML Data Source Objects*

As previously mentioned, Data Source Objects, or DSOs, are ActiveX controls that provide a connection between an object and a data source. The purpose is to provide an easy way to populate forms, fields, tables, edit controls, and so on with data. In most cases, DSOs have the ability to update themselves dynamically. Therefore, users have the experience of a live data connection.

Microsoft's XML DSO allows you to bind XML from data islands with HTML presentation elements. For example, you can populate an HTML table with data from an XML stream. That means your Web pages can update themselves as new XML data streams arrive. To see how this works, consider the following HTML document containing an XML data island:

```
<HTML>
   <HEAD>
      <TITLE>Data Source Object Example 1</TITLE>
   </HEAD>
   <BODY>
      <XML ID="contactDB">
         <?xml version="1.0" ?>
         <contacts>
            <contact>
               <name>Joe Butler</name>
               <phone>123-456-7890</phone>
               <email>joe@somedomain.com</email>
```

```
            </contact>
            <contact>
                <name>Joe Butler</name>
                <phone>987-654-3210</phone>
                <email>bbutler@somedomain.com</email>
            </contact>
        </contacts>
    </XML>

<TABLE datasrc="#contactDB">
<tr>
    <td><div datafld="name"></div></td>
    <td><div datafld="phone"></div></td>
    <td><div datafld="email"></div></td>
</tr>
</TABLE>

    </BODY>
</HTML>
```

The key part of this listing is in the <TABLE> element. First, the table element assigns the name of our data island to the datasrc attribute. This is the same name that was defined in the ID attribute for the <XML> element. Note here that the name of the data island is preceded by the pound sign (#). Next, we create a DIV element within each cell of the table. We use DIV so that we can assign an arbitrary value to an attribute. The XML DSO recognizes the datafld attribute, checks its value, then populates the cell with its associated value.

The DSO also formats additional rows automatically. In other words, we do not have to know how many rows to create in our HTML table. Much like XSL's for-each construct, Internet Explorer iterates through each <contact> instance, automatically creates the additional rows, and populates each cell as we've specified in the <TABLE> element. That saves us from having to script such a feature.

Finally, the XML DSO automatically creates a field called $Text, which contains the fields in the current record. The fields are concatenated together. With that in mind, we could dump all of the fields into a table using the following code:

```
<HTML>
   <HEAD>
      <TITLE>Data Source Object Example 2</TITLE>
   </HEAD>
   <BODY>
      <XML ID="contactDB">
         <?xml version="1.0" ?>
       <contacts>
        <contact>
           <name>Joe Butler</name>
           <phone>123-456-7890</phone>
           <email>joe@somedomain.com</email>
        </contact>
        <contact>
           <name>Joe Butler</name>
           <phone>987-654-3210</phone>
           <email>bbutler@somedomain.com</email>
        </contact>
       </contacts>
      </XML>

   <TABLE datasrc="#contactDB">
   <tr>
       <td><div datafld="$Text"></div></td>
   </tr>
   </TABLE>

   </BODY>
</HTML>
```

This example is the same as the previous example, with the exception that it displays all of the fields from each record instead of just name, phone, and email.

6.1.2.1 Instantiating the XML DSO

The XML DSO is an ActiveX control. As such, it is like any component that can be inserted into a Web page. According to the HTML specification, you can insert any object into a Web page using the <OBJECT> element. For the XML DSO, use the following code:

```
<OBJECT width=0 height=0
    classid="clsid:550dda30-0541-11d2-9ca9-0060b0ec3d39"
    id="xmldso">
</OBJECT>
```

The `classid` attribute contains a namespace that explicitly identifies the XML DSO. The `id` attribute acts as an alias, allowing us to refer to this object by a much shorter name.

The next step is to bind the DSO to your XML. The following JScript code loads our XML document and exposes its elements through the DOM API:

```
<SCRIPT for=window event=onload>
    var sourceDoc = xmldso.XMLDocument;
    sourceDoc.load("contactdb.xml");
    if (sourceDoc.documentNode == null)
    {
        // Place error handling routine here
    }
</SCRIPT>
```

Microsoft has also extended the object element type to accept in-line XML. The following example instantiates the XML DSO, embeds a contact record, and loads it through a script:

```
<HTML>
  <HEAD>
    <TITLE>Data Source Object Example</TITLE>
    <OBJECT width=0 height=0
     classid="clsid:550dda30-0541-11d2-9ca9-0060b0ec3d39"
     id="xmldso">
     <contacts>
     <contact>
       <name>Joe Butler</name>
       <phone>123-456-7890</phone>
       <email>joe@somedomain.com</email>
     </contact>
     </contacts>
    </OBJECT>
  </HEAD>
  <BODY>
```

```
<SCRIPT for=window event=onload>
    var sourceDoc = xmldso.XMLDocument;
    sourceDoc.load(xmldso.altHtml);
    if (sourceDoc.documentNode == null)
    {
        // Place error handling routine here
    }
</SCRIPT>
</BODY>
</HTML>
```

6.1.2.2 Paging Through Data

With larger sets of data, you will likely want to limit the number of records displayed at any given time. Otherwise, your visitors will have to scroll through very long lists to get to a particular record. You can do this easily by setting the DATAPAGESIZE attribute in the <TABLE> element:

```
<TABLE datasrc=#contactDB DATAPAGESIZE="8">
    <!-- table code here -->
</TABLE>
```

Since your application won't be displaying all of the data at once, you will need a way to page through your data. The XML DSO provides four methods that allow you to page through data sets: nextPage, previousPage, firstPage, and lastPage. The following code puts everything together into a single example:

```
<HTML>
  <HEAD>
    <TITLE>Data Source Object Example</TITLE>
    <OBJECT width=0 height=0
     classid="clsid:550dda30-0541-11d2-9ca9-0060b0ec3d39"
     id="xmldso">
    </OBJECT>
  </HEAD>
  <BODY>

  <SCRIPT for=window event=onload>
```

```
        var contactDB = xmldso.XMLDocument;
        contactDB.load("contactDB.xml");
        if (contactDB.documentNode == null)
        {
            HandleError(doc);
        }
    </SCRIPT>

    <INPUT TYPE="button" VALUE="First"
            ONCLICK="myTable.firstPage();">
    <INPUT TYPE="button" VALUE="Next"
            ONCLICK="myTable.nextPage();">
    <INPUT TYPE="button" VALUE="Previous"
            ONCLICK="myTable.previousPage();">
    <INPUT TYPE="button" VALUE="Last"
            ONCLICK="myTable.lastPage();">

    <TABLE ID=myTable DATAPAGESIZE=20 datasrc=contactDB>
    <tr>
        <td><div datafld="name"></div></td>
        <td><div datafld="phone"></div></td>
        <td><div datafld="email"></div></td>
    </tr>
    </TABLE>
    </BODY>
</HTML>
```

After initializing the XML DSO and loading it with data, the <BODY> of this Web document sets up four buttons that allow the user to go to the first page of data, advance to the next page, page back, and go to the last page. Each button's ONCLICK property points to a method that navigates to the appropriate page. The methods are prefixed with the name myTable. This is the name given in the ID attribute of the subsequent <TABLE> element.

The <TABLE> element also sets DATAPAGESIZE so that 20 records will be shown in a page view at a time. In addition, the datasrc is set to contactDB. Note that there is no pound sign (#) prefixing the data source name. The reason is that we are not using a data island, but are instead referring to the document contactDB object created in the <SCRIPT> portion of the document. Now, all that's left is to fill the rows with data from contactDB.xml.

6.1.2.3   Assigning Elements to Tables

In assigning elements and attributes to table cells, the XML DSO follows a specific procedure. In general, the XML DSO traverses the tree structure created when parsing your XML document and assigns cells in "document order." The root or document element is never included in the table. The XML DSO uses this procedure for converting the subelements:

1. Each subelement and attribute corresponds to a column in some rowset in the hierarchy.

2. In general, the element type or attribute name is assigned to the name of the column. One exception is when the parent and child nodes have the same name. In this case, the subelement's column name is prefixed with an exclamation point ("!").

3. Each column is either a simple column containing scalar values (usually strings) or a rowset column containing subrowsets.

4. Columns corresponding to attributes are always simple.

5. Columns corresponding to subelements are rowset columns if either the subelement has its own subelements and/or attributes, or the subelement's parent has more than one instance of the subelement as a child. Otherwise the column is simple.

6. When there are multiple instances of a subelement (under different parents), its column is a rowset column if any of the instances imply a rowset column; its column is simple only if all instances imply a simple column.

7. All rowsets have an additional column named $Text.

While the XML DSO was available in Internet Explorer 4, it has been necessarily modified to keep up with changing standards and subsequent support. The problem with change is that your code may break in certain versions of the browser. So, if you plan to support IE4, you will want to set a flag, called JavaDSOCompatible, to true. Setting this flag makes the Internet Explorer 5 XML DSO compatible with the Java DSO supplied with Internet Explorer 4.0. You can set this flag when creating a new instance of the XML DSO. For instance, the <XML> element accepts the flag as an attribute as shown below:

```
<xml id="xmldata" JavaDSOCompatible=true>
   <!-- XML markup goes here -->
</xml>
```

Of course, inline XML was not available in Internet Explorer 4.0. If you don't want to use inline XML, you can instead set the flag when using the <OBJECT> element to instantiate the XML DSO ActiveX control. The following code does just that:

```
<OBJECT width=0 height=0
   classid="clsid:550dda30-0541-11d2-9ca9-0060b0ec3d39"
   id="xmldso">
 <PARAM NAME="JavaDSOCompatible" value="true">
</OBJECT>
```

So far, none of the previous examples assume the existence of a document type definition. When you introduce a DTD, the rules for converting elements and attributes into rows and columns change a bit:

1. Each subelement type and attribute named by the DTD corresponds to a column in some rowset in the hierarchy.

2. The name of the column is the same as the name of the subelement type or attribute, unless the parent element type has an attribute and a subelement with the same name, in which case a "!" is added as a prefix to the subelement's column name.

3. Each column is either a simple column containing scalar values (usually strings), or a rowset column containing subrowsets.

4. Columns corresponding to attributes are always simple.

5. Columns corresponding to subelements are rowset columns if either the DTD allows the subelement to have its own subelements and/or attributes, or the DTD allows the subelement's parent to have more than one instance of the subelement as a child. Otherwise the column is simple.

6. All rowsets have an additional column named `$Text`.

7. Content corresponding to the content model "ANY" is not included in the rowset hierarchy.

6.1.3 *Channel Definition Format*

If you have ever seen the channel bar on the desktop of Windows 98 or in Internet Explorer 5, then you have seen XML in action. The Channel Definition Format (CDF) is an XML vocabulary that is supported directly in both Internet Explorer (4 and 5) and on the Active Desktop of Windows 98. Simply put, the CDF allows you to define push channels for your Web site. Thus, using a very simple markup language, you can create channels that your visitors can subscribe to. As subscribers, your visitors can automatically receive notifications, updates, and navigational information from your Web site on a regularly-scheduled basis. The benefits are that you can create a loyal community of followers that visit your site on a regular basis.

The way it works is that you first create a CDF file describing your channel or channels. The syntax used to describe your channels is based on a simple collection of tags created in XML. Ultimately, this file is placed on your Web site and is updated anytime your site changes. Once posted to your Web site, this file can be read and parsed by Internet Explorer and the results displayed in Internet Explorer's Channel Bar. To subscribe to a channel, a button is placed on your Home Page informing your visitors that an Active Channel is available. When the user selects the button, a script (that you write) checks the client's browser to ensure IE 4.0 or greater is running. Assuming this test passes, the browser installs the channel in the channel bar and a red "gleam" appears over the channel. This gleam indicates that there's new content at the site.

There are three different types of channels you can create: notification, sitemap, and offline content caching. A Notification channel simply notifies the client when new content is made available. The user also has the choice of having email sent when new content is posted. The second type of channel, sitemap, allows you to send information about a hierarchy of related pages. This can be used for navigation within the Channel bar, itself. For example, you could combine a notification with a sitemap to notify clients of new content and offer a preview of what's waiting at the site. Finally, clients can opt to download all new content as it is posted by selecting offline content.

The CDF allows you to schedule updates of your content to client machines while minimizing loads on the server. Another feature allows you to collect page-hit information from offline users just as you currently do with online visitors. As the client views the offline pages, a local log file is created. That log file is uploaded to a specified directory on your server the next time the client updates the channel. There's also a mechanism to password-protect channels, and you can personalize channels using cookies. You can also create HTML pages that can be used as a screen saver, which can then be associated with specific channels. Finally, there is additional support in the CDF for Active Desktop, but that's beyond the scope of this book.

6.1.3.1   The XML Channel

To show how you can develop your own channels, let's create a channel called the XML channel. Within this channel, we can create three subchannels to cover XML, XSL, and DTDs. Keep in mind that each subchannel can contain one or more related stories.

In creating any channel, you must first decide which type of channel you want to create. To make it interesting, the XML channel will include both a notification and a sitemap. Because the notification will display a miniature site map, or structure, of the updated content, the next step is to design the structure for the channel. In our case, the structure consists of a top level channel, "The XML Channel," three subchannels, and potential instances for each subchannel. As a general rule of thumb, you should limit the number of items (or subchannels) within a channel to roughly eight. Any more than eight items tends to take over the Channel Bar and can potentially overwhelm your viewers.

You should also take bandwidth into consideration when designing your channel. This is especially important when the subscriber is caching content for offline use. In general, you should limit the amount of content to be downloaded to about one-half Megabyte per channel. Keep in mind that .5 Megabyte will take at least six minutes to download over a 28.8K connection. You should also make sure that all resources necessary for viewing the content are delivered. You don't want to force the client to log on to access images for offline viewing.

Once these considerations have been dealt with, you are ready to create your CDF file. Within this file, you create a new channel using the `<Channel>` element, and individual items can be generated using `<Item>` elements, like so:

```
<Channel>
    <Item></Item>
    <Item></Item>
    <Item></Item>
</Channel>
```

The `<Channel>` element has five attributes: `Base`, `HREF`, `LastMod`, `Level`, and `Precache`. `Base` defines a base URL which is used to resolve relative URLs. `HREF` tells the browser where to go when a channel is activated. `LastMod` specifies the date and time the channel was last modified. `Precache` sets a Boolean value that determines whether content should be downloaded and cached. If `Precache` is set to "yes," you can use `Level` to limit the number of levels at which the site should be crawled.

The `<Item>` element also defines attributes for `HREF`, `LastMod`, `Level`, and `Precache`. Table 6-1 provides a summary of the CDF element types.

Table 6-1   Element types included in the Channel Definition Format vocabulary

Character	*Description*
?xml	XML declaration indicating the version of XML supported and the character set.
A	Your basic anchor element, which defines a hypertext link. The URL specified in HREF will be displayed in the browser channel pane if the TITLE element is not present.
Abstract	Used to provide description of your channel, which is displayed in a ToolTip.
Channel	Defines a Channel or subchannel.
EarliestTime	Species the first date and time that an update can occur.
HTTP-EQUIV	Used with the <u>LOGTARGET</u> element to indicate that an HTTP header parameter should be added.
IntervalTime	Determines the update interval, or the number of updates to occur within the range of times specified by <u>EarliestTime</u> and <u>LatestTime</u>.
Item	Defines an item in a channel, usually a Web page.
LatestTime	Defines the last date and time an update can occur.
Log	Indicates the URL of the parent ITEM element to be recorded in the page-hit log file.
Login	Used to set up user authentication.
Logo	Specifies the URL of the logo to be displayed for Channel or Item element.

Table 6-1 Continued

Character	Description
LogTarget	Indicates where to upload the CDF client page-hit log file.
PurgeTime	Used to set the earliest date that page hits will be recorded. Page hits older than the time specified in this element are not reported in the log file.
Schedule	Used to schedule updates.
Title	Test string displayed in the Channel Bar for a channel or item.
Usage	Specifies that an item can be used as a channel, email, a desktop component, screen saver, or software update.

The following example .cdf file uses the elements from Table 6-1 to implement our channel:

```
<?XML version="1.0"?>
<!--
    CDF for The XML Channel
    Michael Floyd (c), 1999

    To run this sample channel, change the URLs to match
    your system and post this file in the cdf Directory.
-->

<CHANNEL HREF="http://www.beyondhtml.com/cdf/index.html"
    BASE="http://www. beyondhtml.com/cdf/">
    <TITLE>The XML Channel</TITLE>
    <ABSTRACT>This channel broadcasts the latest XML
        news and articles from BeyondHTML.com.
    </ABSTRACT>
    <LOGO HREF="logo_big.gif" STYLE="IMAGE-WIDE"/>
    <LOGO HREF="logo_med.gif" STYLE="IMAGE"/>
    <SCHEDULE EndDate="1999-12-31" StartDate="1999-10-01">
            <INTERVALTIME DAY="30" />
    </SCHEDULE>
    <ITEM HREF="workbench.html">
```

```
        <LOGO HREF="gifs/xml3.gif" STYLE="ICON"/>
        <TITLE>Build Your XML Workbench</TITLE>
        <ABSTRACT>
            Create UI widgets with Java Studio
        </ABSTRACT>
    </ITEM>
    <ITEM HREF="xsl.html">
        <LOGO HREF="gifs/xsl3.gif" STYLE="ICON"/>
        <TITLE>Patterns in XSLT</TITLE>
        <ABSTRACT>
            Learn to use XSL Patterns to walk the
            document tree.
        </ABSTRACT>
    </ITEM>
    <ITEM HREF="beyond.html">
        <LOGO HREF="beyond3.gif" STYLE="ICON"/>
        <TITLE>Vocabularies Abound</TITLE>
        <ABSTRACT>
            New XML vocabularies are changing the way we
            use the Web.
        </ABSTRACT>
    </ITEM>
</CHANNEL>
```

Our channel definition starts by specifying the start page for the channel using HREF and the root directory (Base). This is also the directory where your .cdf file should be posted. The text within the <Title> element designates the name of the channel, which is displayed in the Channel Bar. <Title> also takes an attribute, XML-Space, which allows you to control the formatting of the text string. By default, XML-Space is set to "Default", which means in our example that white-space characters such as tabs, spaces and newline characters can be ignored. Setting XML-Space to "Preserve" maintains all white-space characters. The <Abstract> text is displayed as a ToolTip whenever a user holds the mouse over the title. The <Abstract> element also makes use of the XML-Space attribute.

The Logo element specifies one of three logos that are used. You use the Style attribute to specify an Icon, Image, or Image-Wide logo. Image logos are displayed in the Channel Bar next to the channel's title. The image size for this logo must be 32 (H) × 194 (W). In addition, a 16 × 16 Icon image can be displayed next to individual items within the channel. The third image style, `Image-Wide`, is used for logos displayed on the Active Desktop. The `Image` and `Image-Wide` styles are used within the definition of the channel and must occur before any `<Item>`s. The Icon style should be used with `<Item>` elements. Most standard graphics formats including GIF and JPEG are supported. Whatever the style type, an `HREF` attribute specifies the location of the image file. Also, a relative URL can be used, so long as a base URL was given in the `<Channel>` element.

Finally, you can schedule updates using the `<Schedule>` element. Of course, updating thousands of users simultaneously could cause problems for your server. So, the `<Schedule>` element contains `<Earliest-Time>` and `<LatestTime>` attributes that define a range of times for the update to occur. Internet Explorer generates a random time within this time frame to perform the update. You can use the `TimeZone` attribute to designate an absolute time, which is specified as an offset between local time and Universal Time Coordinated (UTC). If no `TimeZone` is given, the client machine's local time is used. Likewise, `StartDate` and `EndDate` attributes can be used to define the dates on which an update can occur. In most cases, `EndDate` should be used sparingly: While it is useful for content with a short shelf life, you could unwittingly prevent some readers from getting updates if they haven't logged on for a while. Finally, you can set the interval at which updates occur using the `IntervalTime` attribute. Our example sets the time frame to between October 1 and December 31, with an update scheduled every 30 days.

The final step is to create the subchannels using the `<Item>` element. In this example, we specify the HTML page to navigate to, a title, abstract, and icon image for the Channel Bar.

6.1.3.2   Implementing Your Channel

The CDF file is only one of several files you'll need to create. You'll need a start page for your channel. This is where your visitors will be taken when they click on the main channel. And of course, you'll also need to create the content pages that your visitors will navigate to. Finally, you'll need to create the logo images for each channel and subchannel you've defined. Post the start page in the file designated by the `<Channel>` element's HREF attribute and the .cdf in the top-level directory as defined by the Base attribute. The other pages and images should be placed in their appropriate directories as specified in the .cdf file.

Next, you need to notify your site visitors that an active channel is available and provide the mechanism for them to subscribe. Microsoft suggests that you use its "Add Active Channel" button to provide a common interface among all Active Channel-enabled Web sites. The button contains some useful code that performs browser detection and if the browser doesn't support Active Channels, points visitors to the latest version of Internet Explorer. To use this button, though, you must become a SiteBuilder Network member (Level One is free) and fill out an agreement.

You can alternatively create a basic button that performs the browser detection and bails out if Active Channels are not supported.

6.1.4   *Open Software Description*

OSD, or Open Software Description, is an XML vocabulary that allows you to describe software components. A software component could be an ActiveX control, a Java bean, or a full-fledged application. OSD follows a classic publish and subscribe model, where the publisher sends out notifications and subscribers respond to these notifications. Using OSD, you can describe how to install ActiveX Controls, Java packages, and Java class files. This allows INF files to be used during the setup process, thus facilitating the ability to install components on the fly.

You can take things a step further by including OSD in your CDF files. This allows you to describe specific software components to be distributed over a channel, providing an effective means for advertising the availability of your software by sending notifications to subscribers. Additionally, OSD is a subset of the Microsoft Internet Component Download (MSICD). That is, you can use the elements defined in the msicd DTD to further describe a software component.

OSD is easy to use and is fully supported by both version 4 and 5 of the Internet Explorer browser. The vocabulary, osd.dtd, defines element types that allow you to describe a component in terms of its version, underlying structure, and its dependence on other components. The basic structure starts with a standard XML document prolog. The `<!DOCTYPE>` declaration identifies the OSD DTD and references the root object, SOFTPKG, as shown here:

```
<?XML version="1.0"?>
<!DOCTYPE SOFTPKG SYSTEM
"http://www.microsoft.com/standards/osd/osd.dtd">
```

You describe your software component as an `<IMPLEMENTATION>` of a `<SOFTPKG>`. There are subelements for describing the platform and operating system your software runs on, where the code base can be found, dependencies on other components, and for internationalization purposes, the language supported. The basic structure is:

```
<SOFTPKG>
    <IMPLEMENTATION>
        <CODEBASE
          VALUE="http://www.beyondhtml.com/foo.cab"
        />
        <LANGUAGE VALUE="en"/>
        <OS VALUE="Win95"/>
        <PROCESSOR VALUE="x86"/>
    </IMPLEMENTATION>
</SOFTPKG>
```

This example describes a component, which happens to be written in C++, whose cab file can be found on the server at foo.cab. Further, it only supports 80×86 processors, runs on Windows 95, and supports English.

The `<SOFTPKG>` element accepts several attributes. The first, AUTOINSTALL, is only valid within CDF files. Setting AUTOINSTALL="Yes" tells the browser to automatically download the distribution unit. When you install a SOFTPKG, the HREF attribute specifies the URL where the package resides. You can also provide a name of up to 260 characters long for your software component using the NAME attribute, and you can describe a product's version including major, minor, custom, and build version numbers using the VERSION attribute.

You can also set a PRECACHE attribute that tells the browser to download the distribution and leave it in the cache without running the auto-installation program. Like the AUTOINSTALL attribute, this attribute is only recognized in CDF files. In addition, AUTOINSTALL takes precedence over PRECACHE.

Finally, when working in conjunction with CDF files, you can specify how a distribution should be downloaded and installed. Microsoft offers two alternatives. The first approach is to use the Microsoft Internet Component Download (MSICD) to download distribution units. The browser will then look to the OSD file for processing instructions. You can instruct the browser to use MSICD by setting the STYLE attribute to "MSICD". Alternatively, you can instruct the browser invoke Microsoft's "Active Setup" engine to install the package by setting the STYLE attribute to "ActiveSetup".

Table 6-2   Element types included in the Open
Software Description vocabulary

Character	*Description*

Abstract	Used to summarize or describe the parent IMPLEMENTATION or SOFTPKG. In the CDF, Abstract is used to describe of your channel.
	
	`<Abstract>XMLEdit Pro allows you to exit`
	`XML documents</Abstract>`

CODEBASE	Specifies the location of the file or distribution unit to be installed.
	
	`<CODEBASE`
	`    FILENAME="file"`
	`    HREF="url"`
	`    SIZE="n"`
	`    STYLE="ActiveSetup" | "MSICD"`
	`/>`

Table 6-2 Continued

Character	Description
DEPENDENCY	Describes an additional component required by the software distribution SOFTPKG to function correctly. **Usage:** `<DEPENDENCY ACTION="Assert" | "Install">`
DISKSIZE	Not implemented at the time of this writing
IMPLEMENTATION	Defines the configuration required by the current software distribution.
LANGUAGE	Used for international distribution, this element specifies a semicolon-delimited list of RFC1766 language codes. **Usage:** `<LANGUAGE VALUE="language" />`
LICENSE	Currently not implemented, this element will be used to describe the software license associated with the distribution.
MEMSIZE	Not implemented at the time of this writing.
OS	Specifies the operating system the software supports. **Usage:** `<OS VALUE="Mac" | "Win95" | "Winnt" />`

PROCESSOR	Describes which processor(s) the software runs on.
	Usage:
	`<PROCESSOR`
	`VALUE= "Alpha" | "MIPS" | "PPC" | "x86"/>`

SOFTPKG	Root object for describing a software package:
	Usage:
	`<SOFTPKG`
	`    AUTOINSTALL="No" | "Yes"`
	`    HREF="url"`
	`    NAME="string"`
	`    PRECACHE="No" | "Yes"`
	`    STYLE="ActiveSetup" | "MSICD"`
	`    VERSION="a,b,c,d" >`

TITLE	Defines the name used in the title bar when downloading, installing, etc.

Now, let's embellish our previous example a bit. Table 6-2 presents a complete list of the element types we can use. For example, you can add TITLE and ABSTRACT elements to name and summarize the distribution like so:

```
<?XML version="1.0"?>
<!DOCTYPE SOFTPKG SYSTEM
"http://www.microsoft.com/standards/osd/osd.dtd">
<?XML::namespace
href="http://www.microsoft.com/standards/osd/msicd.dtd"
    as="msicd"?>

<SOFTPKG NAME="EditPro" VERSION="1,0,0,0" STYLE="MSICD">
    <TITLE>XML EditPro</TITLE>
    <ABSTRACT>XML EditPro is an ActiveX component that
        works in conjunction with your browser to allow you
        to edit XML files.
    </ABSTRACT>
    <IMPLEMENTATION>
        <CODEBASE
          VALUE="http://www.beyondhtml.com/xmlpro.cab" />
        <LANGUAGE VALUE="en"/>
        <OS VALUE="Win95"/>
        <PROCESSOR VALUE="x86"/>
    </IMPLEMENTATION>
</SOFTPKG>
```

This last example uses MSICD to download the software package. Notice that there is a processing instruction that establishes the msicd namespace. This is a required step. There are also three distinct sections you can use to describe installation instructions for Java code, native code (meaning it runs on a specific platform), and dependency code (one program is used by another). The typical OSD file is arranged like this:

```
<?XML version="1.0"?>
<!DOCTYPE SOFTPKG SYSTEM
"http://www.microsoft.com/standards/osd/osd.dtd">
<?XML::namespace
href="http://www.microsoft.com/standards/osd/msicd.dtd"
    as="msicd"?>
```

```
<SOFTPKG NAME="EditPro"
         VERSION="1,0,0,0"
         STYLE="MSICD">
   <MSICD::JAVA>
      <PACKAGE ...>
         <IMPLEMENTATION>
            <CODEBASE .../>
         </IMPLEMENTATION>
      </PACKAGE>
   </MSICD::JAVA>

   <MSICD::NATIVECODE>
      <CODE ...>
         <IMPLEMENTATION>
            <CODEBASE .../>
         </IMPLEMENTATION>
      </CODE>
   </MSICD::NATIVECODE>

   <DEPENDENCY>
      <SOFTPKG ...>
         <IMPLEMENTATION>
            <CODEBASE ... />
         </IMPLEMENTATION>
      </SOFTPKG>
   </DEPENDENCY>

</SOFTPKG>
```

Of course, you would not include all three sections in the same application.

Finally, it is also important to keep processing order in mind. For example, CODE items under NATIVECODE are processed in the order in which they appear in the OSD file. However, they are installed and registered in the reverse of their appearance in the OSD file. That means you should place dependent files after the CODE items that depend on them being available/installed. Also, packages under JAVA are installed before CODE items under NATIVECODE.

6.2 | DOM Extensions

Chapter 5 provided a thorough introduction to the Document Object Model (DOM) Application Programming Interface (API). This API is designed to provide a standard means for accessing and processing elements of the document tree. Microsoft has extended the DOM API with a few proprietary interfaces.

The first, XMLDOMParseError, allows you to get error information back from the MSXML parser when it parses a document. The way it works is that when you initialize the parser, you have the option of setting a flag, validateOnParse, that enables parser validation. Then, any errors that occur during the parsing process are returned via XML-DOMParseError. The information returned includes the line number and character position where the error occurred, along with a text description describing the error. The next chapter demonstrates how you can use this interface to write your own XML validator.

XMLHttpRequest is a Microsoft extension to the W3C DOM that supports communication with HTTP servers. Table 6-3 summarizes the methods and properties you can use in association with this object.

Table 6-3 Properties and Methods for the XMLHttpRequest object

Property	*Description*
onreadystatechange	Specifies the event handler to be called when the readystate property changes.
readystate	Represents the state of the request.
responseBody	Represents the response entity body as an array of unsigned bytes.
responseStream	Represents the response entity body as an IStream.
responseText	Represents the response entity body as a string.
responseXML	Represents the response entity body as parsed by the MSXML XMLDOM parser.

Table 6-3   Continued

Property	Description
status	Represents the HTTP status code returned by a request.
statusText	Represents the HTTP response line status.

Method	Description
abort	Cancels the current HTTP request.
getAllResponseHeaders	Retrieves the values of all the HTTP headers.
getResponseHeader	Retrieves the value of an HTTP header from the response body.
open	Initializes a Microsoft.XMLHTTP request, and specifies the method, URL, and authentication information for the request.
send	Sends an HTTP request to the server and receives a response.
setRequestHeader	Specifies the name of an HTTP header.

Finally, the XTLRuntime interface implements methods that can be called from XSL style sheets. Additional information on these interfaces can be found at Microsoft's Developer's Network Web site at msdn.microsoft.com/xml.

6.2.1 | *Schemas*

Document Type Definitions, or DTDs, define the structure and order of your element types, as well as the rules for using them. The downside is that DTD syntax differs from and can be more complicated than the XML instance markup we have been using.

6.2.1.1 Structure in Schemas

One of the many things XML Schema proposes is the use of XML to describe the structure and rules for using elements. Thus, schemas define the element types that can appear within a document, what attributes an element may have, whether elements and attributes are required or optional, and the number of occurrences a subelement may have. They also define which element types may be child elements of a particular parent element, the type of content of an element, default values for attributes, and so on. More importantly, you create your schemas directly in XML.

As an example, the following listing is a simple schema that models records in a guestbook database:

```
<?xml version="1.0"?>
<Schema name="guestbookSchema"
        xmlns="schemas-microsoft-com:xml-data">
  <ElementType name="name" />
  <ElementType name="address" />
  <ElementType name="phone" />
  <ElementType name="fax" />
  <ElementType name="email" />

  <ElementType name="guestbook" model="closed">
    <element type="name" />
    <element type="address" />
    <element type="phone" />
    <element type="fax" />
    <element type="email" />

    <AttributeType name="href" />
    <attribute type="href" />
  </ElementType>
</Schema>
```

As you can guess, the `<Schema>` element is the document or root element for the schema definition. The `<Schema>` element takes a name attribute that can be used to name your schema. In addition, `<Schema>` requires the `xml:data` namespace. In this last example, we have made the Schema namespace the default namespace so that the schema definition vocabulary can be used without a cumbersome prefix.

The other steps in creating your schema definition involve declaring and defining the elements and attributes of your schema. You use `<ElementType>` and `<AttributeType>` to define a class of elements. In other words, `<ElementType>` defines the element types your schema uses. In the guestbook example, we define basic element types for name, address, phone, fax, and so on. Now, these basic element types can be used to build new, more complex element types.

To use these element types in another `ElementType` definition, you must identify them within an `<element>`. So returning to the example, the `<guestbook>` element is defined in an `<ElementType>`, and it is made up of `<name>`, `<address>`, `<phone>`, `<fax>`, and `<email>` elements. In addition, `<guestbook>` accepts an `href` attribute.

So far, so good. However, we have not fully specified the content models for these element types, the number of occurrences allowed for a particular element, and so on. In addition, we may want to take advantage of another feature of XML Schemas. Namely, data types. Let's rewrite the previous example:

```
<?xml version="1.0"?>
<Schema name="guestbookSchema"
        xmlns="schemas-microsoft-com:xml-data">
  <ElementType name="name" />
  <ElementType name="address" />
  <ElementType name="phone" />
  <ElementType name="fax" />
  <ElementType name="email" />

  <ElementType name="guestbook"
               content="eltOnly"
               model="open">
    <element type="name"
             [minOccurs="1"]
             [maxOccurs="1"]
    />
    <element type="address" [minOccurs="0"] />
    <element type="phone" [minOccurs="0"] />
```

```
            <element type="fax" [minOccurs="0"] />
            <element type="email"
                    [minOccurs="1"]
                    [maxOccurs="*"]
            />

            <AttributeType name="href" />
            <attribute type="href" />
        </ElementType>
    </Schema>
```

Now our `<guestbook>` element must contain one and only one `<name>` element. The elements for address, phone, and fax are optional as designated by `minOccurs="0"`. Finally, we want to require that the user enter at least one email address. So, `minOccurs` is set to 1. However, the user may want to provide alternative email addresses, so we set `maxOccurs="*"` to indicate an unlimited number of occurrences. Details for using XML Schema elements are included in Table 6-4.

Table 6-4 XML Schema element reference

Character	*Description*

attribute	Creates an attribute for an element as defined in ElementType.
	
	Usage:
	
	``<attribute
	    default="default-value"
	    required="{yes | no}" >```

AttributeType	Specifies an attribute type.
	
	Usage:
	
	``<AttributeType
	    default="default-value"
	    dt:type="primitive-type"
	    dt:values="enumerated-values"
	    name="idref"
	    required="{yes | no}" >```

Table 6-4   Continued

Character	*Description*
datatype	Specifies the data type for either an attribute or an element.

Usage:

```
<datatype
    dt:type="datatype" >
```

description	Used for documentation purposes, this element allows you to add descriptive information to a schema.
element	Declares the use of an element type in a content model.

Usage:

```
<element
    type="element-typename"
    [minOccurs="{0 | 1}"]
    [maxOccurs="{1 | *}"]
    >
```

ElementType	Defines an element type.

Usage:

```
<ElementType
    content="{empty | textOnly
             | eltOnly | mixed}"
    dt:type="datatype"
    model="{open | closed}"
    name="element-type name"
    order="{one | seq | many}" >
```

group	Organizes content into a group to specify a sequence, set, or choice.

Usage:

```
<group
    maxOccurs="{1 | *}"
    minOccurs="{0 | 1}"
    order="{one | seq | many}" >
```

Schema	Root element for a schema definition document.

Usage:

```
<Schema
    name="schema-name"
    xmlns="namespace" >
```

There is one other important point to note about this last example. Notice that the `<ElementType>` definition for `"guestbook"` designates `model="open"`. This demonstrates a very flexible feature of XML Schema. Namely, XML Schema allows you to include content that is not explicitly defined in the schema. You do this using the model attribute. Setting model to open allows us to extend the content model of the `<guestbook>` element. This could be useful if we were to pull data from, say, a secondary source and didn't know the names of the element types in advance. On the other hand, setting the model to closed is similar to the standard DTD in that it restricts the schema to the content model specified.

6.2.2 *Data Types in Schemas*

Another feature XML Schema proposes is the introduction of data types to XML. Data typing is extremely useful in computing values, determining formats for database fields, and a lot more. Suffice it to say that data types are an important, albeit missing, part of XML.

To use data types in XML Schema, you must first define the following namespace in the `<Schema>` element:

```
xmlns:dt="urn:schema-microsoft-com:datatypes"
```

Data types can be specified for element types or attributes. Taken from Microsoft's "XML Data Types Reference," Table 6-5 presents all the data types that are supported for elements. Note, however, that IE5's current XML parser and DOM only support a subset of these for attributes. That is, you can only specify a string, id, idref, idrefs, nmtoken, nmtokens, entity, entities, enumeration, or notation on an attribute, just as when using DTD declarations.

Data types can be specified in one of two ways within an XML Schema file. The first method is to specify the data type using an attribute of the element type. For example, we could define a date field in our guestbook that lets us know when the user filled in the record:

```
<ElementType name="userDate"
             dt:type="date"/>
```

Table 6-5   Data types supported by XML Schema

Character	Description
bin.base64	MIME-style Base64 encoded binary BLOB.
bin.hex	Hexadecimal digits representing octets.
boolean	0 or 1, where 0 == "False" and 1 =="True."
char	Either a character or a character string
date	Date in a subset ISO 8601 format, without the time data. For example: "1994-11-05."
dateTime	Date in a subset of ISO 8601 format, with optional time and no optional zone. Fractional seconds can be as precise as nanoseconds. For example, "1988-04-07T18:39:09."
dateTime.tz	Date in a subset ISO 8601 format, with optional time and optional zone. Fractional seconds can be as precise as nanoseconds. For example: "1988-04-07T18:39:09-08:00."
fixed.14.4	Same as "number" but no more than 14 digits to the left of the decimal point, and no more than 4 to the right.
float	Real number, with no limit on digits; can potentially have a leading sign, fractional digits, and optionally an exponent. Punctuation as in U.S. English. Values range from $1.7976931348623157E+308$ to $2.2250738585072014E-308$.
int	Number, with optional sign, no fractions, and no exponent.
number	Number, with no limit on digits; can potentially have a leading sign, fractional digits, and optionally an exponent. Punctuation as in U.S. English. (Values have same range as most significant number, R8, $1.7976931348623157E+308$ to $2.2250738585072014E-308$.)
time	Time in a subset ISO 8601 format, with no date and no time zone. For example: "08:15:27."
i1	Integer represented in one byte. A number, with optional sign, no fractions, no exponent. For example: "1, 127, -128."
i2	Integer represented in one word. A number, with optional sign, no fractions, no exponent. For example: "1, 703, -32768."

Table 6-5   Continued

Character	Description
i4	Integer represented in four bytes. A number, with optional sign, no fractions, no exponent. For example: "1, 703, -32768, 148343, −1000000000."
r4	Real number, with no limit on digits; can potentially have a leading sign, fractional digits, and optionally an exponent. Punctuation as in U.S. English. Values range from 3.40282347E+38F to 1.17549435E-38F.
r8	Same as "float." Real number, with no limit on digits; can potentially have a leading sign, fractional digits, and optionally an exponent. Punctuation as in U.S. English. Values range from 1.7976931348623157E+308 to 2.2250738585072014E-308.
ui1	Unsigned integer. A number, unsigned, no fractions, no exponent. For example: "1, 255."
ui2	Unsigned integer, two bytes. A number, unsigned, no fractions, no exponent. For example: "1, 255, 65535."
ui4	Unsigned integer, four bytes. A number, unsigned, no fractions, no exponent. For example: "1, 703, 3000000000."
uri	Universal Resource Identifier (URI). For example, "urn:schemas-microsoft-com:Office9."
uuid	Hexadecimal digits representing octets, optional embedded hyphens that are ignored. For example: "333C7BC4-460F-11D0-BC04-0080C7055A83."

Alternatively, you can specify a datatype using a datatype specification element within your element type definition, as shown below:

```
<ElementType name="userDate">
  <datatype dt:type="date"/>
</ElementType>
```

We will examine XML Schemas, and particularly the use of data types, in detail in Part 4 of this book. In the meantime, this section should provide a sufficient introduction to begin using XML Schemas as a replacement for the more arcane DTD syntax.

6.3 | Closing Thoughts

Possibly, the greatest endorsement of the future of XML is Internet Explorer 5. Microsoft's support for this emerging technology goes far beyond the early standards to provide a more natural way to write DTDs, and to enable developers to write more robust applications through the use of data types. Built-in technologies such as the Channel Definition Format and Open Software Description show that Microsoft is doing more than giving lip service to XML. It is using XML in practical ways that can enhance your Web site and provide your visitors with a better user experience. The next step is to put these new features to work. And that is just what the next chapters do.

6.4 | References

1. XML Data Types Reference.
http://msdn.microsoft.com/xml/reference/schema/datatypes.asp

Projects for
Internet Explorer

In my early days as a writer and developer, I had the good fortune to work at NASA's Ames Research Center at Moffet Field, California. While there, our team leader told a story about the demonstration of a new supercomputer which was about to be brought online. The system was accessed remotely over Milnet, the military's version of Arpanet. (Later these and other networks would collectively be referred to as the Internet.) Needless to say, countless dollars and man hours had been spent in preparation for this day, the unveiling. The moment of truth was just minutes away. With a few moments to spare, my team leader, being the curious sort, walked up to the terminal that was to control the demonstration to ask a question. As he reached out to the keyboard, he asked, "What is this key for?" When he pressed the key, the remote supercomputer crashed, and it took more than two weeks to bring the system back online.

The moment of truth for any new technology is that moment when the first user reaches out and hits that first keystroke. After all of the research, preparation, design, and coding, everything rests on the shoulders of the user. That's what this chapter is all about. This is where theory ends and usage begins. It is where the rubber meets the road.

The projects presented in this chapter have two purposes. First and foremost, they are designed to enhance your practical knowledge of XML and programming with the DOM. However, these are real-world examples that you should be able to put to use in your own development efforts. In the process, you will learn how to access the document tree and report on elements within your documents. You will also learn how to apply this knowledge to build useful utilities that document structure, validate XML documents, and dynamically generate navigation information. Whatever the application, the first step is to access the document object. And that's where this chapter begins.

7.1 | Accessing the Document Object

Just as we discussed in the last chapter, Internet Explorer includes an XML parser that reads an XML document, parses it into a document tree, and exposes the nodes of that tree through the DOM API. This first example shows how to load an external XML document, parse it, and report on its root element. The basic steps are to:

1. Create an HTML document.

2. Add a form that allows the user to enter the URL of an XML document.

3. Write a script that loads an XML document, parses it and exposes its elements.

4. Report on the document object.

The following code implements these requirements:

```
<!DOCTYPE HTML PUBLIC "-//W3C//DTD HTML 4.0//EN">

<HTML>
  <HEAD>
    <TITLE>Loadxml</TITLE>
  </HEAD>
```

```
<BODY>
  <P>Enter a filename<BR></P>
  <FORM>
     <INPUT NAME="Filename" SIZE="40">
     <BR><BR><BR>

     <INPUT TYPE="BUTTON"
        NAME="ParseButton"
        VALUE="Parse XML File"
        ONCLICK="Parse(Filename.value)">
  </FORM>

<SCRIPT>
var BrowserWin;
var Page;

// Map node types to their string names
function getTypeStr(type)
{
  if (type == 1)
     return "ELEMENT_NODE";
  if (type == 2)
     return "ATTRIBUTE_NODE";
  if (type == 3)
    return "TEXT_NODE";
  if (type == 4)
    return "CDATA_NODE";
  if (type == 5)
    return "ENTITY_REFERENCE_NODE";
  if (type == 6)
    return "ENTITY_NODE";
  if (type == 7)
    return "PROCESSING_INSTRUCTION_NODE";
  if (type == 8)
    return "COMMENT_NODE";
  if (type == 9)
    return "DOCUMENT_NODE";
  if (type == 10)
    return "DOCUMENT_TYPE_NODE";
  if (type == 11)
    return "DOCUMENT_FRAGMENT_NODE";
  if (type == 12)
    return "NOTATION_NODE";
  else
    return "";
}
```

```
function Parse(xmlFilename)
{

 // Create a Document object and report the results.
 var xmlDocument = new
          ActiveXObject("Microsoft.XMLDOM");
 xmlDocument.async = false;
 xmlDocument.load(xmlFilename);

 var docRoot = xmlDocument.documentElement;
 if (docRoot == null)
    alert("Document is null");

 else {
    BrowserWin = window.open("", "XMLReport");
    Page = BrowserWin.document;

    Page.writeln("<HTML>");
    Page.writeln("<TITLE>XML Output</TITLE>");
    Page.writeln("<BODY>");
    Page.writeln("<PRE>");

    var Name = docRoot.nodeName;
    var numChildren = xmlDocument.childNodes.length;
    var firstChildName = docRoot.firstChild.nodeName;
    var firstChildVal = docRoot.firstChild.nodeValue;
    var firstChildType = docRoot.firstChild.nodeType;
    var lastChildName = docRoot.lastChild.nodeName;
    var sibling = docRoot.firstChild.nextSibling;

    typeStr = getTypeStr(firstChildType);

    Page.writeln("<H3>Statistics for ",
                 xmlDocument.url, "</H3><BR>");
    Page.writeln("Number of Child Nodes:",
                 numChildren, "<BR>");
    Page.writeln("Node Name:", Name, "<BR>");
    Page.writeln("First child Name:", firstChildName,
                 "<BR>");
    Page.writeln("Node child value:", firstChildVal,
                 "<BR>");
    Page.writeln("Node child type:", typeStr, "<BR>");
    Page.writeln("Sibling of first child:",
                 sibling.nodeName, "<BR>");
```

```
    var attributes = docRoot.firstChild.attributes;
    if (attributes != null)
    {
        for (var child = attributes.nextNode();
          child != null; child = attributes.nextNode())
        {
          attributeName = child.nodeName;
          attributeVal = child.nodeValue;
          Page.writeln("attr Name:", attributeName,
                    "<BR>");
          Page.writeln("attr Value:", attributeVal,
                    "<BR>");
        }
    }


    // Report on the last node
    Page.writeln("Last Node child:", lastChildName,
                "<BR>");
    attributes = docRoot.lastChild.attributes;
    if (attributes != null)
    {
        for (var child = attributes.nextNode();
          child != null; child = attributes.nextNode())
        {
          attributeName = child.nodeName;
          attributeVal = child.nodeValue;
          Page.writeln("attr Name:", attributeName,
                    "<BR>");
          Page.writeln("attr Value:", attributeVal,
                    "<BR>");
        }
    }


    Page.writeln("</BODY>");
    Page.writeln("</HTML>");
    xmlDocument = null;              // Reset xmlDocument
                                     // for future use


  } // else
 } // Parse
 </SCRIPT>

 </BODY>
</HTML>
```

The first step, creating the HTML document, is straightforward. Within that document, you want to create a form with an edit field that the user can use to input a URL. The form should also include a Submit button that triggers our script.

The entry point into the script is the `Parse()` function. `Parse()` is triggered when the parse button's ONCLICK event occurs: that is, when the user clicks on the parse button. This function's first chore is to create a new document object instance and initialize the MSXML parser. This is easily done by calling:

```
new  ActiveXObject("Microsoft.XMLDOM")
```

and assigning the result to the `xmlDocument` variable. It should be noted that the W3C suggests that a document object be embedded within an HTML page using the `<OBJECT>` element. However, the syntax Microsoft employs in relation to `<OBJECT>` is quite a bit more cumbersome, as you'll see later in the chapter. For now, just note that while the `new ActiveXObject()` syntax is shorter, it is also Microsoft specific.

Once you have instantiated the `xmlDocument` object, you can begin calling methods from the DOM API using JavaScript's familiar dot notation. For example, we call the DOM's `load()` method to load an external XML document using:

```
xmlDocument.load(xmlFilename);
```

Once you have the document, you can access its root (or document) element through the DOM's `documentElement` property. In this case, `Parse()` creates a new variable called `docRoot` variable and assigns the value to it. From this point, you can traverse the document, access individual document elements, and manipulate the document in any way you wish.

As a general measure, `Parse()` ensures that there is indeed a document object. If not, the function informs the user and bails out. The rest of the code queries the other properties exposed by the DOM and reports the results in the browser Window. All of these properties are documented in Chapter 5.

Finally, you may recall from Chapter 5 that the DOM defines node types such as element nodes, attribute nodes, and so on, in terms of integer values (see Table 5-2). These integers can be mapped to a set of string constants, which are also defined in the DOM specification. The getTypeStr() function performs these mappings. Thus, you can call getTypeStr() to get a more readable string value. For example, Parse() calls getTypeStr() to display a node's type to the user.

To test this example, load it into Internet Explorer as an HTML page. (You'll find this example on the accompanying CD, located in the listings/Chap07 directory.) The browser will display an edit box with a prompt to enter a filename. Enter the filename or URL of an XML document and click on the submit button. Assuming the URL points to a valid document, you will see a second browser window containing the results. As a test case, I have included the following XML document (also located on the CD with its associated DTD):

```
<?xml version="1.0"?>
<!DOCTYPE article SYSTEM "\listings\Chap07\news.dtd">

<article>
   <headline>News&amp;Views</headline>
   <deck>New Web Graphics Standard Emerges</deck>
   <byline>Michael Floyd</byline>
   <pubDate>April 1, 1999</pubDate>

   <aBody>
      <para1>
         <dropCap>W</dropCap>hile XML has primarily been used
for text, the <bold>World Wide Web Consortium (W3C)</bold>
released the first public working draft of the <ital>Scalable
Vector Graphics</ital> (SVG) format, which is defined in XML.
SVG is intended to be a vendor-neutral, cross-platform format
for XML vector graphics over the Web. The working draft
status indicates that the W3C is making the proposal public
and openly soliciting feedback.</para1>

      <para>The use of vector graphics means that Web
designers will be able to reuse images more effectively
and that images can be easily resized, cropped and
printed at different resolutions. Because it is defined
in XML, the SVG format can be read by any existing XML
```

```
parser, and programmers and script developers will be able
to access SVG documents through any DOM API to, for
example, create animations. Text within images, such as
figure captions, will be maintained as text, so it can
easily be searched by search engines. And Webmasters will
be able to apply style sheets equally well to XML text
and SVG.
      </para>

      <para2>Members of the W3C's SVG Working Group include
Adobe, IBM, Apple, Microsoft, Sun, HP, Corel, Macromedia,
Netscape, and  Quark. For those interested, a public mailing
list, www-svg@w3.org, has been started. You can get more
information on SVG at www.w3.org/Graphics/SVG/.
      </para2>
   </aBody>

   <copyright>Copyright (c) 1999, Michael Floyd. All Rights
Reserved</copyright>
</article>
```

The resulting output is shown below:

```
Statistics for file:///listings/Chap07/news.xml

Number of Child Nodes:3
Node Name:article
First child Name:headline
Node child value:null
Node child type:ELEMENT_NODE
Sibling of first child:deck
Last Node child:copyright
```

7.2 | A Utility for Documenting Structure

Now that you can load an XML document and access the root object, you will want to traverse the document tree. Our next example is important for two reasons. First, it demonstrates how to walk the source tree using the DOM API. Second, this example is a useful utility for documenting the structure of an XML document. This could be particularly useful for understanding documents without an associated DTD or other formal schema.

This example extends the first with a method, `displayTree()`, which reports on all elements within the document tree. For example, this method reports whether a node is an element node, attribute node, text node, and so on. If it is an element node, `displayTree()` reports on its first child and last child within the child node list. For text nodes, the content of the element is given. For attribute lists, all attribute/value pairs are reported. In all cases, the node's name is given.

```
<!DOCTYPE HTML PUBLIC "-//W3C//DTD HTML 4.0//EN">

<HTML>
  <HEAD>
    <TITLE>Loadxml</TITLE>
  </HEAD>

  <BODY>
    <P>Enter a filename<BR></P>
    <FORM>
       <INPUT NAME="Filename" SIZE="40">
       <BR><BR><BR>

       <INPUT TYPE="BUTTON"
          NAME="ParseButton"
          VALUE="Parse XML File"
          ONCLICK="Parse(Filename.value)">
    </FORM>

    <SCRIPT>
    var BrowserWin;
    var Page;

    function getTypeStr(type)
    {
      if (type == 1)
        return "ELEMENT_NODE";
```

```
      if (type == 2)
        return "ATTRIBUTE_NODE";
      if (type == 3)
        return "TEXT_NODE";
      if (type == 4)
        return "CDATA_NODE";
      if (type == 5)
        return "ENTITY_REFERENCE_NODE";
      if (type == 6)
        return "ENTITY_NODE";
      if (type == 7)
        return "PROCESING_INSTRUCTION_NODE";
      if (type == 8)
        return "COMMENT_NODE";
      if (type == 9)
        return "DOCUMENT_NODE";
      if (type == 10)
        return "DOCUMENT_TYPE_NODE";
      if (type == 11)
        return "DOCUMENT_FRAGMENT_NODE";
      if (type == 12)
        return "NOTATION_NODE";
      else
        return "";
    }

    function displayTree(node, N)
    {
      var child;
      var i, length;

      length = node.childNodes.length;
      Name = node.nodeName;
      Value = node.nodeValue;
      typeStr = getTypeStr(node.nodeType);
      numChildren = node.childNodes.length;

      Page.writeln("<P><B>Node Name:", Name,"</B>");
      Page.writeln("   Node type:", typeStr);

      if ( numChildren != 0)
      {
        firstChildName = node.firstChild.nodeName;
        firstChildVal = node.firstChild.nodeValue;
        firstChildType =
```

```
            getTypeStr(node.firstChild.nodeType);
    lastChildName = node.lastChild.nodeName;
    lastChildVal = node.lastChild.nodeValue;
    lastChildType =
        getTypeStr(node.lastChild.nodeType);

    Page.writeln("   First child Name:",
                    firstChildName);
    Page.writeln("   First child value:",
                    firstChildVal);
    Page.writeln("   First child type:",
                    firstChildType);
    Page.writeln("   Last child Name:",
                    lastChildName);
    Page.writeln("   Last child value:",
                    lastChildVal);
    Page.writeln("   Last child type:",
                    lastChildType);

}

// — Get Attribute information —
var attributes = node.attributes;
if (attributes != null)
{
    Page.writeln("   <I>Attributes:</I> ");
    for (var childAttr = attributes.nextNode();
          childAttr != null;
          childAttr = attributes.nextNode())
    {
        attributeName = childAttr.nodeName;
        attributeVal = childAttr.nodeValue;
        Page.writeln("        ", attributeName, " = ",
                    attributeVal);
    }
}

if (typeStr == "TEXT_NODE")
{
    Page.writeln("   Node value:", Value);
}

// If the element has children, call displayTree
// recursively.
if (node.childNodes != null)
```

```
        {
            for (i = 0; i < node.childNodes.length; i++)
        {
            if (N = numChildren)
                N = N + 1;
            child = node.childNodes.item(i);
            displayTree(child, N);
        }
    }

}

function Parse(xmlFilename)
{

 // Create a Document object and report the results.
 var xmlDocument =
         new ActiveXObject("Microsoft.XMLDOM");
 xmlDocument.async = false;
 xmlDocument.load(xmlFilename);

 var docRoot = xmlDocument.documentElement;
 if (docRoot == null)
    alert("Document is null");

 else {
    BrowserWin = window.open("", "XMLReport");
    Page = BrowserWin.document;

    Page.writeln("<HTML>");
    Page.writeln("<TITLE>XML Output</TITLE>");
    Page.writeln("<BODY>");
    Page.writeln("<PRE>");
    Page.writeln("<H3>Statistics for ", xmlDocument.url,
                "</H3><BR>");

    displayTree(docRoot, 0);

    Page.writeln("</BODY>");
    Page.writeln("</HTML>");
    xmlDocument = null;            // Reset xmlDocument for
                                  // future use
```

```
    } // else
    } // Parse
  </SCRIPT>

  </BODY>
</HTML>
```

The `displayTree()` method is called from `Parse()` and takes a node object and an integer value (N) as its parameters. On the initial call, the node will be the document object and N is zero. You get the value for the document object by querying the document's `root` property, as with our previous example. The purpose of N is to keep track of the level you are at in the hierarchy.

After declaring local variables, `displayTree()` begins by retrieving the properties of the current node. Next, the function checks to see if there are any child nodes. If so, we grab the first and last child nodes in the node list and report the results. Next, the routine queries the attributes property and returns the result in a nodelist. You can access this list using the `item()` method. Thus, the code uses a `for` loop to iterate through the list and report the attribute/value pairs.

The final step is to check to see if there are additional child nodes. If there are, the code must perform the entire process again. I do this by iterating through each element in the collection and calling `displayTree()` recursively. This has the effect of performing a "depth-first search" where each branch of the tree is fully explored before moving on to the next branch. Note here that N is incremented only if its value is different from the current branch level within the tree. Since this is a depth-first search and we are traversing the tree from top to bottom, I only need to increment N when a child branch is encountered. And because of the nature of recursion, I don't have to worry about restoring (or decrementing) the value of N after searching the branch. The reason is that as the recursion "unwinds" to the previous level, the value of N is restored automatically.

To test the code, I have run this example against the news.xml documented presented earlier. The result is a report that details every node in the document tree. The following is an excerpt from the output window generated by our new utility:

```
Statistics for file:///news.xml
Node Name:article
    Node type:ELEMENT_NODE
    First child Name:headline
    First child value:null
    First child type:ELEMENT_NODE
    Last child Name:copyright
    Last child value:null
    Last child type:ELEMENT_NODE
    Attributes:
Node Name:headline
    Node type:ELEMENT_NODE
    First child Name:#text
    First child value:News&Views
    First child type:TEXT_NODE
    Last child Name:#text
    Last child value:News&Views
    Last child type:TEXT_NODE
    Attributes:
Node Name:#text
    Node type:TEXT_NODE
    Node value:News&Views
Node Name:deck
    Node type:ELEMENT_NODE
    First child Name:#text
    First child value:New Web Graphics Standard Emerges
    First child type:TEXT_NODE
    Last child Name:#text
    Last child value:New Web Graphics Standard Emerges
    Last child type:TEXT_NODE
    Attributes:
Node Name:#text
    Node type:TEXT_NODE
    Node value:New Web Graphics Standard Emerges
Node Name:byline
    Node type:ELEMENT_NODE
    First child Name:#text
    First child value:Michael Floyd
```

```
      First child type:TEXT_NODE
      Last child Name:#text
      Last child value:Michael Floyd
      Last child type:TEXT_NODE
      Attributes:
   Node Name:#text
      Node type:TEXT_NODE
      Node value:Michael Floyd
   Node Name:pubDate
      Node type:ELEMENT_NODE
      First child Name:#text
      First child value:April 1, 1999
      First child type:TEXT_NODE
      Last child Name:#text
      Last child value:April 1, 1999
      Last child type:TEXT_NODE
      Attributes:
   Node Name:#text
      Node type:TEXT_NODE
      Node value:April 1, 1999
```

7.3 | Web Site Navigation

Most Web sites embed navigation information right into the pages
that are displayed on a site. The problem is that if these are static Web
pages, making changes to the navigational structure means modifying
every page on the site. Our next example shows how you can solve
this problem by creating an XML document that defines the navigational structure of your Web site. This document can then be used to
automatically generate navigation bars for all of the pages on your
Web site, and to create a site map, topic index, or table of contents.
The beauty of this approach is that you only need to modify one file
to effect the change throughout the site.

The way it works is that you create an XML file that describes your
navigational structure. Then, a JavaScript passes this description to
the browser's XML parser. The parser returns the structure with all of
its elements exposed by the DOM API. You can then access each ele-

ment's attributes to construct the navigation bar. Ultimately, you could write another script to crawl your directory structure and generate this XML file automatically.

The first step is to design a suitable vocabulary. Keep in mind that the goal in designing the vocabulary is to keep it general. So, you must resist the temptation to specialize into categories like Major Topic, Minor Topic, Article Entry, and so on. As you might imagine, any such specializations make the vocabulary application and/or site specific. The idea is to reuse your content description in other Website applications, such as a site map, topic index, or table of contents.

The vocabulary employs a container element called `<SiteNav>`, which contains the elements for describing navigation entries. The only other element is `<ItemEntry>`. You describe all list entries using this single element. You can nest an ItemEntry within another to create subcategories and individual article entries. The syntax for `<Site-Nav>` is shown below:

```
<SiteNav>
   <ItemEntry HREF=URL
      Title=Title_text
      [Description=Descriptive_text]>
      <ItemEntry HREF=URL
         Title=Title_text
         [Description=Description text]>
         <ItemEntry HREF=URL
           . . .

         </ItemEntry>
      </ItemEntry>
   </ItemEntry>
</SiteNav>
```

An `<ItemEntry>` takes several attributes. The HREF attribute defines a link to the document in question. The Title attribute is the title that will be presented in the navigation bar. The Description attribute allows you to add descriptive text that could be, for instance, displayed in a text box when the user mouses over the item. Here is a sample

`<SiteNav>` document describing the navigation entries at my Web site at BeyondHTML.com:

```
<?XML version="1.0"?>
<!DOCTYPE SiteNav SYSTEM "sitenav.dtd">

<SiteNav>
    <ItemEntry HREF="dom/index.html"
        Title="Object Model"
        Description=
        "Home page for the Document Object Model">

        <ItemEntry HREF="dom/overview.html"
            Title="Overview"
            Description="DOM Overview">
        </ItemEntry>

    </ItemEntry>

    <ItemEntry HREF="style/index.html"
        Title="Style Sheets"
        Description="Home page for Style Sheets">
    </ItemEntry>

    <ItemEntry HREF="markup/index.html"
        Title="Markup"
        Description="Home page for Markup Languages">
    </ItemEntry>

    <ItemEntry HREF="scripting/index.html"
        Title="Scripting"
        Description="Scripting Home page">
    </ItemEntry>

    <ItemEntry HREF="tools/index.html"
        Title="Tools"
        Description="Get the tools">
    </ItemEntry>

    <ItemEntry HREF="resources/index.html"
        Title="Resources"
        Description="Books, articles, and other sites">
    </ItemEntry>

    <ItemEntry HREF="bio.html"
```

```
      Title="About Us"
      Description="Find out about BeyondHTML.com">
   </ItemEntry>
</SiteNav>
```

For the purposes of display, I have used HTML frames to divide the screen into three window panes: The navigation bar is displayed in one pane which runs vertically down the left-hand side of the screen. A second pane is positioned along the top of the screen and can be used to store banner ads or your Web site's logo. The remainder of the screen constitutes the main window for viewing content. The HTML document that sets up our frames, called the "framing document," is shown below:

```
<!DOCTYPE HTML PUBLIC "-//W3C//DTD  HTML 4.0//EN">
<HTML>
  <HEAD>
    <TITLE>BeyondHTML Home Page</TITLE>
  </HEAD>

  <FRAMESET FRAMEBORDER="0" BORDER="0" COLS="20%,80%">
  <FRAME SRC="Navbar.html" NAME="NavPane"
        MARGINWIDTH="3" MARGINHEIGHT="3"
        SCROLLING="No" NORESIZE="NORESIZE">
  <FRAMESET ROWS="38%,62%">
    <FRAME SRC="Toppane.html" NAME="TopPane"
        SCROLLING="NO" NORESIZE="NORESIZE">
    <FRAME SRC="toc.shtml" NAME="MainPane"
        SCROLLING="AUTO">
  </FRAMESET>
  <NOFRAMES>
    <BODY>
      <!- Code goes here for browsers that are
          not frames aware.
      ->
    </BODY>
  </NOFRAMES>
</HTML>
```

This framing document sets up our three frames. Each frame, or window pane, is given a name identifier. The Navigation bar is called NavPane, the top pane is TopPane, and the main window is MainPane.

The HTML that constructs each frame is stored in a separate HTML document, and the filename for each document reflects the ID name of its associated frame. In other words, the HTML file that creates MainPane, for example, is called mainpane.html.

One unique feature of this example is that I have embedded the JavaScript code, which loads our XML document and generates the navigation bar, all within toppane.html. Here is the code for the Top-Pane frame:

```
<HTML>
   <HEAD>
      <TITLE>BeyondHTML Title Frame</TITLE>
   </HEAD>

   <BODY BGCOLOR="#FFFFFF" ONLOAD="Parse('nav.xml')">
     <P ALIGN="CENTER">
     <IMG SRC="gifs/logo.gif"
          ALT="Jump to Home page"
          ALIGN="MIDDLE"
          WIDTH="426" HEIGHT="112"
          USEMAP="#logomap"
          BORDER="0">
     </P>
     <MAP NAME="logomap">

        <AREA SHAPE="RECT" COORDS="0,1,425,112"
           HREF="http://www.beyondhtml.com"
           TARGET="_top" ALT="Jump back to the Home page">
     </MAP>

<SCRIPT>
   function displayNavbar(node, N)
   {
   var child;
   var i, length;

     Name = node.nodeName;
     typeStr = getTypeStr(node.nodeType);

     // Guarantee a document object exists
     if (node == null)
     {
        alert("No Document Object for this file!");
     }
```

```
// Get the number of child elements
if (node.childNodes != null)
   length = node.childNodes.length;
else
   length = 0;

// Display the element information; ignore the
// SiteNav object.
if ((typeStr == "ELEMENT_NODE") && (Name != "SiteNav"))
{
   HREFAttr = node.getAttribute("HREF");
   TitleAttr = node.getAttribute("Title");
   DescAttr = node.getAttribute("Description");
   parent.NavPane.document.writeln("<P><B>
         <A HREF=\"", HREFAttr, "\"
            TARGET=\"MainPane\">",
            TitleAttr, "</A></B></P>");
}


// Call displayNavbar recursively to display all top
// level elements
if ((Name == "SiteNav") && (node.childNodes != null))
{
      for (i = 0; i < node.childNodes.length; i++)
   {
      if (N = length)
         N = N + 1;
      child = node.childNodes.item(i);
      displayNavbar(child, N);
   }
}
}


function getTypeStr(type)
{
  if (type == 1)
    return "ELEMENT_NODE";
  if (type == 2)
    return "ATTRIBUTE_NODE";
  if (type == 3)
    return "TEXT_NODE";
  if (type == 4)
    return "CDATA_NODE";
  if (type == 5)
    return "ENTITY_REFERENCE_NODE";
```

```
  if (type == 6)
    return "ENTITY_NODE";
  if (type == 7)
    return "PROCESING_INSTRUCTION_NODE";
  if (type == 8)
    return "COMMENT_NODE";
  if (type == 9)
    return "DOCUMENT_NODE";
  if (type == 10)
    return "DOCUMENT_TYPE_NODE";
  if (type == 11)
    return "DOCUMENT_FRAGMENT_NODE";
  if (type == 12)
    return "NOTATION_NODE";
  else
    return "";
}


function Parse()
{

 // Create a Document object.
 var xmlDocument =
     new ActiveXObject("Microsoft.XMLDOM");
 xmlDocument.async = false;
 xmlDocument.load("nav.xml");


 var docRoot = xmlDocument.documentElement;
 if (docRoot == null)
    alert("Can't load file: ");


 else {
    parent.NavPane.document.writeln("<HTML>");
    parent.NavPane.document.writeln("<TITLE>
            XML Navigation Bar</TITLE>");
    parent.NavPane.document.writeln("<BODY>");
    parent.NavPane.document.writeln("<PRE>");
    parent.NavPane.document.writeln("<P><B>
        <FONT SIZE=\"+1\">InSite</FONT></B> </P>");


    displayNavbar(docRoot, 0);


    parent.NavPane.document.writeln("</BODY>");
    parent.NavPane.document.writeln("</HTML>");
```

```
      xmlDocument = null;
   } //else
}
</SCRIPT>

  </BODY>
</HTML>
```

Again, the Parse() method should look familiar. The only change is that Parse() now calls a new method, called displayNavBar().

The displayNavBar() function starts by querying the node's properties and gathering information about the node including its name, length, and type. After that, the routine begins the processing. The first element we're going to see is <SiteNav>, which is simply a container for our list of items. It's a good idea to verify that we have this object and provide suitable error handling if we don't. Next, we want to process all "element" nodes except <SiteNav>. (Recall, <SiteNav> is simply a container element and requires no specific processing.) The following if statement checks for these conditions:

```
if ((typeStr == "ELEMENT_NODE") && (Name != "SiteNav"))
```

Next, getAttribute() is a DOM method that takes the name of an element's attribute and returns its value. Since we know that we're at an <ItemEntry> in the tree, getAttribute() gets the values for HREF, Title, and Description. Once we have the attributes, we can write the hypertext link out to the NavPane using a writeln(). The only tricky point here is that double quotes and other special characters must be prefaced with a backslash (\). Otherwise, the JavaScript will interpret the double quote as the end of the string. The last step is to check to see if there are additional child elements in the tree, and if there are make a recursive call to displayNavbar() to process them.

7.4 | A Quick and Dirty XML Validator

When you invoke Internet Explorer's XML parser, you have the option of setting a property that turns validation on or off. Then, by checking the results of the parse, you can determine whether the document is well formed, valid, or both. The following example does just that:

```
<!DOCTYPE HTML PUBLIC "-//W3C//DTD HTML 4.0//EN">
<HTML>
  <HEAD>
    <TITLE>XML Validator</TITLE>
  </HEAD>

  <BODY>
    <P>Enter a filename<BR></P>
    <FORM>
      <INPUT NAME="Filename" SIZE="40">
      <BR><BR><BR>

      <INPUT TYPE="BUTTON"
        NAME="ParseButton"
        VALUE="Parse XML File"
        ONCLICK="Parse(Filename.value)">
    </FORM>

  <SCRIPT>

  function Parse(xmlFilename)
  {

    // Create a Document object and report the results.
    var xmlDocument =
        new ActiveXObject("Microsoft.XMLDOM");
    xmlDocument.async = false;
    xmlDocument.load(xmlFilename);

    xmlDocument.validateOnParse = true;
    if (xmlDocument.parseError. errorCode != 0)
```

```
    {
       document.writeln("Parse Error: ",
                  xmlDocument.parseError.reason,"<BR>");
       document.writeln("occurred at line: ",
                  xmlDocument.parseError.line,"<BR>");
       document.writeln("------------<BR>");
       document.writeln("source: ",
                  xmlDocument.parseError.srcText);
    }
    else
    {
       document.writeln("This document is
                     well formed<BR>");
       document.writeln("If a DTD was given, this document
                     is also valid");
    }

  } // Parse
  </SCRIPT>

  </BODY>
</HTML>
```

When an error occurs, this example outputs the error in the browser window. For example, the following error is reported when the `<?xml …?>` processing instruction is inadvertently upper cased with the string "XML":

```
Parse Error: The name 'xml' is reserved and must
be lower case.
occurred at line: 1
------------
source:
```

7.5 | Supporting Internet Explorer 4

You may have heard that Internet Explorer 4 also supports XML. Unfortunately, the support for XML was added prior to the XML 1.0 recommendation and is relatively limited. Nevertheless, you can provide some of the same functionality described in this chapter to your IE4 users.

7.5.1 *Loading a Document*

The following example shows how you can load an XML document and retrieve general information about it. The good news is that this example will run in both versions 4 and 5 of Internet Explorer:

```
<HTML>
   <HEAD>
      <TITLE>Example 1</TITLE>
   </HEAD>
   <BODY>

   <OBJECT
      ClassID="clsid:CFC399AF-D876-11D0-9C10-00C04FC99C8E"
      ID="MSXML"
      Name="xmlDoc">
   </OBJECT>

   <P>Enter a filename</P><BR>
   <INPUT Name="Filename" size=40>
   <BR><BR>

   <INPUT TYPE = "BUTTON"
      Name = "ParseButton"
      Value = "Parse XML File"
      onClick = "Parse(Filename.value)">

   <SCRIPT>
   var BrowserWin;
   var Page;

   function Parse(xmlFilename)
   {
    var xmlDocument;

    BrowserWin = window.open("", "XMLReport");
    Page = BrowserWin.document;
```

```
    Page.writeln("<HTML>");
    Page.writeln("<TITLE>XML Output</TITLE>");
    Page.writeln("<BODY>");
    Page.writeln("<PRE>");

// Create a Document object and report the results.
    xmlDocument = MSXML;          // Create a new object
                                  // instance
// Assign the URL from the value entered by the user
    xmlDocument.URL = xmlFilename;

    Page.writeln("<H3>Statistics for ",
               xmlDoc.URL, "</H3><BR>");

// Get the document's Root element
    var DocumentRoot = xmlDocument.root;

// Access documents attributes and write out the results
    Page.writeln("XML Version: ", xmlDocument.version);
    Page.writeln("Character set supported: ",
                 xmlDocument.charset);
    Page.writeln("Document type: ", xmlDocument.doctype);

    // The following are documented but not Supported:
    //
    // Page.writeln("File Size: ", xmlDocument.fileSize);
    // Page.writeln("Date Modified: ",
                    xmlDocument.fileModifiedDate);
    // Page.writeln("Updated: ",
                    xmlDocument.FileUpdatedDate);
    // Page.writeln("Mime Type: ", xmlDocument.mimeType);

    Page.writeln("</BODY>");
    Page.writeln("</HTML>");

// Reset xmlDocument for future use
    xmlDocument = null;                                 }

  </script>
  </BODY>
</HTML>
```

One big difference between this example and the first example in this chapter is it starts by creating an object using HTML 4's <OBJECT>

element. The <OBJECT> element is a generalized mechanism for inserting things like multimedia objects, plug-ins, Java applets, and COM objects into an HTML document. The <OBJECT> element takes several optional attributes. We are particularly interested in ClassID, ID, and Name. Generally, speaking, the ClassID attribute specifies a URL indicating where the implementation of the object can be found. In Internet Explorer, ClassID acts as an identifier for the object type. The long string of characters assigned to the ClassID attribute references the MSXML parser. The clsid: portion of the string tells Internet Explorer that the rest of the string refers to an ActiveX control. The ID attribute is a unique identifier that you define and use to reference the parser object from within your script.

When you run the example against this XML document you should get the following results:

```
Statistics for file:///news.xml
XML Version: 1.0
Character set supported: UTF-8
Document type:
```

7.5.2 *Documenting Structure in IE4*

The second example in this chapter can also be rewritten to run in IE 4, albeit with limited reporting capability. So in this revised example, the displayTree() method outputs the element details in a visual manner that mimics the structure of the document. Thus, you can see at a glance that, for example, <headline> is a child node of <article>.

```
<HTML>
  <HEAD>
    <TITLE>xmlParse</TITLE>
  </HEAD>

  <BODY>
    <P>
```

```
      <IMG SRC="/htdocs/gifs/logosmall.gif"
          ALT="Jump to Home page"
          WIDTH="200" HEIGHT="52"
          USEMAP="#logosmall" BORDER="0">
  </P>
  <MAP NAME="logosmall">
    <AREA SHAPE="RECT"
          COORDS="0,1,199,52"
          HREF="http://www.beyondhtml.com"
          ALT="Jump to Home page">
    <AREA SHAPE="default"
          HREF="http://www.beyondhtml.com">
  </MAP>

  <OBJECT
    CLASSID="clsid:CFC399AF-D876-11D0-9C10-00C04FC99C8E"
    ID="MSXML"
    NAME="xml1Document">
  </OBJECT>

  <P>Enter a filename<BR></P>
  <FORM>
    <INPUT NAME="Filename" SIZE="40">
    <BR><BR><BR>

    <INPUT TYPE="BUTTON"
        NAME="ParseButton"
        VALUE="Parse XML File"
        ONCLICK="Parse(Filename.value)">
  </FORM>

<SCRIPT>
var BrowserWin;
var Page;

function displayTree(docObject, N)
{
  var child;
  var i, length;
  var indentStr;
  var A, Attr, AttrList;

  // Guarantee a document object exists
  if (docObject == null)
  {
```

```
      alert("No Document Object for this file!");
      BrowserWin = Page;
   }


   // Indent string for displaying child nodes
   indentStr = "";
   for (i = 1; i <= N; i++)
      indentStr = indentStr + "   ";

   // Get the number of child elements
   if (docObject.children != null)
      length = docObject.children.length;
   else
      length = 0;

// Display the element information, indenting child nodes.
   if (docObject.type == 0)        // Only display elements
   {
      Page.writeln(indentStr, "=====");
      Page.writeln(indentStr, "Element Type: ",
                  GetTypeStr(docObject.type));
      Page.writeln(indentStr, "Tag Name: ",
                        docObject.tagName);


      // This only looks for "ID" attributes
      Attr = docObject.getAttribute("ID");


      Page.writeln(indentStr, "Attribute: ", Attr);
      Page.writeln(indentStr, "Number of Children: ",
                  length);


      // skip text for root node
      if (docObject.parent != null)
          Page.writeln(indentStr, "Text: ",
                     docObject.text);
      Page.writeln(indentStr, "=====<BR>");
    }

// If the element has children, call displayTree
// recursively.
   if (docObject.children != null)
   {
        for (i = 0; i < docObject.children.length; i++)
        {
```

```
            if (N = length)
                N = N + 1;
            child = docObject.children.item(i);
            displayTree(child, N);
        }
    }
}

function GetTypeStr(type)
{
    if (type == 0)
    return "ELEMENT";
    if (type == 1)
        return "TEXT";
    if (type == 2)
        return "COMMENT";
    if (type == 3)
        return "DOCUMENT";
    if (type == 4)
        return "DTD";
    else
        return "OTHER";
}

function Parse(xmlFilename)
{
    var xmlDocument;
    BrowserWin = window.open("", "XMLReport");
    Page = BrowserWin.document;
    Page.writeln("<HTML>");
    Page.writeln("<TITLE>XML Output</TITLE>");
    Page.writeln("<BODY>");
    Page.writeln("<PRE>");

    // Create a Document object and report the results.
    xmlDocument = MSXML;                 // Create a new object
                                         // instance
    xmlDocument.URL = xmlFilename;       // Assign the URL from
                                         // the value entered
                                         // by the user

    Page.writeln("<H3>Statistics for ",
                 xmlDocument.URL, "</H3><BR>");
    Page.writeln("XML Version: ", xmlDocument.version);
    Page.writeln("Charcter set supported: ",
```

```
                    xmlDocument.charset);
    Page.writeln("Document type: ", xmlDocument.doctype);

    // The following are documented but not Supported:

    // Page.writeln("File Size: ", xmlDocument.fileSize);
    // Page.writeln("Date Modified: ",
                    xmlDocument.fileModifiedDate);
    // Page.writeln("Updated: ",
                    xmlDocument.FileUpdatedDate);
    // Page.writeln("Mime Type: ", xmlDocument.mimeType);


    // Pass the Document Root to Tree traversal method
    displayTree(xmlDocument.root, 0);
    Page.writeln("</BODY>");
    Page.writeln("</HTML>");


    // Reset xmlDocument for future use
    xmlDocument = null;
}
    </SCRIPT>

  </BODY>
</HTML>
```

Once again, `displayTree()` is called from `Parse()` and takes a document object and an integer value (N) as its parameters. The `displayTree()` function then goes through the normal checks and assuming we have a valid object, creates the indent string used to indent child nodes from their parent nodes.

In IE 4, you can get to child nodes through a collection class called `children`. This class similarly provides an `item()` method to retrieve elements, and a `length` property that lets you determine the number of items in the collection.

The next series of statements print out the element detail in the browser. The first step is to check the current node's type using the `type` property. IE 4 only supports five node types: Element (return value is equal to 0), text (value = 1), comment (value = 2), document (value = 3), or DTD (value = 4). Once again, these values are mapped to their string equivalents in the `getTypeStr()` method. Next, `displayTree()` checks for an element type equal to zero. If found, it writes out the element type, its tag name, and any attributes contained within the element. Also note that the indent string is incorporated into the detail output.

The final step is to check to see if there are any child nodes. If there are, the code performs the entire process again. I do this by iterating through each element in the collection and calling `displayTree()` recursively. The following is the output from our script:

```
Statistics for file:///news.xml

XML Version: 1.0
Character set supported: UTF-8
Document type:
=====
Element Type: ELEMENT
Tag Name: ARTICLE
Attribute: undefined
Number of Children: 6
=====
                =====
                Element Type: ELEMENT
                Tag Name: HEADLINE
                Attribute: undefined
                Number of Children: 1
                Text: News&Views
                =====
                =====
                Element Type: ELEMENT
                Tag Name: DECK
                Attribute: undefined
                Number of Children: 1
                Text: New Web Graphics Standard Emerges
                =====
                =====
                Element Type: ELEMENT
                Tag Name: BYLINE
                Attribute: undefined
                Number of Children: 1
                Text: Michael Floyd
                =====
                =====
                Element Type: ELEMENT
```

```
        Tag Name: PUBDATE
        Attribute: undefined
        Number of Children: 1
        Text: April 1, 1999
        =====

        =====
        Element Type: ELEMENT
        Tag Name: ABODY
        Attribute: undefined
        Number of Children: 3
        Text: While XML has primarily been used for
text, the World Wide Web Consortium (W3C) released the first
public working draft of the Scalable Vector Graphics (SVG)
format, which is defined in XML. SVG is intended to be a
vendor-neutral, cross-platform format for XML vector graphics
over the Web. The working draft status indicates that the W3C
is making the proposal public and openly soliciting feedback.
The use of vector graphics means that Web designers will be
able to reuse images more effectively and that images can be
easily resized, cropped and printed at different resolutions.
Because it is defined in XML, the SVG format can be read by
any existing XML parser, and programmers and script
developers will be able to access SVG documents through any
DOM API to, for example, create animations. Text within
images, such as figure captions, will be maintained as text,
so it can easily be searched by search engines. And
Webmasters will be able to apply style sheets equally well to
XML text and SVG. Members of the W3C's SVG Working Group
include Adobe, IBM, Apple, Microsoft, Sun, HP, Corel,
Macromedia, Netscape, and Quark. For those interested, a
public mailing list, www-svg@w3.org, has been started. You
can get more information on SVG at www.w3.org/Graphics/SVG/.
            =====
        =====
        Element Type: ELEMENT
        Tag Name: PARA1
        Attribute: undefined
        Number of Children: 6
        Text: While XML has primarily been used for text, the
World Wide Web Consortium (W3C) released the first public
working draft of the Scalable Vector Graphics (SVG) format,
which is defined in XML. SVG is intended to be a vendor-
neutral, cross-platform format for XML vector graphics over
the Web. The working draft status indicates that the W3C is
making the proposal public and openly soliciting feedback.
```

```
=====
    =====
        Element Type: ELEMENT
        Tag Name: DROPCAP
        Attribute: undefined
        Number of Children: 1
        Text: W
    =====
    =====
        Element Type: ELEMENT
        Tag Name: BOLD
        Attribute: undefined
        Number of Children: 1
        Text: World Wide Web Consortium (W3C)
    =====
    =====
        Element Type: ELEMENT
        Tag Name: ITAL
        Attribute: undefined
        Number of Children: 1
        Text: Scalable Vector Graphics
    =====
=====
    Element Type: ELEMENT
    Tag Name: PARA
    Attribute: undefined
    Number of Children: 1
    Text: The use of vector graphics means that Web
designers will be able to reuse images more effectively and
that images can be easily resized, cropped and printed at
different resolutions. Because it is defined in XML, the SVG
format can be read by any existing XML parser, and
programmers and script developers will be able to access SVG
documents through any DOM API to, for example, create
animations. Text within images, such as figure captions, will
be maintained as text so it can easily be searched by search
engines. And Webmasters will be able to apply style sheets
equally well to XML text and SVG.
    =====
    =====
        Element Type: ELEMENT
        Tag Name: PARA2
        Attribute: undefined
        Number of Children: 1
        Text: Members of the W3C's SVG Working Group include
```

```
Adobe, IBM, Apple, Microsoft, Sun, HP, Corel, Macromedia,
Netscape, and Quark. For those interested, a public mailing
list, www-svg@w3.org, has been started. You can get more
information on SVG at www.w3.org/Graphics/SVG/.
        =====
                =====
                Element Type: ELEMENT
                Tag Name: COPYRIGHT
                Attribute: undefined
                Number of Children: 1
                Text: Copyright (c) 1999, Michael Floyd. All
Rights Reserved
                =====
```

7.6 | Conclusion

In this chapter, I have shown how to load documents and use the DOM
to access elements and attributes, walk the document tree, and exploit
features specific to Internet Explorer. You have also seen how these
techniques can be used in real-world projects. Ultimately, this chapter
presents some useful utilities that will help you document your XML
structures, validate your source documents, and automate Web site
navigation. However, the journey does not stop here. Most Web developers will want to know how to present XML in more useful ways that
we have presented here. That is the subject of the next chapter.

Presenting XML in the Client

If you doubt the power of presentation, consider that the Web did not see widespread interest until the birth of Mosaic, the first graphical browser for viewing HTML pages. With the graphical browser came the ability to present rich media types such as graphic images, animations, and sound. The ability to control the layout of these rich media types with suitably formatted text was a boon to a whole new era in user interface design. The "great wall of text" had finally been torn down.

Suffice it to say that presentation is a primary concern for Web developers. As it turns out, there are a number of ways you can present XML. For example, you can use browser-specific features to bind XML data to HTML elements such as tables, edit fields, and other form elements. You can use the DOM, as we did in the last chapter, to access source elements and dynamically generate presentation elements. You can even use XSL formatting objects to format XML directly. This chapter examines these different approaches to presenting XML. In the process, you will learn the benefits and drawbacks of each strategy and when a particular approach is warranted.

8.1 | Presentation Strategies

When considering how to present XML, your first thought might be to use XSL style sheets to format your XML documents for display. After all, XSL provides a collection of formatting objects, which are analogous to the style rules used in Cascading Style Sheets (CSS). These formatting objects allow you to directly control the formatting of your XML elements. However, simple formatting is not necessarily the reason XSL was created. Instead, XSL was given more general features that allow you to write your own style sheet language, just as XML allows you to create your own markup language.

What XSL brings to the table is the ability to access, process, and format virtually any piece of data that has been described by XML. For Web deployment, the most common scheme will likely use XSL to transform XML to HTML. The HTML generated will make use of CSS to control the formatting details.

To see how this might work, let's create a boilerplate document based on the news story from the last chapter. The structure of this boilerplate document is intended to emulate that of most articles on your Web site. Thus, all you need to do is fill in the blanks to have a working XML document.

```
<?xml version="1.0"?>
<!DOCTYPE article SYSTEM "news.dtd">
<?xml-stylesheet
    type="text/xsl"
    href="news.xsl"?>


<article>
   <headline>Some Headline</headline>
   <deck>Supplemental headline</deck>
   <byline>Author Name</byline>
   <pubDate>Month X, 1999</pubDate>

   <aBody>
     <para1>
        <dropCap>T</dropCap>his is a sample first paragraph
to be used in this template. Simply replace this text with
your own.</para1>
```

```
<para>This type of paragraph can be inserted anywhere within
the body of your document. As with the &lt;para1&gt; type,
you can use various formatting styles including
<bold>bold</bold> and <ital>italics</ital>. </para>

<para2>This final paragraph type should be used in the final
paragraph in your page. Right now, it functions the same as
the &lt;para1&gt; element. However, it could be used to
create consistent endings for documents.</para2>
   </aBody>

   <copyright>Copyright (c) 1999, holder name. All Rights
Reserved</copyright>
</article>
```

The first thing you will notice about this boilerplate is that it relies
on two other files. The first, which is referenced in the `<!DOCTYPE>`
declaration, is the DTD (news.dtd) that defines our elements. Here
are the definitions from news.dtd:

```
<!ELEMENT article  (headline , deck , byline , pubDate ,
          aBody , copyright )>
<!ELEMENT headline  (#PCDATA )>
<!ELEMENT deck  (#PCDATA )>
<!ELEMENT byline  (#PCDATA )>
<!ELEMENT pubDate  (#PCDATA )>
<!ELEMENT aBody  (para1 , para , para2 )>
<!ELEMENT para1  (#PCDATA | dropCap | bold | ital)*>
<!ELEMENT dropCap  (#PCDATA )>
<!ELEMENT bold  (#PCDATA )>
<!ELEMENT ital  (#PCDATA )>
<!ELEMENT para  (#PCDATA | dropCap | bold | ital)*>
<!ELEMENT para2  (#PCDATA | dropCap | bold | ital)*>
<!ELEMENT copyright  (#PCDATA )>
```

The second entity is an XSL style sheet, which is referenced in the
`<?xml-stylesheet>` processing instruction. Here is our style sheet:

```
<?xml version="1.0"?>

<xsl:stylesheet
   xmlns:xsl="http://www.w3.org/TR/WD-xsl"
   xmlns="http://www.w3.org/TR/REC-html40"
   result-ns="">
```

```
<!- Root template ->
<xsl:template match="/">
  <HTML>
    <HEAD>
      <META http-equiv="Content-Type"
            content="text/html; charset=iso-8859-1"/>
      <STYLE TYPE="text/css">

        <!- Navigation Bar Styles ->

        A:link {
            COLOR:  Navy;
            text-decoration: none }
        A:visited { COLOR: Navy }
        A:active { COLOR: blue }

        #NavText {
            font-weight: bold;
            font-size: 14px;
            text-decoration: none;
            font-family: "Times New Roman",
                         "Garamond", "serif" }

        #NavHead {
            font-weight: bold;
            text-align: center;
            font-size: 24px;
            text-decoration: none;
            font-family: "Times New Roman",
                         "serif", "Garamond";
            color: white;
            display: block;
            background-color: navy;
            border-style: outset;
            margin-left: 2%; margin-right: 5% }

        <!- Document Styles ->

        .headline {
            color: #FF0000;
            background-color: #FFFFFF;
            text-transform: Capitalize;
            text-align: Left; }
```

```
.deck {
   font-style: italic;
   font-size: 14px;
   font-weight: bold;
   color: black;
   margin-left: 64px;
   font-family: Arial, helvetica, sans-serif;}

.byline {
   color: Navy;
   font-weight: bold;
   font-size: 14px;
   font-family: Arial, helvetica, sans-serif;}

.pubDate {
   color: Red;
   font-weight: normal;
   font-size: 12px;
   font-family: Arial, helvetica, sans-serif;}

.copyright {
   color: Red;
   font-weight: normal;
   font-size: 12px;
   font-family: Arial, helvetica, sans-serif;}

.aBody { display: block;
   font-weight: normal;
   font-size: 12px;
   font-family: "Arial", "Garamond", "serif"; }

.dropCap { background: white;
   color: red;
   float: left;
   vertical-align: text-top;
   font-size: 24px;
   font-style: bold;
   border: none; }

.bold { font-style: bold; }
.ital { font-style: italic; }

#BoxCopy { color: white;
   background-color: red;
```

```
            vertical-align: text-bottom;
            font-size: 24px;
            font-style: bold;
            font-family: "Times New Roman",
                        "serif", "Garamond";
            color: white;
            padding-left: 1px;
            padding-right: 3px;
            text-decoration: none;
            border: none; }

      #BoxCopy1 { color: white;
            background-color: gray;
            vertical-align: text-top;
            font-size: 24px;
            font-style: bold;
            text-decoration: none;
            border: inset }

      .BoxCopy2 { color: navy;
            background-color: white;
            float: right;
            vertical-align: text-top;
            font-size: 20px;
            font-style: bold;
            border: none; }
  </STYLE>
  <TITLE>
    <xsl:value-of select="article/headline"/>
  </TITLE>

 </HEAD>
 <BODY>

<TABLE WIDTH="100%">
  <TR>
    <TD WIDTH="121" HEIGHT="211"
        BACKGROUND="gifs/navBackground.jpg"
        VALIGN="TOP">

    <Span id="NavHead">InSite</Span>

    <P>
    <A HREF="present/index.shtml" TARGET="_top">
        <SPAN id="NavText">Presentation</SPAN>
```

```
   </A></P>

   <P>
   <A HREF="markup/index.shtml" TARGET="_top">
      <SPAN id="NavText">Markup</SPAN>
   </A></P>

   <P>
   <A HREF="markup/xml/index.shtml" TARGET="MainPane">
      <SPAN id="NavText">XML</SPAN>
   </A></P>

   <P>
   <A HREF="scripting/index.shtml" TARGET="_top">
      <SPAN id="NavText">Scripting</SPAN>
   </A></P>

   <P>
   <A HREF="tools/index.shtml" TARGET="_top">
      <SPAN id="NavText">Tools Database</SPAN>
   </A></P>

   <P><SPAN id="NavText">Bookshelf</SPAN></P>

   <P>
   <A HREF="resources/index.shtml" TARGET="_top">
      <SPAN id="NavText">Archives</SPAN>
   </A></P>

   <P>
   <A HREF="bio.shtml">
      <SPAN id="NavText">About Us</SPAN>
   </A></P></TD>

   <TD WIDTH="35" HEIGHT="211" BGCOLOR="#FFFFFF"
      VALIGN="TOP"></TD>
   <TD WIDTH="442" HEIGHT="211" BGCOLOR="#FFFFFF"
      VALIGN="TOP">

<MAP NAME="logosmall">
   <AREA SHAPE="RECT" COORDS="0,1,199,52"
         HREF="http://www.beyondhtml.com"
         ALT="Jump to Home page">
   </AREA>
```

```
        <AREA SHAPE="default"
            HREF="http://www.beyondhtml.com">
        </AREA>
    </MAP>

    <P><BR></BR>
        <IMG SRC="gifs/logo.gif"
            ALT="BeyondHTML Logo" ALIGN="MIDDLE"
            WIDTH="426" HEIGHT="112">
        </IMG>
    </P>

            <Span ID="BoxCopy">
                <xsl:value-of select="article/headline"/>
            </Span><BR></BR>

            <DIV Class="deck">
                <xsl:value-of select="article/deck"/>
            </DIV>
            <BR></BR>

            <DIV Class="byline">
                By
                <xsl:value-of select="article/byline"/>
            </DIV>
            <BR></BR>
            <DIV Class="aBody">
                <P><xsl:value-of
                    select="article//aBody/para1"/></P>
                <P><xsl:value-of
                     select="article//aBody/para"/></P>
                <P><xsl:value-of
                    select="article//aBody/para2"/></P>
            </DIV>
        </TD></TR>
    </TABLE>

    <P ALIGN="CENTER"><FONT SIZE="-1"> [<A
HREF="/present/index.shtml">Presentation</A>]
    [<A HREF="/markup/index.shtml">Markup</A>] [<A
HREF="/markup/xml/index.shtml">XML</A>]
    <A HREF="/scripting/index.shtml">[Scripting</A>] [<A
HREF="/xmlTools.html">Tools
        Database</A>] [<A
HREF="/archives/index.shtml">Archives</A>] [<A
HREF="/bio.shtml">About
```

```
        Us</A>]</FONT> </P>
     <HR></HR>

     <P><xsl:value-of select="article/copyright"/></P>

     <P><FONT SIZE="-1"><I>Last Modified:
       <!-#echo var="LAST_MODIFIED"-></I></FONT></P>

        </BODY>
      </HTML>
  </xsl:template>


  <xsl:template match="aBody">
     <P>
        <xsl:apply-templates/>
     </P>
  </xsl:template>


  <xsl:template match="dropCap">
     <DIV Class="dropCap">
        <xsl:apply-templates />
     </DIV>
  </xsl:template>


  <xsl:template match="bold">
     <B>
        <xsl:apply-templates/>
     </B>
  </xsl:template>


  <xsl:template match="italic">
     <I>
        <xsl:apply-templates/>
     </I>
  </xsl:template>


  <xsl:template match="byline[@Email]">
     <A HREF="mailto:mfloyd@BeyondHTML.com">
        <xsl:apply-templates/>
     </A>
  </xsl:template>


</xsl:stylesheet>
```

As we described in Chapter 3, the root template rule does most of the work. This rule generates the opening HTML elements and creates our CSS style sheet. For a production system, you will want to replace these styles with styles of your own. For the purposes of demonstration, this example creates a navigation bar on the left-hand side of the browser window and uses the rest of the window to view the document. Thus, the first set of style rules provide formatting for the navigation bar, while the second set of rules define formatting for the XML document.

Further down in the template, we generate HTML that creates a table along the left hand side of the screen. This is where the navigation bar is placed. Next, the example uses the `<xsl:value-of>` statement to place the title, deck, byline, and the rest of the article on the page. The result is shown in Figure 8-1.

DETERMINING BROWSER SUPPORT

Assuming your users have Internet Explorer 5, you can use the strategy described in this chapter to deploy XML files just as you would HTML files. You can link to these documents and users will be able to view them, hyperlink to other documents, and so on. At the same time, you can maintain your site more easily and provide a more consistent look and feel.

The key to this is, of course, guaranteeing that your users are running IE5. The following script determines whether the client browser supports XML. If XML is supported, then the XML document is presented; otherwise, an HTML version of the document is selected.

```
<HTML>
<HEAD><TITLE>Detecting the browser type</TITLE></HEAD>
<BODY>

<SCRIPT LANGUAGE="JavaScript">
if (navigator.appVersion.indexOf("MSIE 5.0") >= 1)
    window.location.href = 'news.xm';
  else
    window.location.href = 'news.html';
</SCRIPT>
```

```
<NOSCRIPT>
Sorry, your browser doesn't support client-side
scripting, so we are unable to display this
document.
</NOSCRIPT>
</BODY>
</HTML>
```

As soon as this page loads, the script takes over. First it checks the AppVersion property to see if it contains the "MSIE 5.0" string. If so, we know that the browser will support the viewing of our XML document. The real trick here is that we simulate a redirect using `window.location.href`. *Thus, the news.xml file (or news.html, as the case may be) is loaded automatically with no intervention from the user. Finally, a* `<NOSCRIPT>` *clause is included in case the user has turned scripting off.*

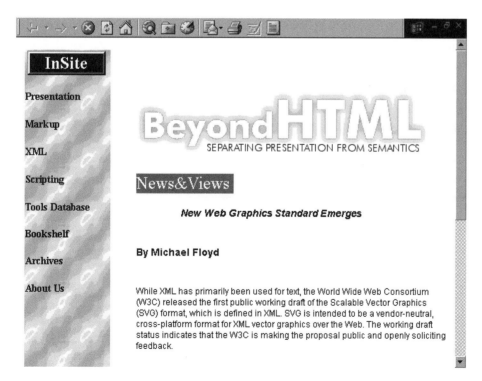

Figure 8–1   The result of displaying news.xml in Internet Explorer 5. `news.xsl` performs the transformation to HTML.

8.2 | Selecting From Multiple Style Sheets

In creating a specific set of styles for your Web site, it is important to note that not all styles are created equally. That is, what may look good on your Solaris workstation running Navigator within a 19-inch monitor may not translate well to a Windows 98 machine running Internet Explorer with 13 inches of viewable area. The reasons for these deviations vary, ranging from differences in the way browsers map color palettes, to the fonts that are installed on your machine. As a result, I occasionally receive email from my site visitors suggesting that a particular font is too small, or a given set of colors didn't map well on that user's browsing platform.

One way you could solve this problem is by giving your site visitors the ability to customize the styles used to present the site's content. That allows your users to view your site in an optimal way under any number of configurations, while offering a level of personalization most sites don't provide.

This next example solves that very problem. The example loads a Web page, our previous news story, using a default set of styles. The user is then presented with three buttons, each of which is wired to a different style sheet. When the user selects a button, a different theme is loaded.

```
<HTML>
  <HEAD></HEAD>

  <SCRIPT FOR="window" EVENT="onload">
    {
      source = new ActiveXObject("Microsoft.XMLDOM");
      source.async = false;
      style = new ActiveXObject("Microsoft.XMLDOM");
      style.async = false;

      source.load("news.xml");
      style.load("style1.xsl");
      xslTarget.innerHTML = source.transformNode(style);
```

```
    }
  </SCRIPT>

  <BODY>
    <FORM>
      <INPUT TYPE="BUTTON"
        NAME="StyleButton"
        VALUE="Change Styles"
        ONCLICK="changeXSL('style1.xsl')">
      <INPUT TYPE="BUTTON"
        NAME="StyleButton"
        VALUE="Change Styles"
        ONCLICK="changeXSL('style2.xsl')">
      <INPUT TYPE="BUTTON"
        NAME="StyleButton"
        VALUE="Change Styles"
        ONCLICK="changeXSL('style3.xsl')">
    </FORM>

  <SCRIPT>
    var source;
    var style;

    // --- Scripts to control XSL Processing ---

    function changeXSL(xslStyle)
    {
        style.load(xslStyle);
        xslTarget.innerHTML = source.transformNode(style);
    }

  </SCRIPT>

    <DIV id="xslTarget"></DIV>

  </BODY>
</HTML>
```

This script differs from others presented thus far in that this one checks the onload event and runs immediately upon loading the page. When the page loads, the script creates two DOM objects. The first object, xmlDocument, will represent the XML document and the other represents the XSL style sheet. Next, the onload script loads news.xml into the XML DOM.

We have defined three style sheets, each capable of displaying news.xml in a different style. Initially, the `onload` script loads style1.xsl into our newly created `stylesheet` object. To associate the style sheet with the XML document, I take advantage of the `transformNode()` method, which is a Microsoft extension to the DOM. In general, the `transformNode()` method takes a DOM node (or set of nodes) with an associated style sheet and transforms the node according to the style sheet. In this case, transform the entire document and assign it to the `innerHTML` property.

If you are unfamiliar with `innerHTML`, it is a DHTML property that allows you get and set HTML dynamically within a Web document. In this case, we assign this property to the user-defined `xslTarget` object. In the document `<BODY>` we use a `<DIV>` element to display the contents of the innerHTML property, which is the transformation of our XML document and associated style sheet.

I should mention that there is one *huge* drawback to this approach. Apparently, the `innerHTML` property does not properly handle the HTML `<STYLE>` element. That means our CSS styles will not be applied to the transformed HTML. To get around this problem, you can rewrite your transformations by placing each style to be applied within a `<DIV>` block. For example, the news.xsl style sheet presented earlier in this chapter contains the following transformation:

```
<STYLE TYPE="text/css">

        <!-- Navigation Bar Styles -->
   ...
        #NavHead {
            font-weight: bold;
            text-align: center;
            font-size: 24px;
            text-decoration: none;
            font-family: "Times New Roman",
                          "serif", "Garamond";
            color: white;
            display: block;
```

```
      background-color: navy;
      border-style: outset;
      margin-left: 2%; margin-right: 5% }
 ...
</STYLE>
```

The ellipses represent surrounding code. The purpose of the `#Nav-Head` style rule is to format the navigation bar's title, which is called "InSite." As you can see from Figure 8-1, this rule places white text on a navy blue background and uses the `outset` border style to give the title a raised, 3-D appearance.

Because the `innerHTML` property doesn't properly apply CSS styles, this rule will be ignored. You can work around this problem by applying the STYLE attribute within a `<DIV>` block, like so:

```
<DIV STYLE="font-weight: bold;
      text-align: center;
      font-size: 24px;
      text-decoration: none;
      color: white;
      display: block; background-color: navy;
      border-style: outset;
      margin-left: 2%; margin-right: 5%">InSite</DIV>
```

This approach works, but note that the content of the `<DIV>` element is the navigation bar's title. The implication is that this style cannot be reused. In addition, rewriting all of your styles in a non-standard way is not a desirable solution.

There are (at least) two alternatives to associating a style sheet with an XML document. The first is to read the source XML document into a DOM object, use DOM method calls to create the `<xsl:stylesheet>` processing instruction, and write the whole thing back out to the result tree. This has the effect of mapping the style sheet to the source document dynamically. The potential drawbacks are that it can consume additional processing time and require additional trips to the server to fetch the style sheet.

The other approach is far less elegant. Essentially, you create multiple versions of the source document, each of which contains an

`<?xml-stylesheet>` processing instruction pointing to a different style sheet. For example, you might have three source documents named source1.xml, source2.xml, and source3.xml. The source1.xml document would contain the processing instruction pointing to style1.xsl.

```
<?xml-stylesheet type="text/xsl" href="style1.xsl"?>
```

source2.xml would contain a similar processing instruction pointing to style2.xsl, and so on. All that needs be done at this point is to provide the user with a means for selecting different style sheets, such as a Submit button or a hyperlink. Under the hood, you simply point the URL to the appropriate source document.

8.3 | Presenting Data

Possibly the most frequently asked question I receive is: "How do I populate a table with fields from a database?" In fact, there are three approaches you can take. The choice you make depends on the complexity of the data, how you need to process it, and the capabilities of your users. Your choices are, in order of difficulty: to use a data source object (either through a data island or by instantiating the DSO ActiveX control), to create an XSL style sheet, or to load the XML document into a DOM object and access the data through the DOM API. Let's look at the simple case first.

Our example takes an XML data stream that represents database records. The records are from a database of XML tools. The data stream could have been sent by the server in response to a database query. To test our example, here's a sample data stream containing three records from the XML Tools database:

```
<?xml version="1.0"?>
<?xml-stylesheet type="text/xsl" href="tools1.xsl"?>
```

```
<productDB>
   <product category="authoring">
      <prodName>XML Toolbox</prodName>
      <company name="BeyondHTML">
         <address>
            <street1>123 West Fourth Street</street1>
            <street2>Suite 5</street2>
            <city>Anytown</city>
            <state>CA</state>
            <province/>
            <country>USA</country>
         </address>
         <phone>123-456-7890</phone>
         <fax>123-987-6543</fax>
         <website href="http://www.beyondhtml.com"/>
      </company>
      <version>1.0</version>
      <price>99.95</price>
      <sys-requirements>
          Any Java Platform
      </sys-requirements>
      <description>
         XML Toolbox is a collection of tools for creating
         and processing XML documents.
      </description>
      <prodURL
      href="http://www.beyondhtml.com/toolbox.html"/>
   </product>


   <product category="parser">
      <prodName>xml4j</prodName>
      <company name="IBM">
         <address>
            <street1>123 West Fourth Street</street1>
            <street2>Suite 5</street2>
            <city>Anytown</city>
            <state>CA</state>
            <province/>
            <country>USA</country>
         </address>
         <phone>123-456-7890</phone>
         <fax>123-987-6543</fax>
         <website href="http://www.beyondhtml.com"/>
      </company>
      <version>1.1.1.4</version>
```

```
    <price>Freely available</price>
    <sys-requirements>
       Any Java platform
    </sys-requirements>
    <description>
       xml4j is an XML processor that is compliant with
       the XML 1.0 working draft specification
    </description>
 </product>

 <product category="parser">
    <prodName>MSXML</prodName>
    <company name="Microsoft/DataChannel">
       <address>
          <street1>123 West Fourth Street</street1>
          <street2>Suite 5</street2>
          <city>Anytown</city>
          <state>CA</state>
          <province/>
          <country>USA</country>
       </address>
       <phone>123-456-7890</phone>
       <fax>123-987-6543</fax>
       <website href="http://www.beyondhtml.com"/>
    </company>
    <version>N/A</version>
    <price>Freely available</price>
    <sys-requirements>
       Any Java platform
    </sys-requirements>
    <description>
       MSXML is an XML processor that is compliant with
       the XML 1.0 working draft specification
    </description>
 </product>
</productDB>
```

Each of the three records is contained in a `<product>` element. Each product contains information about the product as well as details about the company offering the product. The entire data stream is wrapped in a `<productDB>` element.

Also, note that an XSL style sheet is referenced in the XML data stream. This style sheet is used to transform the data stream to

HTML for presentation in any XML-aware browser. However, since we are using Internet Explorer 5, we can create an HTML table that automatically binds the XML data to it. This table will override any styles established by the stylesheet. The following HTML file shows how to create this table:

```
<HTML>
    <HEAD>
        <TITLE>Data Source Object Example</TITLE>
    </HEAD>
    <BODY>

     <P>DSO Example</P>

        <XML ID=productDB src="tools1.xml">
        </XML>

       <TABLE datasrc=#productDB BGCOLOR="66CCFF">
       <CAPTION ALIGN="left"
                STYLE="background-color: 0066CC;
                       color:CCFFFF;">
          <B>Search Results</B>
       </CAPTION>
       <THEAD>
          <TR><TH align="left">Product Name</TH>
          <TH align="left">Version</TH>
          <TH align="left">Price</TH></TR>
       </THEAD>
       <TBODY>
       <tr>
          <td><div datafld="prodName"></div></td>
          <td><div datafld="version"></div></td>
          <td><div datafld="price"></div></td>
       </tr></TBODY>
        </TABLE>
    </BODY>
    </HTML>
```

This example uses the <XML> element to create an XML data island. The src attribute specifies the URL for the database result set, which is loaded into the data island. The ID attribute allows us to reference the data island through script. By creating a data island, we automatically

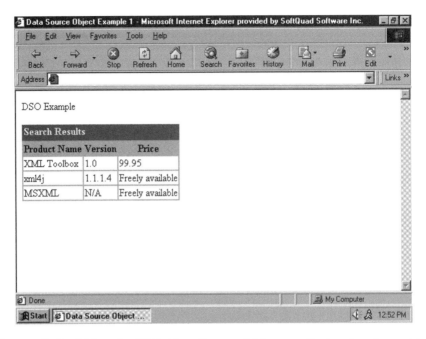

Figure 8–2   Using the XML Data Source Object to display data in a table.

create a new data source object and load it with the XML data stream, thus avoiding the <OBJECT> tag syntax.

More importantly, the XML DSO allows us to map our data to a number of HTML elements including tables. All we need to do is map the table to the data source using the datasrc attribute. The value used in the datasrc attribute must be prefixed with the pound sign, and is the value that was created in the ID attribute of the data island. After that, populating the table is a simple matter of specifying the record field names. The result is shown in Figure 8-2.

8.3.1   *Filtering Your Result Set*

Our next example shows how you can access all of the elements in your document, including their attributes. In this example, we will use an XSL style sheet to filter out portions of the database. Specifically, the

XML Tools database categorizes tools into five areas: authoring tools, vocabularies and DTDs, interfaces and APIs, parsers, and miscellaneous tools. Using a style sheet, we can examine each product element and check its category attribute. If the category matches that specified by the user, it is included in the result set. Here is an XSL style sheet that filters out all of the tools except authoring tools:

```
<?xml version="1.0"?>

<xsl:stylesheet
   xmlns:xsl="http://www.w3.org/TR/WD-xsl"
   xmlns="http://www.w3.org/TR/REC-html40"
   result-ns="">

  <!- Root template ->
  <xsl:template match="/">
    <HTML>
     <HEAD>
       <META http-equiv="Content-Type"
             content="text/html; charset=iso-8859-1"/>
      <TITLE>
        XML Tools Database
      </TITLE>

    </HEAD>
    <BODY>
    <TABLE BGCOLOR="66CCFF">
    <CAPTION ALIGN="left"
            STYLE="background-color: 0066CC;
                   color:CCFFFF;">
      <B>Search Results</B>
    </CAPTION>
    <TBODY>
        <TR>
          <TD><B>Product</B></TD>
          <TD><B>Company</B></TD>
          <TD><B>Price</B></TD>
        </TR>
        <xsl:for-each select="productDB/product">
          <TR>
          <xsl:if test="@category[.='authoring']">
              <TD><xsl:value-of select="prodName"/></TD>
              <TD>
```

```
            <xsl:value-of select="company/@name"/>
            </TD>
            <TD><xsl:value-of select="price"/></TD>
        </xsl:if>
        </TR>

      </xsl:for-each>
    </TBODY>
    </TABLE>

    </BODY>
  </HTML>
  </xsl:template>
</xsl:stylesheet>
```

This style sheet performs the filtering and transformations at the same time. First the table is created and formatted. Then, an <xsl:for-each> element processes each row of the table. The key to the filtering process is an <xsl:if> element, which instructs the processor to check the @category attribute. If this attribute equals "authoring," then a new row is created in the table; otherwise, this record is ignored and the processor moves on to the next record.

Additional style sheets are created for the other categories. To display the results in an HTML page, we simply reload the XML data stream with the appropriate style sheet. Here's the code:

```
<HTML>
  <HEAD></HEAD>

  <SCRIPT FOR="window" EVENT="onload">
    {
      source = new ActiveXObject("Microsoft.XMLDOM");
      source.async = false;
      style = new ActiveXObject("Microsoft.XMLDOM");
      style.async = false;

      source.load("tools1.xml");
      style.load("authoring.xsl");
      xslTarget.innerHTML = source.transformNode(style);
    }
  </SCRIPT>
```

```
<BODY>
<SCRIPT>
  var source;
  var style;

  // --- Scripts to control XSL Processing ---


  function changeXSL(xslStyle)
  {
      style.load(xslStyle);
      xslTarget.innerHTML = source.transformNode(style);
  }

  // --- Function to filter out by category ---
  function filter(cat)
  {
    if (cat == "authoring")
       changeXSL("authoring.xsl");
    if (cat == "parser")
       changeXSL("parser.xsl");
    if (cat == "interfaces")
       changeXSL("interfaces.xsl");
    if (cat == "vocabularies")
       changeXSL("vocabularies.xsl");
    if (cat == "misc")
       changeXSL("misc.xsl");
  }
</SCRIPT>

  <FORM Method="post">
   <SELECT NAME="category">
      <OPTION VALUE="prodName">--select a category--
      <OPTION VALUE="authoring">authoring
      <OPTION VALUE="parser">parser
      <OPTION VALUE="interfaces">interfaces
      <OPTION VALUE="vocabularies">vocabularies
      <OPTION VALUE="misc">misc
    </SELECT>

      <INPUT TYPE="BUTTON"
             NAME="ChangeView" Value="Filter"
             ONCLICK="filter(category.value)">
    </FORM>
```

```
<DIV id="xslTarget"></DIV>

</BODY>
</HTML>
```

The resulting display is shown in Figure 8-3. In this example, the user has elected to view all of the parsers in the database. Of course, this is just a sample data set: the real XML tools database (available at BeyondHTML.com) lists more than a dozen parsers.

Finally, it should be noted this solution is not particularly elegant since it hardwires the filter into the style sheet, and it requires another trip to the server to retrieve the appropriate style sheet. A production system would most likely provide all of the filtering in a single style sheet using a series of `<xsl:if>` statements. However, this requires that the server software be able to intercept the filter request and process the stylesheet accordingly. In addition, it still requires another trip to the server to process the request.

If traffic on the server is an issue, you might choose to send the style sheet just once and let the browser do all the processing. That's where our third (and next) approach using the DOM comes in.

8.3.2   *Searching*

The simplicity of the data island syntax makes it easy to load XML documents and bind the data to HTML controls. However, this approach is best for smaller sets of data when little processing other than basic presentation is required. For example, note in our XML data stream that the `product` element contains a `category` attribute. The problem is that the simple syntax used in these bound controls does not allow us to access and present an element's attributes.

Certainly style sheets can be used to process navigation requests, but the style sheet must be reloaded each time a new request is made. In a heavily-used database, it may be desirable to offload such processing to the browser. Our next example shows you how.

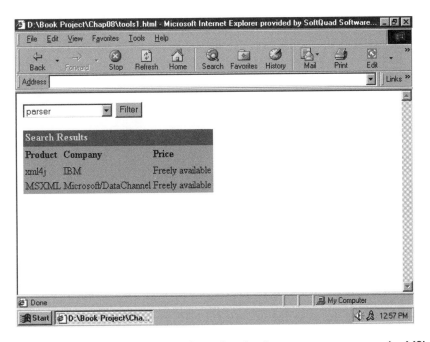

Figure 8–3 Filtering out all tools in the database except parsers. An XSL style sheet performs the filtering, then transforms the result to HTML. The XML DSO is used to populate both the table and the drop-down list box.

```
<HTML>
  <HEAD></HEAD>

  <SCRIPT FOR="window" EVENT="onload">
    {
      source = new ActiveXObject("Microsoft.XMLDOM");
      source.async = false;
      style = new ActiveXObject("Microsoft.XMLDOM");
      style.async = false;

      source.load("tools1.xml");
      style.load("tools1.xsl");
      xslTarget.innerHTML = source.transformNode(style);
    }

  </SCRIPT>

  <BODY>
```

```
<SCRIPT>
  var source;
  var style;

  // ----- Swap XSL Style Sheets ------
  function changeXSL(xslStyle)
  {
      style.load(xslStyle);
      xslTarget.innerHTML = source.transformNode(style);
  }

 function search(searchStr)
 {
  var docRoot = source.documentElement;
  if (docRoot == null)
     alert("Document is null");

  else {

    Name = source.nodeName;
    Value = source.nodeValue;

    node = docRoot.selectSingleNode("/productDB/product/
    prodName");
    products = docRoot.selectNodes("/productDB/product/
    prodName");
    len = products.length;

    for (i = 0; i < len; i++)
    {
       prod = docRoot.selectNodes("/productDB/product/
       prodName").item(i).text;
       if ( prod == searchStr )

       company = prod.selectNodes("../price").item(0).text;

   xslTarget.innerHTML = prod + found! + xslTarget.innerHTML;

    }

  }

 }
```

```
</SCRIPT>

   <P>Enter a search phrase<BR></P>
   <FORM>
      <INPUT NAME="searchStr" SIZE="40">
      <BR><BR><BR>

      <INPUT TYPE="BUTTON"
         NAME="searchButton"
         VALUE="Search"
         ONCLICK="search(searchStr.value)">
   </FORM>

   <DIV id="xslTarget"></DIV>

   </BODY>
</HTML>
```

This example is similar to the last example. It loads the XML Tools database and calls `changeXSL()` to load a style sheet. This time, however, we place an edit field on the screen that the user can use to enter a search phrase. When the user presses the "search" button, the `search` method is invoked.

The search method demonstrates how you can use `selectNodes()` to access any element in the document. `selectNodes()` takes a pattern (see Chapter 3) as an argument and selects the set of nodes that matches the pattern. In this case, we have selected all nodes that have been tagged as a `prodName`. A node list is returned in the products variable. From here, you can use the `length` property to determine the number of nodes that have been selected. We use this number in a `for` loop to iterate through the list. The loop first tests to see if the current product name is equal to the search string entered by the user. If it is, the loop simply reports that the entry has been found. In practice, you will likely pull up the entire record.

If the current product name doesn't match the search string, the loop skips the printing step. Either way, the loop continues through the list, yielding all possible matches. The search lacks most features you'd find in a typical search such as case mapping, pattern matching, and so on. You will also want to add the ability to search other fields. Those steps are left as an exercise for the reader.

8.4 | Conclusion

When it comes to presenting XML in Internet Explorer, you have several alternatives to choose from. For simple tasks involving smaller data sets, you can use the XML Data Source Object to bind HTML elements. Presenting regular data, such as database records in a table, is particularly easy to implement. Internet Explorer even exposes properties and methods that make it easy to display and page through larger record sets.

Unfortunately, simplicity comes at a price. When you need to present elements in an order other than document order, or you need finer control over presentation, you should consider using XSL style sheets. As we have presented them in this chapter, style sheets are mainly used to access specific elements in the document tree and to transform their content into HTML. Deployment takes a file-based approach in which you can store your XML and XSL files in a directory structure, just as you currently do with HTML files. As long as your visitors are using Internet Explorer, you can point them directly to the .xml file and let the browser process the style sheet and display the document.

For the ultimate in flexibility, you can load your XML streams into a DOM object and access them programmatically. This allows you to modify the data, make calculations, and so on, after it arrives in the browser. This approach also allows you to maintain live connections to your data streams and to dynamically generate presentation elements. We will revisit some of these topics again as we shift our focus to server-side XML in Part 3. See you there.

Part Three

- XML on the Server
- Serving XML with Java
- XML and Active Server Pages

Server Side XML

XML on the Server

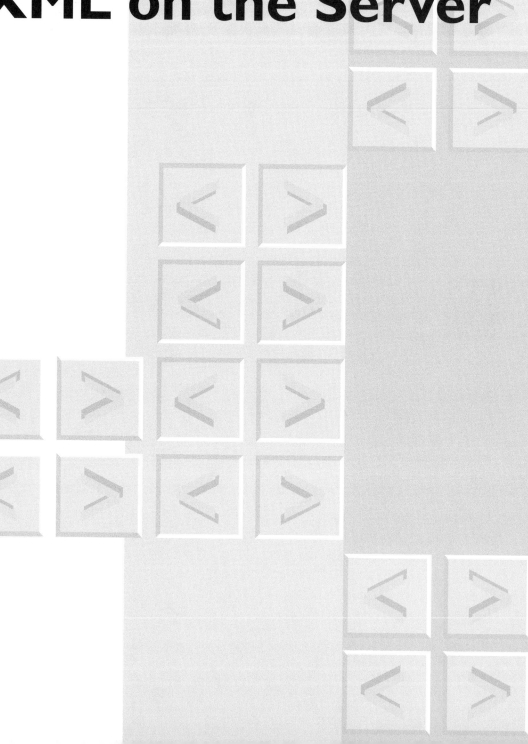

P ossibly the greatest hurdle in Web development is getting Web pages to look and behave the same way in, say, 90 percent of the browsers visiting your site. It is the old Balkanization problem described back in Chapter 1. For all of its features and promise, Internet Explorer may not necessarily be the best place to process XML. The obvious reason is that the solutions presented only run in one browser.

It so happens that not only can you solve the Balkanization problem, but you can improve the situation dramatically. The approach is simple: First, store your Web documents in XML format instead of HTML. Then create a set of style sheets, each tuned to output HTML (or XML, or a combination of both) for a specific browser type. Lastly, create a "gateway" program to detect the browser, select an appropriate style sheet, create the transformation, and send it back to the user. The net result is that you only have to write your style sheets once, updating with new styles is easy, and your users gain an interface customized for their environment. Figure 9-1 shows the overall architecture.

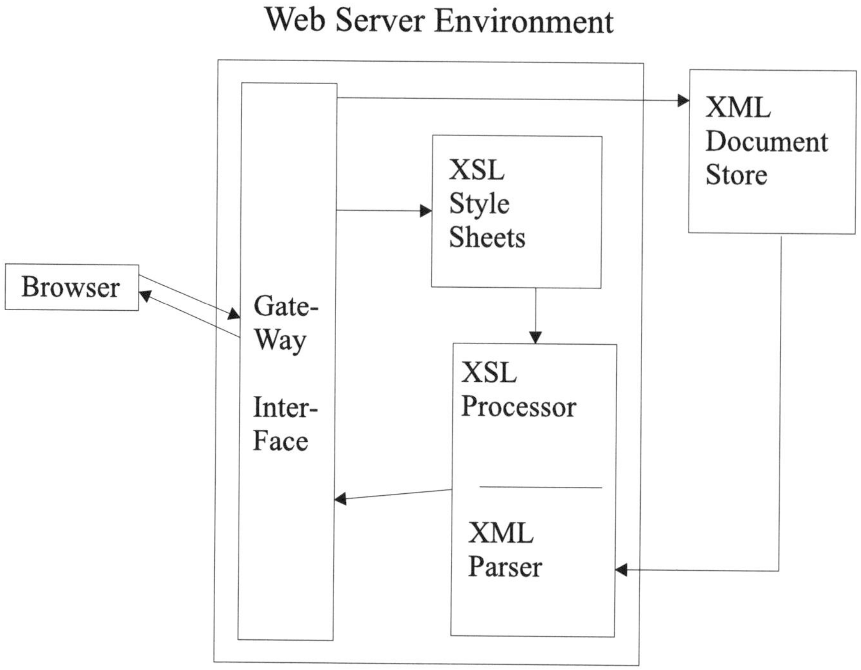

Web Server Environment

Figure 9–1 Serving customized HTML from XML documents.

When you view the Web as a three-tier architecture, processing XML on the middle tier Web server makes sense. Consider a database application where you want to view, search, sort, and modify database records from a client browser. The database resides on a backend server (the third tier) that is accessible from the Web server (the middle tier). In effect, the Web server acts as a "portal" to the database. All of the logic that accepts and processes requests resides on this middle tier. Increasingly, the business and program logic of an application is kept in another tier that is between the Web server and the database server, supported by middleware known as a Web application server (packages such as Netdynamics, Silverstream, Weblogic, and Netscape Application Server). So, it makes sense to process XML at this stage.

These reasons are so compelling that you may be wondering why you would consider processing XML on the client at all. There are, in fact, good reasons for pushing the processing onto the client. However, the architecture you require will ultimately be the determining factor. In this chapter, we will look at various technologies for serving XML and explain the strengths and weaknesses of each approach. Ultimately, the road you take will depend on many factors including the type of problems your development project aims to resolve, the technologies already in use, the skills you possess, the resources at hand, and even your personal preference.

9.1 | Solving the Basic Problem

When I start on a new problem, the first question I ask is: "What do I want to accomplish?" In general terms, you want to:

■ Communicate between the client browser and the Web server.

■ Send XML as a stream from the client to the server.

■ Send transformed XML from the server to the client.

Each point has a different set of issues associated with it. For example, the general mechanism for communicating between browser and server is HTTP. However, there is currently no direct support for XML built into HTTP servers. Therefore, you need to extend the HTTP server in some way. There are several methods for extending a server including CGI, server APIs, and Java servlets. So, the method for extending your server's functionality to support XML will be the first decision you must make.

The second point, sending an XML stream to the server may or may not be a requirement. For example, a simple document server that stores XML documents and serves appropriately formatted HTML back to the client has no compelling need to receive XML. From the browser's perspective, it is business as usual. On the other hand, a browser that is submitting an update to a database may want to process XML, then send the resulting text back to the server. The benefit is that you avoid server-side transformations, and as a bonus you could perform client-side validation for "data scrubbing" before hitting the database. Therefore, the decision to handle incoming XML is specific to your particular problem.

At a minimum, however, you will want to send transformed XML from the server to the client. The data stream may be transformed HTML, or it could be dynamically generated XML. To perform this level of XML processing, you will need to install both an XML parser to read XML documents and expose them through the DOM, and an XSL processor to handle the transformations. Your choices here involve the processors. The most popular processors are written in either Java or C/C++. However, there are processors that have been written in Python, Perl, and even JavaScript. Again, the choice you make will most likely be based on performance, functionality, skill set, and personal preference.

You must also put the problem into context. How much money and resources do you have to throw at the problem? Can you gain more from a canned solution? To that end, we will later look at some solutions that are commercially available. First, let's consider the methods you can use to extend your server in order to support XML.

9.2 | Extending Web Servers

No matter which Web server platform you are working with, the bottom line is that you must in some way extend its capabilities. As with everything else on the Web, there are several methods for doing this. The first and most universal method for extending Web server functionality is CGI, or Common Gateway Interface.

As a Web developer, you know CGI programs are server-side programs or scripts that take a request and pass control to an external program on the server. The external program's output is then sent back to the browser in response to the request. To invoke the CGI program, the browser usually makes a request using a URL that points to the program or script. For example, the browser could make a request in response to the user clicking on a hyperlink to yourScript.cgi. When the Web server gets a request for the script's URL, it creates a new process and establishes a set of environment variables containing information about the server, the browser making the request, and the request itself. The server then executes the script, intercepts everything the script prints, and sends it back to the client browser. Finally, the server ends the process that the script ran in.

The response that is sent back to the client must be readable by the browser. Therefore, the response must be suitably formatted HTML. In effect, the CGI script creates a virtual HTML document containing the output of the server program's operation. Web developers quickly learned to exploit this feature to create dynamically generated HTML. In fact, generating HTML on the fly is a primary technique used by CGI programmers today.

Another benefit of CGI scripts is that virtually all Web servers support the CGI interface. Further, the most popular language for writing CGI scripts, Perl, is supported on most server platforms. So, you could write a CGI script that takes a request for an XML document, passes the request to a program that loads the document into an XML parser, processes the document, and sends back the result. Best of all, you can write that CGI program knowing that it is portable to other Web server platforms.

On the downside, you may have noted from our discussion that the process terminates after the script finishes its work. Once the process is terminated, all environment variables are cleared, and the server knows nothing of the script's previous state. If the browser makes another request, the server must create a whole new process. This one process per request method means serious overhead for highly interactive sessions. In addition, plain CGI is inherently slow because of its interpretive nature. Fortunately, in roads have been made with technologies like FastCGI, which attempt to improve the number of requests that can be handled within a process.

9.3 | The XML::Parser Module

If you plan to take the CGI approach using Perl, then you will want to install the XML::Parser module. The XML::Parser module provides an interface to Expat, a popular XML parser written by James Clark. The module was co-developed by Larry Wall, Perl's inventor, and Clark Cooper. XML::Parser requires Perl 5.004, and you can find XML::Parser along with several other useful modules for XML development at your local CPAN (C Perl Archive Network) such as http://www.perl.com/CPAN.

To use XML::Parser, you must first install the package. See the documentation for details. Once it is installed, you can include the module in your scripts by writing:

```
use XML::Parser;
```

Next, you can create a new parser object instance and invoke the parser using the following lines:

```
$xmlDocument = new XML::Parser(Style => 'Debug');
$xmlDocument->parse('<myElementType>Hello
World</myElementType>');
```

This last example parses a short XML element of the type `<myElementType>`. More often, however, you will want to load an XML document from a file. You can do that using the following:

```
$xmlDocument = new XML::Parser(Style => 'Debug');
$xmlDocument->parsefile('myFile.xml');
```

Now, the `$xmlDocument` variable contains a parser object representing the document's tree structure. Thus, you can call any of Expat's parsing methods to traverse the tree, access elements and attributes, and so on. Each time you call to one of the parsing methods, a new instance of XML::Parser::Expat is created. This is a lower-level module that is used to parse the document. You can also set options to control how the parser is invoked, including the ability to toggle validation and to specify handlers. For instance, the previous example invokes the parser in debug mode using a style handler.

You can parse an incoming XML data stream directly using the following approach:

```
$xmlStream = new XML::Parser(Handlers => {
            Start => \&handle_start,
            End   => \&handle_end,
            Char  => \&handle_char});
$xmlStream->parse($socket);
```

As a final example, the following program taken from the XML::Parser samples distribution shows how to walk the document tree and report on elements and attributes:

```
#!/usr/local/bin/perl -w
#
# $Revision: 1.5 $
#
# $Date: 1998/10/28 04:30:23 $

package Elinfo;

sub new {
    bless { COUNT   => 0,
            MINLEV  => undef,
            SEEN    => 0,
            CHARS   => 0,
            EMPTY   => 1,
            PTAB    => {},
            KTAB    => {},
            ATAB    => {} }, shift;
}


package main;

use English;
```

```perl
use XML::Parser;

my %elements;
my $seen = 0;
my $root;

my $file = shift;

my $subform =
    '        @<<<<<<<<<<<<<<         @>>>>';
die "Can't find file \"$file\""
  unless -f $file;

my $parser = new XML::Parser(ErrorContext => 2);
$parser->setHandlers(Start => \&start_handler,
                     Char  => \&char_handler);

$parser->parsefile($file);

set_minlev($root, 0);

my $el;

foreach $el (sort bystruct keys %elements)
{
    my $ref = $elements{$el};
    print "\n===============\n$el: ", $ref->{COUNT}, "\n";
    print "Had ", $ref->{CHARS}, " bytes of character data\n"
    if $ref->{CHARS};
    print "Always empty\n"
    if $ref->{EMPTY};

    showtab('Parents', $ref->{PTAB}, 0);
    showtab('Children', $ref->{KTAB}, 1);
    showtab('Attributes', $ref->{ATAB}, 0);
}

################
## End of main
################

sub start_handler
{
    my $p = shift;
```

```perl
    my $el = shift;

    my $elinf = $elements{$el};

    if (not defined($elinf))
    {
    $elements{$el} = $elinf = new Elinfo;
    $elinf->{SEEN} = $seen++;
    }

    $elinf->{COUNT}++;

    my $partab = $elinf->{PTAB};

    my $parent = $p->current_element;
    if (defined($parent))
    {
    $partab->{$parent}++;
    my $pinf = $elements{$parent};

    # Increment our slot in parent's child table
    $pinf->{KTAB}->{$el}++;
    $pinf->{EMPTY} = 0;
    }
    else
    {
    $root = $el;
    }

    # Deal with attributes

    my $atab = $elinf->{ATAB};

    while (@_)
    {
    my $att = shift;

    $atab->{$att}++;
    shift; # Throw away value
    }

}  # End start_handler

sub char_handler
```

```perl
{
    my ($p, $data) = @_;
    my $inf = $elements{$p->current_element};

    $inf->{EMPTY} = 0;
    if ($data =~ /\S/)
    {
        $inf->{CHARS} += length($data);
    }
}  # End char_handler

sub set_minlev
{
    my ($el, $lev) = @_;

    my $elinfo = $elements{$el};
    if (! defined($elinfo->{MINLEV})
        or $elinfo->{MINLEV} > $lev)
    {
    my $newlev = $lev + 1;

    $elinfo->{MINLEV} = $lev;
    foreach (keys %{$elinfo->{KTAB}})
    {
    set_minlev($_, $newlev);
    }
    }
}  # End set_minlev

sub bystruct
{
    my $refa = $elements{$a};
    my $refb = $elements{$b};

    $refa->{MINLEV} <=> $refb->{MINLEV}
    or $refa->{SEEN} <=> $refb->{SEEN};
}  # End bystruct

sub showtab
{
    my ($title, $table, $dosum) = @_;

    my @list = sort keys %{$table};
```

```
    if (@list)
    {
    print "\n    $title:\n";

    my $item;
    my $sum = 0;
    foreach $item (@list)
    {
        my $cnt = $table->{$item};
        $sum += $cnt;
        formline($subform, $item, $cnt);
        print $ACCUMULATOR, "\n";
        $ACCUMULATOR = '';
    }

    if ($dosum and @list > 1)
    {
        print "                               =====\n";
        formline($subform, '', $sum);
        print $ACCUMULATOR, "\n";
        $ACCUMULATOR = '';
    }
    }

}   # End showtab

# Tell Emacs that this is really a perl script
# Local Variables:
# mode:perl
# End:
```

9.4 | Server APIs

Another method for extending server functionality is through a set of programming interfaces or server APIs. These are proprietary interfaces and are specific to each brand of Web server. The most common server APIs are Netscape's NSAPI and Microsoft's ISAPI. Vendors of these APIs claim that you can do away with CGI scripts because you can write more efficient C or C++ programs that extend the server's base functionality. I mention server APIs only because vendors may support XML directly in them in the future. For now, we will not consider the use of these server APIs. If, however, you want to experiment with a server API, you should install one of the many XML parsers as described by this and subsequent chapters. From there, you simply need to handle HTTP requests and the processing of XML documents on the server, because the XML Parser will actually be the workhorse.

9.5 | Java Servlets

Another way to extend Web servers is through the use of Java servlets. Servlets are Java classes that can be loaded dynamically and used to extend server functionality. They run as server applications within a "servlet engine." Most servlet engines include modules that allow the Web server to "translate" servlet requests and forward them to the engine. As of version 1.2 of the Java Development Kit (JDK), servlets are a standard extension to the Java Language.

Servlets have become popular for several reasons. First, they can be used to generate documents on the fly, thus replacing CGI scripts as a means for creating dynamically generated HTML. In addition, because servlets run as threads within a single Web server process, they overcome the one process per request problem that CGI imposes. You also gain the benefits of Java including built-in support for network sockets, database connectivity, and string manipulation. Finally, your servlets are easily portable to any Java-enabled Web server.

In the next chapter, we will examine two approaches to serving XML through the use of servlets. The first is through extensions to the Apache Web server, dubbed the Cocoon Project. The second approach involves writing your own servlets.

9.6 | Active Server Pages

So far, we have been talking somewhat generically about Web servers with a slight lean toward Unix Web servers, and particularly Apache. If you are working with Microsoft's Internet Information Server (IIS) on Windows NT, then you will most certainly want to consider using Active Server Pages, or ASP. ASP is a Microsoft technology that is built into Internet Information Server. ASP allows you to embed JScript or VBScript into HTML pages that reside on the server. The pages are processed at runtime to generate HTML that is sent to the client. As such, ASPs are Microsoft's principal technology for generating Web content dynamically.

ASP allows you to instantiate a DOM object, load XML documents, and manipulate them using JScript or VBScript in much the same way we have discussed in Part 2. Chapter 11 covers ASP in detail, so an in-depth explanation will be deferred until then.

9.7 | Commercial XML Servers

If creating your own server tools is not your bag, or your company has the resources to spend money on a more robust system, you may want to consider a commercial XML server package. Most server packages include industrial-strength server features including security, transaction processing, and seamless access to back-end systems. While still an emerging market, there are already several approaches to serving XML. DataChannel Rio and WebMethods's B2B both address the high-end enterprise market and include the ability to recognize and process XML. In a slightly different class, Object Design offers its eXcelon XML data server, which combines its object-oriented database technology with Java and XML.

While space does not permit a complete discussion of each of these products, it may be useful to examine one such XML server product that fits well into the Web paradigm, contains robust features, and is easy to set up and use. Bluestone's XML-server is based, in part, on Bluestone's expertise with its Sapphire/Web server—one of the first industrial-strength Web development tools. XML-Server combines Java and XML to create what the company refers to as XML applications. This server features security services and the transaction processing features, thread pooling, and more. XML Server also supports the idea of Data Source Integration Modules (DSIMs) that give a standard method for accessing database data. Interestingly, DSIMs extend the traditional concept of data sources to other sources including APIs and even network protocols. Please note that the following discussion is not an endorsement of this particular product, nor is it a review.

9.7.1   *Bluestone XML-Server*

As Bluestone Software describes it, Bluestone XML-Server is a dynamic XML application server. The server runs in a Java Virtual Machine and offers a number of services that are accessible to Java programmers through an application framework (see Figure 9–2). This approach allows you to develop "XML applications," programs containing logic that can be executed through the server. The server contains several services to support thread pooling, connection pooling, security, and transactions. XML-Server includes full XML and XSL processing support, and additionally includes a set of document handlers for processing XML dynamically.

To develop an XML application, you start by creating an application class, which takes incoming XML documents and passes them to a set of document handlers. The document handlers then process XML documents. In general, you define a document handler for each XML document type your application will process. You can also

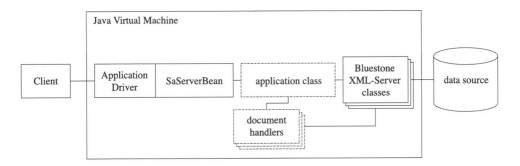

Figure 9–2   Bluestone's XML-Server Architecture.

define a default document handler within the application class. Because document handlers run in the same JVM as the application class that uses it, they can be shared by multiple XML applications. They can also be defined to be private to prevent other XML applications from modifying unknown document types.

Developing an XML application is straightforward for the seasoned Java programmer. However, Bluestone also supplies a visual tool, Visual XML, that can be used to generate an application. The tool is particularly useful for those with less programming experience. However, seasoned developers can also use the tool to avoid a bit of hand coding.

Once the application has been created, it can be called by Bluestone's Load Balance Broker or through an application driver. To invoke the XML application, the client sends an XML document and the name of the Java class file containing an XML application. When the server receives the request, the application driver (or LBB) searches the CLASSPATH of the local machine, and an instance of this class is launched in the JVM. The driver also reads a configuration file containing configuration information for the XML application and sends this along with the XML document to the XML application instance. Next, the appropriate document handlers are selected and the XML document is processed. This also makes the document tree accessible to the document handlers through the DOM.

Borrowed from the Bluestone XML-Server documentation, the following example shows how you can set up an XML application and access it from a client browser over an HTTP connection. On the client side, the example instantiates an SaServerBean and sends it a simulated HTTP request. The arguments are sent as part of a posted form.

```
// create a server bean
SaServerBean bean = (SaServerBean) Beans.instantiate(null,
"SaApi.SaServerBean");

// set its configuration file
bean.setConfigFileName("D:/sapphire/config/sajava.ini");

// set the application class
bean.setUrlSpec("SaExXmlApp.class");

// simulate form "post"
bean.setPost(true);

// add form arg "SaDocAction" which sets doc method
bean.SaAddArg("SaDocAction", "theDefault");

// add form arg "SaDocType" which sets doc type
bean.SaAddArg("SaDocType", "item-list");

// add form arg "SaDoc" which sets document contents
bean.SaAddArg("SaDoc", "<item-list></item-list>");

// perform request
bean.serviceRequest();

// get the contents
String c = bean.getContents();

// print the results
System.err.println(c);
```

The example sets three parameters—SaDoc, SaDocType, and SaDoAction—and posts them to XML-Server a form. SaDoc and SaDocType contain the names of the XML document and its document type, respectively. SaDoAction names a method that should be called by one of the document handlers. Finally, the example retrieves the resulting output from the server and prints it out.

9.8 | Conclusion

The question of "where" XML should be processed is a more subtle question than "when?" For example, when working with a back-end database, should you store the raw data marked up in XML, or should you process XML independently outside of the system? If you are creating a new database from scratch, storing the markup with the data could allow for better description (and therefore, better manipulation) of data. To gain the full benefit of XML within the database will require specialized software. Who knows, it is even possible that the next wave of technology will include "XML-oriented databases!"

However, it is far more likely that you are working with an existing database, in which case you will want to find a solution that doesn't require modifications to existing systems. The question then is: "How do I get my data into XML?" The first step is to translate your database field names into markup and the raw data into content. At this point, you can simply read your "XML data stream" into a DOM object and process as usual. The larger issues that loom involve how data is described.

When it comes to client interaction, the question is when should the client send XML? This offloads work from the server while taking advantage of the client's ability to format and process XML. Of course, this requires an XML-aware browser, so you are by definition limiting your audience or requiring specialized resources. Either way, these decisions affect the approach you take in developing your server software.

Whatever you decide, the first question is: "How will you marshal the requests on your server?" In this chapter, we have looked at a

CGI-based approach. We have also touched upon server APIs and application servers. In the following chapters, we will examine two alternatives: Java Servlets and Active Server Pages.

9.9 | Resources

Java Development Kit
http://java.sun.com

Java Servlet Development Kit
http://java.sun.com

Java ProjectX
http://java.sun.com

XML for Java Processor
http://www.AlphaWorks.ibm.com

LotusXSL
http://www.AlphaWorks.ibm.com

XML Enabler
http://www.AlphaWorks.ibm.com

9.10 | References

"Java Servlet Programming" by Jason Hunter and William Crawford (O'Reilly: Sabastapol, CA, 1998).
"XML-Server API Documentation." Bluestone Software (Mount Laurel, NJ, 1999).

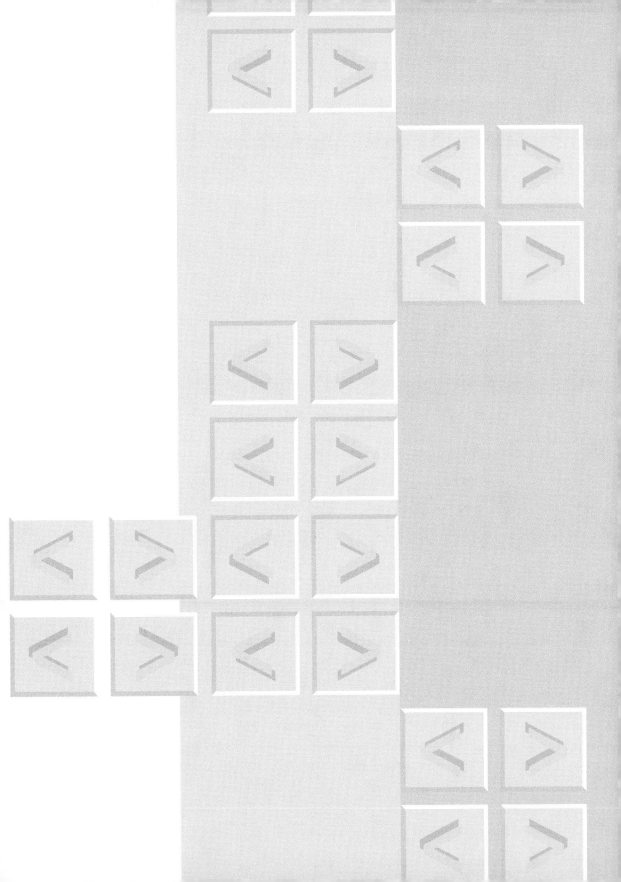

Serving XML Using Java Servlets

Dishing up XML from a Web server seems like it would be a straightforward task. All you need is an XML parser and a way to communicate via HTTP. Indeed, there are dozens of freely available XML parsers that can be downloaded from the Web. There are parsers written in Java, C++, Perl, Python, and even JavaScript. The other half of the equation is your ability to communicate over an HTTP connection. That part is easy—just go to your Web server, right? Well, this is where things become a bit muddled. For one thing, much depends upon the server platform you are running on. For instance, your system may be hosted with a service that is running Red Hat Linux with the Apache server. On the other hand, you may be working in an Intranet environment that uses the Internet Information Server (IIS) on Windows NT.

When it comes to Unix, Java servlets are emerging as a primary means for delivering XML. For example, the Apache Web server uses Java servlets to deliver XML through a project called the Cocoon Project. At the same time, Sun Microsystems is providing enabling technologies such as Java Server Pages (JSP), which allow the dynamic creation of Web pages using Java and Java Project X, which provide core XML capabilities. ProjectX includes a fast XML parser with optional validation and an in-memory object model tree that supports the DOM. Using this package, it is rather easy to write a servlet that intercepts HTTP requests and serves XML documents in response.

Indeed, the servlet scene is heating up. This chapter examines several approaches to serving XML through the use of Java servlets and shows how you can set up your own solution for delivering XML using freely available tools.

10.1 | About Java Servlets

In the last chapter, we looked at a CGI-based approach to delivering XML content, which should work on most Web platforms. With CGI, however, you are limited both in terms of the parsers supported and by the one-process-per-request problem. Not only does this affect performance, it also makes it cumbersome to handle issues of persistence. This, in turn, makes it difficult for the client and server to interact at a finer-grained level.

For example, there are times where you will want to work with portions of a document tree, rather than the entire document. One example might be a workgroup application that allows authors to work on different parts of the same document. The standard way of dealing with this is to allow only one author to "check out" the document and lock out other authors until the document is checked back in. A distributed approach, on the other hand, could allow designers, content authors, and the Webmaster to "check out" portions of the document tree, thus allowing each to work on the same document simultaneously. This is clearly a nontrivial problem using CGI.

Servlets, on the other hand, are Java classes that load dynamically and run inside a servlet engine. What this means is that all of your servlets can run inside a single Java Virtual Machine (JVM). One important consequence is that your servlets can share (or hide) data.

Also, once a servlet is started, it exists as an object instance within the servlet engine. This means that servlets can maintain state in between requests. The final piece of the puzzle is multithreading. Servlets can process multiple requests on a per-thread basis. This is the feature that could, for instance, allow an author to update a portion of the document tree while the Web Master works on another.

Other reasons to consider servlets is that they work hand in hand with the numerous Java XML processors that are readily available. And like CGI, servlets are easily portable to any Java-enabled Web server. If you are convinced that servlets are the way to go, the next question is how do you implement your servlets and integrate them with your XML parser. One answer comes from the Cocoon Project.

10.2 | Cocoon: An XML-enabled Servlet for Apache

Without question, one of the most popular and common Web servers in use is the Apache Web server. In fact, according to a survey by Netcraft Ltd., more than 56 percent of the six-million-plus public Web sites worldwide are running on Apache software. So, I would be remiss if I overlooked XML solutions for this popular Web server. The Cocoon Project consists of a group of developers from the Apache Group that are adding XML capability to Apache. Cocoon, itself, is a Java servlet that specifically supports XML and XSL. Therefore, a prerequisite to using Cocoon is that you enable Apache to run servlets. The Apache group includes the Apache JServ servlet engine for this purpose, and because of their popularity there's a good chance that servlets are already enabled on your server. Installing a servlet engine is beyond the scope of this book, so check with your system administrator for details.

By default, Cocoon uses OpenXML for its XML parser and XSL:P as its style sheet processor. However, it also supports IBM's XML for

Java (xml4j) and LotusXSL processors, and the processors included with Sun's ProjectX. The way Cocoon interacts is that the server receives a request for an XML document, which is then passed to the servlet. For example, the servlet loads the document into the OpenXML parser and calls XSL:P to apply any style sheets that may be referenced. The result can be an HTML transformation or transformed XML to be processed on the client. So, the Cocoon servlet allows for three output types: HTML, XHTML, and XML. (XHTML is a W3C draft standard that forces HTML to be well-formed.) Whatever type is specified, the output is then passed back to the client in that format.

10.2.1 *Installing Cocoon*

Installation of Cocoon assumes that you already have Apache JServ up and running on your server. With servlet support installed, you can download the Cocoon distribution from http://java.apache.org. Once you have the distribution, simply unpack Cocoon into its own directory.

With the files unpacked, you are ready to install the servlet in your servlet engine. First, copy the /bin/cocoon.jar file from the distribution into your servlets directory (the directory specified in your CLASSPATH). You must also add the jar files for the XML and XSL processors you will be using. In this example, we will be installing the OpenXML and XSL:P processors. (Details for installing IBM's xml4j and LotusXSL processors are presented in the next section.)

After physically placing the files within the directory structure, you must add the names of the two packages, xslp.jar and openxml.jar, to your servlet properties file. For example, assuming you've installed Cocoon into a directory called "cocoon," add the following lines to your jserv.properties file:

```
wrapper.classpath=cocoon/bin/xslp.jar
wrapper.classpath=cocoon/bin/openxml.jar
```

Next, you need to inform the engine where the servlet can be found. You do this by adding it to a servlet zone. Servlet zones are referenced in a properties file with a name that is something like my-zone.properties. Within that file, add the following line:

```
repositories=cocoon/bin/cocoon.jar
```

Next, the servlet engine must be able to pass initialization parameters to the Cocoon servlet. These arguments are set in the coocoon.properties file. So, you must add the following line so that the servlet can locate its configuration file (note that because of book formatting, this appears on two lines. In practice, it must be written on a single line in the configuration file):

```
servlet.org.apache.cocoon.Cocoon.initArgs=
properties=cocoon/bin/cocoon.properties
```

At this point, Cocoon should be properly configured. The only thing left to do is to register the XML file type with Apache. This allows the server to direct any call to an XML file (or any other file you want Cocoon to process) to the Cocoon servlet. To do this, you should add the following line to your Apache conf files where you placed the other mod_jserv directives (usually httpd.conf):

```
ApJServAction .xml /servlets/org.apache.cocoon.Cocoon
```

10.2.2   *Working with Cocoon*

As an unfinished work, Cocoon suffers from a number of problems. One such problem involves XML's requirement for elements to be well formed. For example, XML allows empty elements to be specified using a single tag with a trailing slash, as shown here:

```
<BR/>
```

Assuming you specified either the XML or XHTML output type, the transformed document will still contain this empty element syntax. If you then try to display this document in a nonXML aware browser, it will choke on this element because the trailing slash is not recognized in HTML. The obvious workaround is to specify output type to be HTML. Unfortunately, the output type is specified when you invoke the Cocoon servlet, and it cannot be changed once the servlet is running. The net result is that you cannot generate both XML documents and HTML documents using the same instance of the Cocoon servlet. The documentation suggests that you get around this by creating two servlet zones with two different instances of Cocoon running in the same servlet engine.

10.2.3   *Generating XML Dynamically*

Another drawback to Cocoon is that it provides for only static XML. That is, the XML files must already exist on the server (or somewhere accessible over the network). Stated another way, Cocoon currently does not allow you to dynamically generate XML. Members of the Cocoon project have been working on this problem and have proposed two extensions that would allow dynamic processing of XML.

The first, eXtensible Server Pages (XSP), allows you to embed programming logic directly into an XML document. This is similar in concept to the way Active Server Pages (ASP) embeds JavaScript or VBScript into HTML documents, or the model used for Java Server Pages (JSP), which executes Java code that is embedded directly into documents.

XSP defines a DTD for the elements that can be used in your XML documents. These elements are programming constructs that are executed on the server before the document is served. The elements allow you to create an XSP page and define programming structures that can contain includes, variables, program logic, and XML content. So, for example, consider the following XSP document:

```
<?xml version="1.0"?>
<!DOCTYPE page>

<page>
   <headline>Today's Weather Forecast</headline>
   <para>Today's weather forecast calls for <skies/> skies,
with <winds/> winds. Forecast high for today is <high/> and
the predicted low is<low/>.
   </para>
</page>
```

You will notice in this example that the paragraph text contains
empty elements that imply additional content. For instance, the actual sky conditions have been substituted with the `<skies/>` element.
Likewise, wind conditions and the forecast high and low values have
also been substituted with elements. Within the XSP model, these
values will be substituted with their actual values according to an XSL
style sheet. XSP calls these "logic sheets." Here's the logic sheet for
this document:

```
<?xml version="1.0"?>
<xsl:stylesheet
 xmlns:xsl="http://www.w3.org/TR/WD-xsl"
 xmlns:xsp="http://java.apache.org/DTD/WD-xsp"
 result-ns="http://java.apache.org/DTD/WD-xsp"
>

 <!— Process the root node —>
 <xsl:template match="/">
  <xsp:page
   xmlns:xsp="http://java.apache.org/DTD/WD-xsp"
   language="java">

  <xsp:structure>
   <xsp:include>java.io.*</xsp:include>
   <xsp:include>java.text.*</xsp:include>
   <xsp:include>java.util.*</xsp:include>
  </xsp:structure>

  <xsp:logic>
   // These methods would normally do lookups in a
   // database
   public string[] skies() {
```

```
            skies = "partly cloudy";
            return;
      }
      public string[] wind() {
            winds = "light";
            return;
      }
      public string[] windDir() {
            windDir = "Northwest";
            return;
      }
    public int hi() {
            hi = "86";
            return;
    public int low() {
            lo = "59";
            return;
      }
    </xsp:logic>

    <xsp:content>
        <page>
          <xsl:apply-templates/>
        </page>
    </xsp:content>
   </xsp:page>
  </xsl:template>

  <xsl:template match="skies">
   <xsp:eval>skies()</xsp:eval>
  </xsl:template>

<xsl:template match="wind">
  <xsp:eval>wind()</xsp:eval>
</xsl:template>

<xsl:template match="windDir">
  <xsp:eval>windDir()</xsp:eval>
</xsl:template>

<xsl:template match="hi">
  <xsp:eval>hi()</xsp:eval>
</xsl:template>

<xsl:template match="low">
```

```
  <xsp:eval>low()</xsp:eval>
</xsl:template>

<xsl:template match="headline">
  <P><H1>
     <xsl:apply-templates/>
  </H1><P>
</xsl:template>

<xsl:template match="para">
  <P>
     <xsl:apply-templates/>
  <P>
</xsl:template>

</xsl:stylesheet>
```

As with any XSL style-sheet document, the first step is to create the opening `<stylesheet>` tag. Within the tag, you create appropriate namespaces. The first is the familiar `xsl:` namespace. (Note that the value used for this namespace is dependent upon the XML processor you are using, and older processors use a slightly different syntax; see Chapter 3 for details.) The attributes following the `xsl:` namespace show how to define the `xsp` and result namespaces.

Next, you will need to create a template for processing the root element, `page`. Details on syntax for this element were sketchy at the time of this writing. You will notice that the `page` element once again references the `xsp` namespace before declaring the language for this XSP page. The reasons for this redundancy are unclear. However, the `language` attribute is required. The only language supported at the time of this writing is Java. Presumably, XSP will support other languages in the future.

The `<xsp:structure>` element is used to define the includes for your program. Here, we import java.io.*, java.text.*, and java.util.*. Finally, the methods of your program should be placed within the confines of an `<xsp:logic>` element. These are the methods that will be evaluated when the XSP environment resolves the "element calls" from the original XML document. For the purpose of this example, each method simply returns a static value. In a real-world application, these values would likely be retrieved from a back-end database.

As with all typical style sheets, the templates following the root template match with specific elements from the document tree and apply additional formatting. The only difference now is that the formatting comes by evaluating a method as defined in the `<xsl:logic>` element. So, for example, when the processor encounters the `<skies/>` element in the document tree, the "skies" template (that is, `<xsl:template match="skies">`) becomes instantiated. This template uses `<xsp:eval>` to evaluate the `skies()` method. In this case, the method simply returns the string "partly cloudy."

Lastly, XSP is a valid XML document and therefore conforms to a DTD. For completeness (and the sake of the curious), the following is the XSP DTD:

```
<!ELEMENT xsp:page (xsp:structure?, xsp:logic?, xsp:content)>
<!ATTLIST xsp:page
  language CDATA #REQUIRED
  result-ns NMTOKEN #IMPLIED
  default-space (preserve|strip) "preserve"
  indent-result (yes|no) "no"
  xmlns:xsp CDATA #FIXED "http://java.apache.org/cocoon/xsp"
  xml:space (default|preserve) "preserve"
>

<!ELEMENT xsp:structure (xsp:dtd?, xsp:include*)>

<!ELEMENT xsp:dtd (#PCDATA)>
<!ELEMENT xsp:include (#PCDATA)>
<!ELEMENT xsp:variable (#PCDATA)>
<!ELEMENT xsp:content
      (#PCDATA |
       xsp:logic |
       xsp:element |
       xsp:eval |
       xsp:pi |
       xsp:comment)*
>

<!ELEMENT xsp:logic
      (#PCDATA |
```

```
        xsp:eval |
        xsp:content |
        xsp:element |
        xsp:comment |
        xsp:pi)*
>
<!ATTLIST xsp:logic
  xml:space (default|preserve) "preserve"
>

<!ELEMENT xsp:element
        (#PCDATA |
        xsp:attribute |
        xsp:element |
        xsp:logic)*
>
<!ATTLIST xsp:element
  name CDATA #REQUIRED
>

<!ELEMENT xsp:attribute (#PCDATA)>
<!ATTLIST xsp:attribute
  name CDATA #REQUIRED
  xml:space (default|preserve) "preserve"
>

<!ELEMENT xsp:pi (#PCDATA | xsp:eval>
<!ELEMENT xsp:comment (#PCDATA | xsp:eval)>
<!ELEMENT xsp:eval (#PCDATA)>
```

10.3 | Building Your Own XML Server

Another more general approach to serving XML also involves Java servlets. In this case, we will put together a collection of Java tools that will allow you to receive HTTP requests, process XML documents, and return the result. The component that makes this work is a Java servlet, called XML Enabler, which was written by IBM and is distributed freely. The servlet takes a request for an XML document, detects the type of browser that made the request, and attaches a style sheet to the XML document based on the requesting browser. By creating a set of style sheets, each containing HTML transformations that take advantage of a specific browser's features, you can serve HTML that is optimized for that browser.

The approach presented here does not require Java programming expertise. The following sections will guide you through the process of installing the necessary components. However, these sections provide enough information so that Java programmers can load an XML file and access nodes through the DOM API. In addition, the XML Enabler servlet can be replaced with a servlet of your own design.

The arrangement of the tools for your development environment is straightforward. First, you must install the Java Development Kit (JDK). The JDK provides all of the supporting Java extensions, including network support. Second, you will need an XML parser and an XSL processor. Generally, the two processors go hand in hand. That is, the XML parser is integrated with the XSL processor in some way and knows how to invoke the style-sheet engine in order to process style sheets. It is also important to note that the version of the JDK you install is dependent upon these two components.

For our example, we will be using IBM's XML for Java parser (xml4j) and the LotusXSL processor. You can, however, substitute these with any other combination of processors. The following sections show you how you can obtain these tools and walk you through the process of installing and using them.

10.3.1 *Java Development Kit*

The Java Development Kit, or JDK, as it is referred to, needs little introduction. The JDK is the foundation for all Java development, so the first step in building our toolbox is to install the JDK. If you are doing much development work, there is a good chance you already have the JDK installed on your machine. For example, many Java tools set up the JDK as part of their installation. Or you may be doing Java development, in which case the JDK is a part of your development platform.

If you do have the JDK installed on your server, the only caveat is to be sure you have the correct version. For example, the IBM processors used in the following section are mixed in their support of the JDK: The XML for Java processor supports JDK 1.2, but the XSL processor works only under JDK 1.1, so that will be our base platform. Note that you can install multiple versions of the JDK, so you don't have to give up the latest update to build this workbench of tools. If you plan to install both versions, check the JDK for configuration details.

10.3.1.1   Installing the JDK

If you have already installed the JDK, you can skip this section and go on to installing the parser. If you haven't installed the JDK, you will want to go to Sun's Web site at java.sun.com. The precise installation instructions will vary depending upon the operating system you are running. The Windows version comes as an executable archive. Double-clicking on the archive file invokes the JDK installer, which creates the directory structure and unpacks the tools and documentation bundles. On Solaris, you must unpack everything manually. Once you've unpacked the archive, you can delete this file to recover the nearly 9MB of disk space that archive file chews up.

However, unpacking the archive results in a bunch of files including some additional .zip files. Warning: do *not* unpack these .zip files. In particular, you'll find a file named CLASSES.ZIP in the /lib directory. This file contains all of the core Java classes and should not be unzipped. A feature of Java is its ability to locate class files that are stored in archives including JAR (Java ARchive) and .zip files. If you inadvertently delete this .zip file after unpacking it, Java will not be able to locate the classes it needs.

Depending on how you've obtained the JDK (directly from Sun, or through third-party software), you may or may not have to set environment variables. The first is the CLASSPATH environment variable, which stores the paths to the supporting classes your Java programs need. The JDK 1.0 required that you specified the location of core Java classes in the CLASSPATH variable. However, as of version 1.1, the JDK assumes the location of core class files relative to a root directory. So as long as you don't move files around, the environment knows that, for example, CLASSES.ZIP is in the /lib directory. If, on the other hand, you've obtained the JDK as part of a third-party Java development environment, the CLASSPATH variable is automatically set by the installation program.

10.3.2   *Adding a Servlet Engine*

All of the major Web servers support Java servlets. However, servlet support may not be enabled on your server. Check with your system administrator or Web hosting service to determine if your server supports them. If you are lucky enough to have a servlet engine installed, then you may skip to the next section; otherwise, read on.

The servlet API is a standard Java extension and comes as part of the JDK 1.2. If you are using the tools described later, you will be using version 1.1 of the JDK. In that event, you must get the Java Servlet Development Kit (JSDK) 2.0 from Sun's Web site at http://java.sun.com. Once you have the JSDK, unzip the archive to a directory on your hard drive. Assuming you've installed the JSDK in a directory called "jsdk," you will need to include the path to the jsdk/lib/jsdk.jar file in your CLASSPATH.

Setting Your CLASSPATH   *Under Windows 95/98, you can determine the value of your CLASSPATH by opening a DOS window and entering the command:*

    SET

This will list the values for all environment variables that have been set in your system. If you wish to change the value of CLASSPATH, you can enter:

```
SET CLASSPATH="somepath.jar;anotherpath"
```

Note that this destroys the previous CLASSPATH. However, you can preserve the old value using %CLASSPATH%. For example, the following command line appends something.jar and anotherpath to the previously set CLASSPATH.

```
SET CLASSPATH=%CLASSPATH%;somepath.jar;
anotherpath
```

You can also save a CLASSPATH string in a temporary variable, and later use that variable to restore the original CLASSPATH. For example, the following saves the original CLASSPATH, then sets a new one:

```
set savedCLASSPATH=%CLASSPATH%
set CLASSPATH=path1;path2;path3
```

You can later reset the original CLASSPATH using the following:

```
set CLASSPATH=%savedCLASSPATH%
```

Be aware that Windows 95 and 98, unlike Windows NT, sets aside a limited amount of memory to store environment variables, and you can run out of environment space. Therefore, try to limit the length of your environment strings and use them sparingly.

Also note that the order in which you specify your paths is significant. That's because the Java interpreter looks for classes in the order they appear in CLASSPATH. Once a class is found, no other paths are searched. Also, for classes specified in a .zip or .jar file, you must specify the filename: for example, ../myclasses.jar. However, paths to .class files should end with the folder name. In addition, the path to a package should point to the parent directory of that package.

Finally, whenever you call the Java Runtime Environment (JRE), the CLASSPATH variable is temporarily unset. That means you must specify class paths on the command line when running JRE, even if you have set them in CLASSPATH.

The JSDK also provides a simple Java server, ServletRunner, for testing servlets locally before deploying. You can use this or one of the many freely available servlet engines on the Web for this purpose. Either way, you should test your installation by running some sample servlets on both your local development machine and on the server where you'll deploy your servlets.

10.3.3   *The XML Processor*

The next part of your development platform is the XML processor. Currently, there are more than a dozen XML parsers that are freely available over the Web. Of the validating parsers, some are written in C++, but most are written in Java. The best known of these are James Clark's XP, IBM's XML for Java, and Microsoft's MSXML. We will also examine Sun's XML parser, which is part of the Java ProjectX distribution.

For the purposes of this project, you may substitute any of the parsers just mentioned. However, the following discussion is specific to IBM's xml4j. I have chosen this processor because of its thorough and continuing support of emerging XML and XSL standards. I have found that within a few days of a standards release, the IBM team usually makes an xml4j update available. This makes it easy to experiment with newer features such as XSL expressions, which haven't appeared in parsers with longer release cycles.

Currently, the xml4j processor includes a parser that supports the full XML 1.0 Recommendation and an engine that supports the Document Object Model (DOM) Level 1 specification. IBM's xml4j processor also provides support for XML namespaces, and Simple API for XML (SAX) 1.0. In addition, the distribution includes an XPointer package that parses XPointer expressions. In addition, the package can generate an XPointer based on a node in the document tree, and it allows your application to search for nodes referenced by XPointers. The processor supports some 37 encodings (as specified in the `<?xml encoding=…>` declaration), including several variants of UTF, ISO, and EBCDIC encodings. Also, xml4j supports a feature called "validating generation" that allows an application to query a DTD and generate a document with the corresponding structure.

Installing xml4j is straightforward. First, download the xml4j distribution from http://www.alphaworks.ibm.com and unpack it into a new directory. The appropriate version is determined by our next tool LotusXSL, which I'll describe in a moment. To test the installation from Windows, open up a DOS window and issue the command:

```
type data\personal.xml
```

If the personal.xml file is there, it will display on the screen. Next, run the Java Runtime Environment tool (part of the JDK) with the following command line:

```
jre -cp xml4j_1_1_14.jar;xml4jSamples_1_1_14.jar
    samples.XJParse.XJParse -d data\personal.xml
```

Note that the jar files must be specified in the command line. That's because JRE ignores the CLASSPATH environment variable. If all goes well, this command line invokes XJParse, which parses personal.xml and checks the syntax. This command line also regenerates personal.xml. If no error messages are shown, the test has passed and you should be able to display the personal.xml file on the screen again using the DOS type command.

Once you have the processor working, you can begin experimenting with some of the other tools including a Channel Definition Format (CDF) editor, a CDF viewer, and SiteOutliner, which scans a Web site and reports its profile in CDF format. If you have installed the Java Swing library, you can also run the Tree Viewer, which displays a tree structure of an XML document.

10.3.4 *Adding an XSL Processor*

The XSL processor that complements xml4j is LotusXSL, also freely available from IBM. The LotusXSL processor is called by xml4j to process a source tree, apply any transformations and place its output in a result tree. IBM is careful to note that LotusXSL is an experimental tool. However, the tool is very stable and fully supports the XSLT draft specification described in Chapter 3. On the downside, LotusXSL does not currently support XSL formatting objects, a big part of XSL. Recall that XSL formatting objects conceptually parallel the formatting objects in Cascading Style Sheets (CSS). However, an XSL processor supporting XSL formatting objects was not available at the time of this writing.

To install LotusXSL, download the latest release from the Alpha-Works Web site. If you are downloading the Windows version, you will get a .zip file which you should unpack into a new directory. The unpacking process extracts the documentation, source files, and another .zip file containing the binaries. You'll need to unpack this file from the root LotusXSL directory to complete the installation. You can test the installation by opening a DOS window and going to the /testsuite directory, then entering the command line:

```
test test1
```

This invokes a batch file that temporarily resets your CLASSPATH and runs the processor on the style sheet, test1.xsl. If you plan to develop applications using this processor, be sure to add the following to your CLASSPATH:

```
set CLASSPATH=.;..;somePath\js.jar;
somePath\LotusXSL.zip;
somePath\JAVA\LIB\CLASSES.ZIP;
somePath\JAVA\LIB;
somePath\xml4j\xml4j_1_1_14.jar
```

Keep in mind that "somePath" in the above line should be replaced by the directory path in which you installed the JDK.

 Resolving Error Messages   *If you have already verified the installation of xml4j, and are receiving error messages from the LotusXSL processor stating that certain classes could not be found, first check that the version of LotusXSL you are running is compatible with your version of xml4j. This information is contained in the LotusXSL documentation.*

If you still receive errors, ensure that all class and jar files were correctly installed and carefully check that your CLASSPATH has been properly set.

10.3.4.1 Accessing the Parse Tree

For general development, you will want to instantiate a new DOM object, and load and parse an XML file. Here is a short example that shows you how:

```
import com.ibm.xml.parser.*;
  import org.w3c.dom.*;
import java.io.*;

public class loadXMLFile {

public static void main (String args[]) {
   String filename = null;
   if (args.length > 0) {
      filename = args[0];

       if (filename != null) {
          InputStream xmlStream;
          try {
             xmlStream = new FileInputStream(filename);
             } catch (FileNotFoundException notFound) {
                 System.err.println(notFound);
                 return;
             }
          Document xmlDocument = new
             Parser(filename).readStream(xmlStream);
          }
      }
   }
}
```

10.3.5 *XML Enabler*

The final tool, XML Enabler, is a servlet that takes an HTTP request from a browser and uses information in the HTTP header to determine which type of browser made the request. The servlet then selects an XSL style sheet from a collection of style sheets, transforms the data into HTML and sends it back in a response. By customizing different style sheets for various browsers, you can optimize the

HTML output for that specific browser. So now, you'll be able to render XML data in virtually any browser. Once you've installed the tools described here, all you have to do is define a mapping between the browser types you want to support and their corresponding style sheets. Of course, you'll have to define the style sheets themselves.

Assuming you've downloaded the XMLEnabler distribution (see "Resources" at the end of this chapter) and unpacked the file to a new directory, the next step is to add support for your servlet to your Web server. There are many ways to do this depending on your server, so you'll have to rely on your server's documentation for the precise steps. Most servers support a servlet.properties file where you can associate your servlet with its class. If you're using the ServletRunner from the JSDK, or possibly the Java Web Server, add the following line to your servlet.properties file:

```
servlet.xmlenabler.code=
    com\ibm\XMLEnabler\XMLEnabler
```

You must also place the XMLEnabler package in your servlets directory. Then assuming your servlet engine is running, you should now be able to access XMLEnabler through your browser. Currently, you must pass the name of the XML document to be parsed as a parameter in the URL:

```
http://localhost:8080/servlet/com.ibm.XMLEnabler.XMLEnabler?
URL=http://localhost/myDocument.xml
```

10.4 | Java ProjectX

Java ProjectX is a collection of Java classes from Sun's Java division that implements a set of XML services. Java ProjectX includes both validating and non-validating parsers that conform to the XML 1.0 Recommendation. The distribution also supports the Document Object Model (DOM) Level 1 specification, and Simple API for XML (SAX) 1.0.

Java ProjectX defines a set of "core" functionality that includes parsing XML documents and optionally validating them. The parser loads an XML document and makes elements available through either the DOM or SAX APIs. The parser can also take a DOM object and write it out as well-formed XML. However, Java ProjectX currently does not implement an XSL processor, and therefore does not support XSLT transformations. This situation is expected to change in the near future, so check the Java ProjectX Web page for updates.

While Java ProjectX is not specifically a server technology, one can implement the XML server previously described using all Sun technology. In addition, Java ProjectX may fit well in the context of Java Server Pages. It is important to note, however, that Java ProjectX is currently not a standard Java extension. Rather, it is an experimental technology. Be that as it may, it is important for the reader to be aware of Sun's efforts to combine XML with Java. The software is distributed freely (with some restrictions on source code) and is available at Sun's Web site at http://java.sun.com.

10.5 | Conclusion

As this chapter comes to a close, you may be wondering about Microsoft's Active Server Pages, or ASP. ASP is a technology built into Internet Information Server that allows you to embed JScript or VBScript into HTML pages. As such, ASPs are Microsoft's way of generating Web content dynamically. If you are interested in ASP, then this next chapter is for you.

10.6 | Resources

Java Development Kit
http://java.sun.com

Java Servlet Development Kit
http://java.sun.com

Java ProjectX
http://java.sun.com

XML for Java Processor
http://www.AlphaWorks.ibm.com

LotusXSL
http://www.AlphaWorks.ibm.com

XML Enabler
http://www.AlphaWorks.ibm.com

Cocoon
http://java.apache.org/cocoon/

10.7 | References

Hunter, Jason, and Crawford, William. "Java Servlet Programming" (O'Reilly, Sebastopol, CA: 1998).

XML and Active Server Pages

11

When you examine the Web server market, the servers fall into two camps: Apache on Unix, and Microsoft's Internet Information Server (IIS) on Windows NT. Of course, this generalization ignores the high-end Web server software such as Netscape's Enterprise server. Nevertheless, while Web hosting companies vary in their server support, virtually all high-end hosting companies support both server configurations.

When it comes to Intranet sites, the numbers favor Windows NT and IIS. Part of the reason involves the many technologies Microsoft makes available through its operating system, including COM, ActiveX, scriptlet components, and ODBC connectivity. Microsoft embeds these technologies in all of their products, and many third-party vendors also support them.

At the core of Microsoft IIS is Active Server Pages (ASP), which allows developers to generate HTML pages dynamically from the server. ASP can be coupled with a number of different scripting engines that allow you to connect to ODBC databases, wire together ActiveX components, and a great deal more. Thus, ASP is the central starting point for Web application development. The first portion of

257

this chapter introduces ASP concepts and shows how you can build various types of server pages using JScript. Once you have learned the scripting basics and how to make use of IIS's server objects, the chapter shows how you can add support for XML. We will wrap up this chapter by showing how you can query a SQL database from a client browser, and return the results in XML for processing in the browser. Along the way, this chapter also shows how you can implement a flat-file database which is processed completely on the server. First, however, let's examine the ASP basics.

11.1 | Introducing Active Server Pages

As mentioned in Chapter 9, the two Web server software packages that are in widespread use are Apache on Unix systems and Internet Information Server (IIS) on Windows NT. The reason for the popularity of both servers may be attributed to cost. Apache is freely available on the Internet, and Microsoft IIS comes as a part of Windows NT Server edition.

In order to add support for XML to IIS, you must again extend the server's functionality in some way. At the same time, you want to be able to generate XML (possibly transformed to well-formed HTML) dynamically, and add script to handle program logic. Fortunately, IIS can already do most of this through Active Server Pages (ASPs). Essentially, Active Server Pages is an ActiveX component that allows you to embed scripting code into HTML pages. ASP comes with built-in scripting support for JScript or VBScript. However, Microsoft claims that ASP's scripting engine allows you to embed any scripting language (such as Perl or Python) that supports the ASP interface.

In keeping with other parts of this book, this chapter presents its examples using JavaScript. (Actually, this section uses Microsoft's variant of the language, JScript.) Before considering XML and DOM support, however, let's take a quick tour of Active Server Pages.

11.1.1 *Creating Active Server Pages*

An ASP page looks very much like an HTML page with scripting code embedded in it. Such a page typically contains static HTML and script; the scripting code is used to tie together components on the page, gather input from the user, query and retrieve data from the back-end database, and send the results back to the user. Thus, an ASP file is just a text file with an .asp file extension. When the Web server encounters an .asp file, it knows it needs to parse the HTML and process it. This is similar to the parsed (.shtml) files on the Apache Web server.

You can embed script code in your pages using one of two methods. The first method uses the `<%` and `%>` character strings to identify the beginning and end, respectively, of a block of script. You can then place your code within those delimiters. The second method uses HTML's `<SCRIPT>` element to embed code, just as is done with client-side scripting. As you will see, each approach has certain constraints.

Let's start with a basic example. The following example shows how to include a function that sends the string "Hello, World!" back to the browser. The string will include enough HTML markup to display it in the browser.

```
<%@ LANGUAGE=JScript %>
<HTML>
<HEAD></HEAD>
   <BODY>
   <%
     function hello()
     {
        Response.Write("Hello, World!");
     }
   %>
   </BODY>
</HTML>
```

The first line in this example is an ASP processing instruction, which is designated by the @ symbol. This processing instruction sets the scripting language to be used on this page. This line is optional, but, if used, must be the first line in the .asp file. If you do not specify a language (and one has not been defined elsewhere), the language will default to VBScript.

The ASP processing instruction also accepts several other attributes, which are summarized in Table 11-1.

The next few lines in our example set up the HTML tags for the page. Next, the `<%` indicates that a JavaScript follows. The script consists of a single function, `hello()`, whose sole purpose is to output the "Hello, World!" string. It is apparent from this script that this is accomplished using the `Response.Write` method. (You can also send strings from the server outside of script blocks using another directive, which will be presented shortly.)

`Response` is one of the six server objects that are supported in ASP. These built-in objects are `Application`, `Request`, `Response`, `Server`, `Session`, and `ObjectContext`. These objects allow you to gather browser information during a request, send responses, manage cookies, and much more. Table 11-2 summarizes ASP's built-in objects.

In addition to these built-in objects, ASP includes several ActiveX components. Possibly, the most important for our purposes is the Database Access component, which provides access to any database that supports ODBC. Other components include a banner ad rotator, a content rotator, a file access component, an NT server collabo-

Table 11-1   Attributes for the ASP processing instruction

Attribute	*Description*
CODEPAGE	Sets the character encoding for the current page.
ENABLESESSIONSTATE	Enables the current page to use a session state.
LANGUAGE	Sets the scripting language.
LCID	Defines the locale identifier for the current page.
TRANSACTION	Specifies that the current page will run under Microsoft Transaction Server (MTS).

Table 11-2	ASP objects and their methods, properties, events, and collections

Object	Description
Application	Used to set attributes and gather information for the lifecycle of the application.
	Methods: Lock, Unlock
	Events: Application_OnStart, Application_OnEnd
	Collections: Contents, StaticObjects
ObjectContext	Used to commit or abort a transaction.
	Methods: SetComplete, SetAbort
	Events: OnTransactionCommit, OnTransactionAbort
Request	Accesses information sent with an HTTP request, including GET and POST requests, cookies and client certificates.
	Methods: BinaryRead
	Properties: TotalBytes
	Collections: ClientCertificate, Cookies, Form, QueryString, ServerVariables
Response	Sets the data sent back to the user agent.
	Methods: AddHeader, AppendToLog, BinaryWrite, Clear, End, Flush, Redirect, Write
	Properties: Buffer, CacheControl, Charset, ContentType, Expires, ExpiresAbsolute, IsClientConnected, PICS, status
	Collections: Cookies
Server	Used to create objects, access methods, and so on, on the server.
	Methods: CreateObject, HTMLEncode, MapPath, URLEncode
	Properties: ScriptTimeout
Session	Used to set and gather information for the current session.
	Methods: Abandon
	Properties: CodePage, LCID, SessionID, Timeout
	Events: Session_OnStart, Session_OnEnd
	Collections: Contents, StaticObjects

ration object, and a component that allows you to customize output for a specific browser type. In-depth coverage of these objects is beyond the scope of this book. We are specifically concerned with the relationship between XML and ASP here. Therefore, refer to the Active Server Pages documentation or one of the many books that cover ASP for more in-depth coverage.

11.1.2 *Adding Script to Server Pages*

You have already seen a bit of the ASP syntax. The `<%` and `%>` delimiters indicate an ASP script. In general, `<%` indicates that some ASP-related statements follow. The other syntax seen in the first example is `<%@ ... %>`, which indicates a processing directive. ASP supports one other directive, `<%= ... %>`, called the "output directive." The output directive provides a convenient way to output markup in the browser. For instance, our first example outputs the "Hello, World!" string in the browser using the `Response.Write` method. You could rewrite that example much more simply using the following:

```
<HTML>
<HEAD></HEAD>
   <BODY>
   <%= "Hello, World!" %>
</HTML>
</HEAD>
```

You can also use the output directive to send the output of a function to the browser like this:

```
<%@ LANGUAGE=JScript %>
<HTML>
<HEAD></HEAD>
   <BODY>
   <%
     function hello()
     {
        return ("Hello, World!");
```

```
    }
  %>

<P>Today's Greeting is: <%= hello() %>
    </BODY>
</HTML>
```

In this last example, the output directive calls the JavaScript `hello()` function, which simply returns the "Hello, World!" string. This is combined with some static HTML to create this final string: "Today's Greeting is Hello, World!" To summarize these examples: The output directive can be used to produce output from the ASP page, while the `Response.Write` method must be used within your script functions and procedures.

Another point to note from the last example is that ASP allows you to freely mix scripting code with static HTML. This feature isn't restricted to just the output directive. You can, for example, mix If-Then-Else statements with HTML to produce output based on a set of conditions. For example, you could write:

```
<% if Request.Form("myForm") == "True"
{

// Code to process the form's data goes here

}
else %>
<P>The form <%= FormName %> not Found!
```

Just as ASP liberalizes the use of script within HTML, so it does with the use of variables. That is, you can declare, set and modify a variable in one location within your .asp file, and make use of it again later in the file. Of course, these variables must be declared globally outside of a given function or procedure. (The reason is that variables declared inside of a function are, by definition, local to that routine and do not exist outside its context.)

You can also define the scope for variables outside of a particular Active Server Page. In particular, variables can be defined to have session scope, (which exist for the duration of a user's session), or application scope (which exist so long as the application is running). To define either a session or application variable, you associate the variable and its value with that object. For example, the following statement creates a new session variable called `filename` and assigns it the value "`test.xml`":

```
Session("filename") = "test.xml";
```

Now, you can access this variable later in a session. The following statement uses the output directive to send the file's name back to the browser:

```
<%= Session("filename") %>
```

11.1.3 *XML and ASP*

With that bit of background, we can now look at how you would include support for XML in your Active Server Pages. The first step, if you have not already done so, is to install IIS, which comes with Windows NT Server edition. If you are running Windows 95, 98, or NT Workstation, you can still run the following examples using Microsoft's Personal Web Server (PWS). PWS comes with the Windows NT Option Pack, which is freely available at the Microsoft NT Server Web site. If you have PWS for Windows 98 installed on your machine, you will still have to get the NT Option Pack and install Active Server Pages support. Likewise, if you have Peer Web Services installed on NT Workstation (available in the Windows NT Service Pack), you must likewise install the Option Pack to gain ASP support.

Once you have either IIS or PWS with ASP support installed, you can add support for XML. The easiest option here is to install Internet Explorer 5. Installing client software to gain server support may seem a bit strange. However, Internet Explorer contains the engine that drives XML: the MSXML parser and XSL processor. When you install IE, it installs MSXML.DLL (which contains these two components), and registers both the "text/xml" MIME type and the XML file type with the operating system. At this point, the DOM API is available to you through scripting (JavaScript and VBScript) and programming (C++ and Java), and you can send and receive XML from the server over an HTTP connection.

Supporting XML in IIS Without Installing IE

It is possible to support XML in both IIS and Personal Web Server on Windows 98 without using the Microsoft supplied components. For example, you may want to use IBM's XML for Java and Lotus XSL processors and rely on servlets to serve XML data streams. In this case, you must properly register the text/xml MIME type, and the .xml and .xsl file extensions with the operating system. One easy way to do this is to run register-xml.reg, which inserts the appropriate keys into the system's registry. Once you have done this, simply reboot the system for the changes to take effect.

You can also manually enter the XML MIME type from Windows Explorer by selecting "Folder Options" from the "View" menu, then clicking on the "File Types" tab. Next, click on the "New Type" button and enter .xml for the file type and "text/xml" for the Content type. Add another entry for the .xsl file type and you are done.

An alternative approach, which works only with IIS, is to use the Internet Service Manager console to register the XML MIME type. To do so, select the properties button from "Default Web Site," then click on the "HTTP Headers" tab. Next, click on the "File Types" tab and then the "New Type" button. Then simply enter the new types as described above.

Once you have installed the proper software, you will want to test the installation and ensure that the server recognizes your ASP pages. First, ensure that the server process is running (see your documentation for details). If you are attached to a network, this step is easy. Simply point your browser to the home page. This should bring up a page, default.asp, which performs a redirect to welcome.htm in the samples directory.

If, on the other hand, you are not on a network and need to run the Web server locally, there is a bit of trickery you must perform. At the heart of the solution is a file called HOSTS, which allows you to map an IP address to a domain name. Microsoft has set up a special IP address and mapped it to the domain, localhost. This allows you to enter http://localhost/ to access your Home page. The following instructions are specific to Windows NT Workstation 4.0. The process is similar for Windows 95 and 98.

First, go to Control Panel and select the Network application. Then, click on the Protocols tab and select TCP/IP Protocol. If the TCP/IP Protocol icon is not listed in the window, then it must be installed from your Windows system disks. Assuming it is installed, click the Properties button, then select the WINS tab, and ensure that the "Enable LMHOSTS Lookup" checkbox is selected. Also, be sure that "Enable DNS for Windows Resolution" is *not* selected. Click OK, close the dialog and reboot the system.

The next step is to create a file called HOSTS (note, there is no file extension in this file name). The HOSTS file should be placed in a subdirectory below the directory that Windows NT is installed (usually winnt) in the \system32\drivers\etc subdirectory. The file should contain the following line:

```
127.0.0.1  localhost
```

This maps this IP address to your local host directory. Finally, be sure that your Internet Connection options are set to "connect to the Internet using a local area network." (If this doesn't work, try setting this option to use a proxy server.) At this point, you should be able to access the home of your server by entering the URL http://localhost/. Alternatively, you can access the home page using http//127.0.0.1/.

11.1.4   *Scripting XML with ASP*

Finally, the moment of truth is at hand. You should now be able to load XML documents, parse them, transform them, and display them using the methods described throughout this book. There are, of course, some slight syntactic differences. As a first example, let's look at how you might create a new DOM object. Again, we use JavaScript as the scripting language:

```
var xmlDocument = Server.CreateObject("Microsoft.XMLDOM");
```

You can also create a server-side object within the page using HTML's `<OBJECT>` element:

```
<OBJECT RUNAT="server" PROGID="Microsoft.XMLDOM"
id="xmlDocument">
 </OBJECT>
```

Once you have created a new instance of the XML DOM object, you can build new document trees in memory using the DOM API, or you can load a document either from a file or from a stream.

11.1.5   *Processing XML on IIS*

As you might imagine, there are several means for acquiring XML data and the method depends, in part, on how the data is stored. For example, raw data may be stored in a database. In that case, you may want to retrieve the data set in question and construct the document tree in memory using the DOM. Microsoft provides an alternative to this approach using the ActiveX Data Object (ADO) 2.1 or higher. Assuming you are using an ADO-compliant database (such as Microsoft Access), the ADO allows you to import raw data into an XML DOM object. In this case, the database field names are used to assign element names and the fields form the content for their respective elements.

If you are publishing XML documents from your site, you may be using a file-based model similar to the way HTML files are stored on a Web site. In this case, your goal might be to apply a style sheet to a requested document and serve the result document back to the client browser. Another scenario might be a system that communicates through some XML messaging scheme that you have devised. In this case, the user never sees the XML. Instead, the server would receive and send XML as a data stream. In that case, you might want to take the stream and load it into the XML control using the `LoadXML` method described in Part 2.

Finally, there is no rule that says you have to load XML into the parser at all. There may be times when you simply want to scan an XML document for the presence of certain elements. Writing such a scanner is relatively simple and uses fewer resources than firing up the XML control and performing in-memory processing. This scanning process, which is known as "hacking," has been particularly popular with CGI scripters and Perl programmers.

For Web developers, serving XML documents from files stored on the server seems like a fairly typical task. Let's examine how you might accomplish this using IIS and ASP. The following creates a new DOM object instance and loads an XML file:

```
<%@ LANGUAGE=JScript %>
<HTML>
<HEAD></HEAD>
<BODY>
    <%
    var xmlDocument =
        Server.CreateObject("Microsoft.XMLDOM");
    xmlDocument.load(Server.MapPath("homepage.xml"));
    Response.Write(xmlDocument.xml)
    %>
</BODY>
</HTML>
```

First, `Server.CreateObject` is used to create a new DOM object, then the document is loaded into that object using the `load` method. `MapPath` is one of the `Server` objects' methods (see Table 11-2) and is used to construct a fully qualified path from a relative path. The homepage.xml file represents the Web site's Home page.

In order to send the XML document, which is currently in tree form, it must be serialized into a text stream. That is, you cannot send a DOM object directly to the client. The way we accomplish this is by accessing the root element's `xml` property. Then, it is a simple matter of sending the stream back to the client using a `Response.Write`.

One thing you will notice is that there is no loading of a style sheet document. You might expect Internet Explorer to process the style sheet referenced in homepage.xml. However, behavior suggests that you cannot simply let the browser render the document from an incoming XML stream. What you get in the browser is just the content of the elements from the document tree. Therefore, you will have to load the incoming stream back into a DOM tree, then apply the style sheet using the `transformNode` method as described in Chapter 8.

For ordinary browsers, you will want to process the style sheet on the server and serve the resulting transformation. Here is how to do just that:

```
<%@ LANGUAGE=JScript %>
<HTML>
<HEAD></HEAD>
<BODY>
    <%
    var xmlDocument =
        Server.CreateObject("Microsoft.XMLDOM");
    var xslDocument =
        Server.CreateObject("Microsoft.XMLDOM");

    xmlDocument.load(Server.MapPath("homepage.xml"));
    xslDocument.load(Server.MapPath("homepage.xsl"));
    Response.Write(
        xmlDocument.transformNode(xslDocument));
    %>
</BODY>
</HTML>
```

This is similar to the previous example in that we load an XML document from a file. This time, however, the example creates a second DOM object to represent the XSL style sheet, which contains the transformations to HTML. Again, `ServerMapPath` is used to resolve the relative URLs. Finally, we use the `transformNode` method described in Chapter 8 to apply the style sheet transformation to the XML document. Then, the `Write` method sends the result back to the browser.

I should mention one other method, the `transformNodeToObject`, that allows you to write a transformation directly to a stream. (For Java and C++ programmers, this is the `IStream` interface.) The benefit of this approach is that the style sheet is applied in memory and written directly out to the data stream, resulting in better performance on the server side. The following example demonstrates this approach:

```
<%@ LANGUAGE=JScript %>
<HTML>
<HEAD></HEAD>
<BODY>
   <%
     var xmlDocument =
         Server.CreateObject("Microsoft.XMLDOM");
     var xslDocument =
         Server.CreateObject("Microsoft.XMLDOM");

     xmlDocument.load(Server.MapPath("homepage.xml"));
     xslDocument.load(Server.MapPath("homepage.xsl"));
     xmlDocument.transformNodeToObject(
         Server.MapPath("homepage.xsl"), Response);
   %>
</BODY>
</HTML>
```

11.1.6 *Threading Models*

As with Java servlets, the Microsoft approach offers the ability to write threaded applications. For the Web developer, this is handled under the hood. All you have to do is select which version of the XML control you want to use. Microsoft calls the two threading models the rental model and the free-threading model. The "rental model" provides single-threaded access to the XML control. The "free-threading model" allows multiple threads to access the control at the same time. The tradeoffs are user convenience versus performance. Offering a free multi-threaded version of the XML control allows you to process more than one document tree at a time. However, this will cost you in terms of performance.

Virtually all of the examples presented thus far use the rental model. For instance, the previous example creates a new DOM object using:

```
var xmlDocument =
        Server.CreateObject("Microsoft.XMLDOM");
```

The `Microsoft.XMLDOM` part of the call is referred to as the ProgID and refers to the rental model version of the XML control. To select the free-threading model, use the ProgID, `Microsoft.FreeThreadedXMLDOM`. Thus, the previous instantiation becomes:

```
var xmlDocument =
     Server.CreateObject("Microsoft.FreeThreadedXMLDOM ");
```

11.1.7 *Sending XML from the Client*

In Chapters 6, 7, and 8, the emphasis was on receiving and processing XML within the client browser. There will be times when you want to process XML on the client and send it back to the server. An example that immediately comes to mind is a database update: The server sends a data set to the client, allowing the user to modify records which should be posted back to the database.

There are two methods you can use to send data from the client back to the server. The first method relies on an HTML form to post the data. Consider the following example:

```
<FORM METHOD=POST ACTION="someaction">
   <INPUT TYPE="text" NAME="xmlDataStream" SIZE="40">
      <BR><BR><BR>

      <INPUT TYPE="SUBMIT"
         NAME="sendButton"
         VALUE="Send XML to the Server" >
</FORM>
```

This HTML creates a form with an input field and a Submit button. The form allows the user to input XML markup into the edit field. When the user hits the Submit button, the data is sent as a text stream to the server. On the server side, you can use the DOM load method to load the contents of ASP's `Request` object.

```
<%@ LANGUAGE=JScript %>
<HTML>
<HEAD></HEAD>
<BODY>
<%
    var xmlDocument =
        Server.CreateObject("Microsoft.XMLDOM");

    if (Request.ServerVariables("REQUEST_METHOD") == "POST")
    {
     // Load the posted XML data and save it to disk.
     xmlDocument.load(Request);
     xmlDocument.save(Server.MapPath("someFile.xml"));
    }
%>
</BODY>
</HTML>
```

When the user hits the submit button, the XML data that the user entered is posted to the server. So, this last ASP document uses `Request.ServerVariables()` to watch for the form POST. When the POST occurs, we load the contents of the Request object and save the file out to disk. In practice, you will want to verify that this is well-formed XML before saving the file.

If you include an ACTION attribute in the <FORM> element, you can direct the data stream to a script on the server. For example, you can direct the XML stream to a script called myScript in the cgi-bin directory using the following:

```
<FORM METHOD=POST ACTION="/cgi-bin/myScript">
  <!— Code goes here —>
</FORM>
```

Of course, your script must be able to accept parameters and know how to process the XML stream. You can also grab form data in ASP using the `Request.Form` property.

An alternative method is to use the `xmlHttpRequest` object to send data from the client back to the server. This object is a Microsoft extension to the DOM and was covered in Chapter 6. Table 6-3 summarizes `xmlHttpRequest`'s properties and methods.

11.2 | XML and Database Development

One of the more common tasks for Web application developers involves database access. In this section, we look at a sample database application that can be queried from a client browser. The database we will create is a catalog of freely-available XML tools similar to that presented in Chapter 8. This time, however, the XML representation of the database will be processed on the server.

When working with databases, it is also useful to consider two approaches. The first follows the road traveled by thousands of CGI/Perl programmers: the flat-file database. Flat-file databases are common on the Web because they are easy to implement and don't require expensive database tools and expertise.

The second approach will be familiar to Intranet developers working with existing back-end databases. The example uses ASP to connect to and query an ODBC-compliant database. The data returned, which is already formatted with XML markup as shown in the previous section, will be loaded into the MSXML parser. Next, the example uses an XSL style sheet to transform the result set into well-formed HTML, and the result is sent back to the client browser.

11.2.1 *The Flat-File Database*

Creating a flat-file database to be served from an ASP page is amazingly simple to implement. The following is a record from the XML

Tools database. The record is one of many stored in a flat file called
xmltools.xml. Here it is:

```
<?xml version="1.0"?>
<?xml-stylesheet type="text/xsl" href="testdb.xsl"?>

<productDB>
    <product category="Authoring">
      <prodName>Amaya</prodName>
      <company name="World Wide Web Consortium">
        <address>
           <street1></street1>
           <street2></street2>
           <city></city>
           <state></state>
           <province/>
           <country></country>
        </address>
        <phone></phone>
        <fax></fax>
        <website href="http://www.w3.org"/>
      </company>
      <version>1.3 Beta</version>
      <price>Freely available</price>
      <sys-requirements>
          Most
      </sys-requirements>
      <description>
<prodName>Amaya</prodName> is both a <toolType>
browser</toolType> and an <toolType>editing tool</toolType>
and was <use>created as a reference implementation</use> by
the W3C. <prodName>Amaya</prodName> is used to demonstrate
and test many of the new developments in Web protocols and
data formats. <prodName>Amaya</prodName> includes a
<feature>WYSIWYG style interface</feature> and
<feature>supports many of the W3C standards including
<standards>HTML 4</standards>, <standards>CSS2</standards>,
and <standards>XML</standards></feature>.
</description>
        <prodURL
        href=" http://www.w3.org/Amaya/"/>
    </product>
</productDB>
```

This database structure is similar to that presented in Chapter 8 and you may want to refer to that chapter for details of the database design. One difference in this example is that additional markup has been added to the description field. The description field is a "memo" field that contains, from an XML point of view, a fair amount of unstructured data. By adding appropriate markup, you add context and meaning to large fields of unstructured data. The benefits of this approach will become evident when I discuss ODBC databases on the following pages.

For now, let's examine the style sheet that will transform our data into XML.

```
<?xml version="1.0"?>

<xsl:stylesheet
   xmlns:xsl="http://www.w3.org/TR/WD-xsl"
   xmlns="http://www.w3.org/TR/REC-html40"
   result-ns="">

  <!— Root template —>
  <xsl:template match="/">
    <HTML>
     <HEAD>
       <META http-equiv="Content-Type"
             content="text/html; charset=iso-8859-1"/>
      <TITLE>
        XML Tools Database
      </TITLE>

     </HEAD>
     <BODY>

     <TABLE BGCOLOR="66CCFF">
     <CAPTION ALIGN="left" STYLE="background-color: 0066CC;
             color:CCFFFF;">
             <B>Search Results</B>
     </CAPTION>
     <TBODY>
         <TR>
           <TD><B>Product</B></TD>
           <TD><B>Company</B></TD>
```

```
          <TD><B>Price</B></TD>
          <TD><B>Description</B></TD>
        </TR>
        <xsl:for-each select="productDB/product">
          <TR>
          <xsl:if test="@category[.='Authoring']">
              <TD><xsl:value-of select="prodName"/></TD>
              <TD><xsl:value-of
                  select="company/@name"/></TD>
              <TD><xsl:value-of select="price"/></TD>
              <TD><xsl:value-of
                  select="description"/></TD>
          </xsl:if>
          </TR>

        </xsl:for-each>
    </TBODY>
    </TABLE>
  </BODY>
  </HTML>
 </xsl:template>
</xsl:stylesheet>
```

This example brings up another application-design decision. Note that the style sheet includes the surrounding HTML necessary for presenting the database table. As you may recall from earlier examples in this chapter, ASP also allows us to include surrounding HTML. The question is, where's the best place to handle this presentation code? In part, this is a matter of preference. However, maintaining presentation code in your style sheets should always be your first consideration. One compelling reason is that you will have to modify only one .xsl file instead of many .asp files. All we need now is an Active Server Page to handle the request.

```
<%@ LANGUAGE=JScript %>
<HTML>
<HEAD></HEAD>
<BODY>
    <%
    var xmlDocument =
        Server.CreateObject("Microsoft.XMLDOM");
    var xslDocument =
```

```
    Server.CreateObject("Microsoft.XMLDOM");

    xmlDocument.load(Server.MapPath("tools.xml"));
    xslDocument.load(Server.MapPath("tools.xsl"));
    xmlDocument.transformNodeToObject(
        Server.MapPath("tools.xsl"), Response);
    %>
</BODY>
</HTML>
```

11.2.2 *Connecting to ODBC Data Sources*

Since this chapter focuses on IIS and ASP, both Microsoft technologies, I will enlist another proprietary technology that will significantly ease the burden of database programming—namely, ActiveX Data Objects, or ADO. ActiveX Data Objects are designed specifically for the purposes of connecting to ODBC databases (and OLE DB data sources), navigating them, and performing queries and updates on them.

For development purposes, I will be using Microsoft Access and connecting to it through an ODBC data source. The ASP script code for this example uses SQL statements to query the database. Therefore, you should have little difficulty using these same scripts in conjunction with any SQL database such as SQL Server.

Before you can begin writing your scripts, you must tell ADO where to find your database configuration and drivers. In our example, the database is called xmlTools.mdb. To configure this database for ADO, go to the Windows Control Panel and open the ODBC Data Sources application. This will open a dialog box with several tabs at the top. Select the File DSN tab. This window presents a list of available data source names (DSNs). Click on the Add button to create a new DSN, select the Microsoft Access Database driver, and click on the Next button. At this point you will be asked to enter the name of your data source. Assuming you have copied the XML Tools database from the disk that comes with this book, hit the browse button to locate and select this file. Then, simply click the OK button and you are done.

11.2.3   *Making the Connection*

One reason we are using ADO is that it makes the coding process much easier. This is particularly evident when connecting to an ODBC data source. All we have to do is create a new `Server` object instance using the `ADODB.Connection` object.

```
<%
var dbConnection = Server.CreateObject("ADODB.Connection");
dbConnection.Open("xmlTools.mdb");
%>
```

With the connection established, you can begin querying the database. To do so, we will create another ADO object, called a `Recordset`. This object will actually hold the return values from the query, and it includes methods to display rows and records, page through data, modify the database, and so on.

```
<%
var dbConnection = Server.CreateObject("ADODB.Connection");
dbConnection.Open("xmlTools.mdb");

var xmlToolsDB = Server.CreateObject("ADODB.Recordset");
query = "SELECT toolName, author, description FROM
        xmlTools1 WHERE toolName='MSXML'";
xmlToolsDB.Open(query, dbConnection);
Name = xmlToolsDB("toolName");
auth = xmlToolsDB("author");
descr = xmlToolsDB("description");
Response.Write(Name, auth, descr);
%>
```

11.3 | Building a Document From a Query

The next example presents the XML Tools database, which is located on the disk that comes with this book. This data forms the basis for the online catalog of tools presented at my Web site at Beyond-HTML.com. Therefore, you should find the information useful in its own right. The database contains a little less than 50 records listing information about various XML tools. All of the tools are freely available and the database includes their URLs so that you can download them immediately.

For the purpose of this example, I have imported the data into a Microsoft Access database. The table structure includes a field that categorizes tools into one of six categories. This allows you to search for all parsers listed in the database, or possibly all authoring tools. The six categories you can search on are Authoring, Conversion, Parsers, Interfaces, Vocabularies, and Miscellaneous tools.

Let's start with the client side. The following code creates a form that allows the user to search by category:

```
<HTML>
   <HEAD>
      <TITLE>XML Search Page</TITLE>
   </HEAD>
   <BODY bgcolor=antiquewhite>

   <STRONG>Search the XML Tools Database</STRONG>
   <P></P>
   <FORM
    action=http://localhost/db/xmltools.asp method=post>

   <P>To search by category, you must enter one of the
      following categories:</P>

   <P>Authoring, Conversion, Interfaces, Parsers,
      Vocabularies, or Miscellaneous</P>

   <P><INPUT id=qt name=queryText></P>
   <P><INPUT id=submit1 name=submit1
         type=submit value=Submit>
```

```
     <INPUT id=reset1 name=reset1
        type=reset value=Reset></P>
  </FORM>

  </BODY>
</HTML>
```

The form specifies an ASP page in the form's ACTION attribute. When the user hits the Submit button, the server page referenced in the ACTION attribute is invoked. Because this is a submit form, the server page can access the query through the server's Request object. However, I have included both id and name attributes for the <INPUT> element. The id attribute is used internally by IIS. However, the name property is used from within the Active Server Page to access the data in the text-edit field. This may seem a bit redundant for a submit form. However, forms often include multiple text edit controls, list-boxes, checkboxes, radio buttons, and the like. So, you will find the name attribute useful any time you have more than one control on the screen. In any case, Figure 11-1 shows the resulting form.

The next step is to create the Active Server Page. The following code takes the search string posted by the browser's form and queries

Figure 11–1   Form used to search the XML Tools database.

the database. This generates a recordset containing the results of the query. Our goal is to build an XML document from this recordset. From there, we can load the XML document string into a DOM object, apply style sheets and send the result back to the user.

```
<%@ LANGUAGE=JScript %>
<HTML>
<HEAD>
<TITLE>XML Tools Database Example</TITLE>
</HEAD>
<BODY>
    <%

    // Create DOM Objects for the XML document and
    // the Style sheet
     var xmlDocument =
        Server.CreateObject("Microsoft.XMLDOM");
     var xslDocument =
        Server.CreateObject("Microsoft.XMLDOM");

    // Connect to the Access database
    curDir = Server.MapPath("xmltools.mdb");
    xmlConn = Server.CreateObject("ADODB.Connection");
    xmlConn.Open("DBQ="+curDir+";
        Driver={Microsoft Access Driver (*.mdb)};
        DriverId=25;FIL=MS Access;");

    // Build a query string and execute the query
    searchtxt = Request.Form("text1");
    query = "SELECT Product,Company,Description FROM
            xmlTools WHERE Category='" + searchtxt + "'";
    oRs = xmlConn.Execute(query);

    // Construct the XML markup strings
    prolog = "&lt;?xml version='1.0'?>
            &lt;?xml-stylesheet type='text/xsl'
             href='xmltools.xsl'?>";
    rootOpen = "&lt;productDB>";
    rootClose = "&lt;/productDB>";
    prodOpen = "&lt;product>";
    prodClose = "&lt;/product>";
    prodNameOpen = "&lt;prodName>";
    prodNameClose = "&lt;/prodName>";
    coOpen = "&lt;company>";
```

```
coClose = "&lt;/company>";
descOpen = "&lt;description>";
descClose = "&lt;/description>";

// Build the XML Document
xmlStr = prolog + rootOpen;
while (!oRs.eof) {
   xmlStr = xmlStr + prodOpen;
   xmlStr = xmlStr + prodNameOpen +
            oRs.fields.item(0) + prodNameClose;
   xmlStr = xmlStr + coOpen + oRs.fields.item(1) +
            coClose;
   xmlStr = xmlStr + descOpen +
            oRs.fields.item(2) + descClose;
   xmlStr = xmlStr + prodClose;
   oRs.MoveNext();
}
 xmlStr = xmlStr + rootClose;

// Load the document into a DOM object, apply the
// style sheet and ship it off to the browser
xmlDocument.loadXML(xmlStr);
xslDocument.load(Server.MapPath("xmltools.xsl"));
Response.Write(
        xmlDocument.transformNode(xslDocument));

%>

</BODY>
</HTML>
```

The code follows the steps outline previously and is fully commented, so I won't walk through each of the steps again. Also, the style sheet in the last example is similar to the style sheet for the flat-file database, so I won't recreate it again here. (Note that the line of code referencing the Price filed must be removed from that style sheet in order to work properly with this example.) The results of executing the code are shown in Figure 11–2.

However, this is actually the creative part of this exercise. First, you could further massage the recordset by applying filters from within the style sheet. On the presentation side, you could add a mechanism that chooses from one of several style sheets. This would allow you to

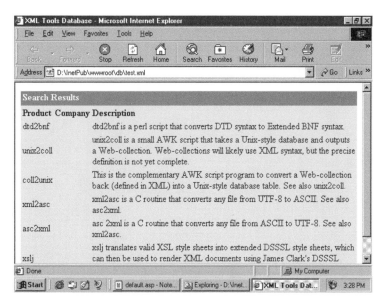

Figure 11–2 Searching the database and filtering the result set.

customize the results based on the browser making the request, as described in Chapter 8. Alternatively, you could set up style sheets representing "themes" that the user could select from. But, that is the fun part. So I will gladly leave these tasks as an exercise for the reader.

11.4 | Conclusion

There is one other item I will refrain from presenting here—the DTD for the XML Tools Database/Document structure. That does not mean DTDs aren't important. Quite the contrary. DTDs are extremely useful when it comes to validating data. Nowhere is this more important than when sending data to another application. However, there's a better alternative to DTDs that I believe will ultimately replace them. That will be the subject of Chapter 13.

Part Four

- Supporting Forms in XML
- Schemas in XML
- Building an XML-Based Web Site

XML and Web Development

Supporting Forms in XML

A side from tables, HTML forms are one of the most widely used features of HTML. Forms are important because they allow you to gather input from the user and post it back to the server. With a bit of scripting, you can also use forms to present information, which has been drawn from the server. A form could be as simple as a logon form used to enter a sensitive area of a Web site, or it could be a data entry screen that allows you to select, navigate, and modify information from several data sources. Indeed, forms are an important part of business. Forms are traded between business partners, clients, government agencies, and educational institutions.

While forms are intuitively simple to grasp, implementing forms, even in HTML, can quickly become a formidable task. Forms must be able to present labels, gather input, post queries to the server, perform field validation, authentication, make calculations, and much more. As strange as it seems, the XML specification makes no provisions for forms. However, a W3C technical note authored by Tim Bray and others suggests a solution, called Extensible Forms Description Language.

This chapter examines two approaches to forms in XML: Extensible Forms Description Language, and another W3C proposal, called the "XML Forms Architecture," that would allow Web application developers to design and create XML forms with the ability to include calculations, presentation elements, and validation in the form object, all while separating presentation from semantics.

12.1 | Extensible Forms Description Language

In a nutshell, the Extensible Forms Description Language, or XFDL, proposes a DTD that defines a specific XML-based language for defining forms. This allows forms documents to be loaded, parsed, and validated against the DTD. It also means that a DOM can be created and made available to applications, and that XSL style sheets can be used to transform them to HTML for display in the browser.

Rather than present the theory behind XFDL, let's take a look at a short example.

```
<?xml version="1.0"?>
<XFDL version="4.1.0">
   <bgcolor content="array">
      <ae>128</ae>
      <ae>128</ae>
      <ae>128</ae>
      </bgcolor>

   <page sid="Contact_Entry_Page">
      <bgcolor content="array">
         <ae>192</ae>
         <ae>192</ae>
         <ae>192</ae>
      </bgcolor>

      <label>Enter Contact Information</label>
```

```
<field sid="Name">
   <label>Enter Contact's Name:</label>
</field>

<field sid="address">
   <label>Address:</label>
</field>

<field sid="phone">
   <label>Phone:</label>
</field>

<field sid="email">
   <label>email:</label>
   <value>yourname@somedomain.com</value>
</field>

<button sid="submit_button">
   <value>Add Contact</value>
   <fontinfo content="array">
      <ae>Times</ae>
      <ae>14</ae>
      <ae>bold</ae>
   </fontinfo>
   <type>done</type>
   <url content="array">
      <ae>
    http://www.beyondhtml.com/cgi-bin/someScript.cgi
      </ae>
   </url>
</button>
   </page>
</XFDL>
```

As with most XML documents, this one begins with a standard XML prolog. In terms of structure, the root element for any XFDL document is <XFDL>. This element requires that the version attribute be specified. Currently, it is unclear from the W3C Technical Note which versions are supported. However, the proposed specification is XFDL 4.

Within the root element, you define one or more pages using <page> elements, and create individual forms by grouping together elements that represent various objects. For example, you can associate a set of radio buttons and their labels together with a submit button to create a form. The individual objects include a verbose set of GUI objects including radio buttons, checkboxes, input fields, and so on. However, you can also define nonGUI elements that can carry information, such as a word processing document or a digital signature. The general format for these items is:

```
<itemType sid="itemTag">

  <!-- option definitions here -->

</itemType>
```

The `sid` attribute is called a "scope identifier." The sid uniquely identifies an element within the scope of its logical parent. So in our first example, `<field>` is an item type that defines a text-edit field that can be used to enter one or more lines of data. Each field contains a scope identifier that uniquely identifies each field within the context of that page. Table 12-1 summarizes most of the items included in XFDL. I say "most" because the list of items to be included was not fully specified at the time of this writing.

The other element you may have noticed is the `<ae>` element. This element refers to an array element. In our example, `<ae>` is used to set the RGB colors for the `<bgcolor>` element. Notice that `<bgcolor>` contains a content attribute with the value set to "array." It turns out that `<bgcolor>` is defined in terms of an element array, so this attribute is required for this element. You can also assign names to array elements, which allows you to use more logical names than "ae." For example, you could write:

```
<bgcolor content="array">
  <red>255</red>
  <green>248</green>
  <blue>220</blue>
</bgcolor>
```

Table 12-1   List of GUI objects supported by XFDL

Component	Description
action	Defines a task, such as print, cancel, submit, and so on. Actions can be scheduled to fire either after a certain period of time or with a regular frequency.
box	Creates a rectangular area. Typically used to visually group a set of other GUI widgets on the page.
button	Creates a button item and allows a task (similar to an action) to be associated with the button.
cell	Defines a single entry in a list, popup or combobox. Selecting a cell can also trigger an action.
check	Defines a checkbox.
combobox	Defines a combo box.
data	Used to carry binary information using base-64 encoding.
field	Defines an edit control.
help	Defines the text for help associated with a given item.
label	Defines a label to be used with a control.
line	Draws a horizontal line, such as when you create a visual separator.
list	Creates list box.
popup	Specifies a popup menu.
radio	Defines a radio button.
signature	Stores a digital signature.
spacer	Used for positioning other items.
toolbar	Defines the position, window, and items for a toolbar.

12.1.1 *Setting Options*

The `<XFDL>` element can contain zero or more "option" elements followed by at least one `<page>` element. Options are used to define properties for entire pages, a form, or a single item. You can think of options as scoped variables where page and form options are global to their respective element types, and item options are local to that item. Also, local options override global options of the same name. Table 12-2 summarizes the various options you can set.

Table 12-2 List of options supported in XFDL

Option	*Description*
activated, focused and mouseover	These values are set by the processing software (not the author).
bgcolor, fontcolor, labelbgcolor and labelfontcolor	Sets the colors for an item or its label using either a name or RGB value.
borderwidth and labelborderwidth	Defines a 3D border for either an item or label, respectively.
coordinates	Returns the coordinates of a mouse click on an image.
data and datagroup	Creates an association between data items and buttons.
delay	Specifies the timing for an event in an action item and whether it should be repeated.
editstate	Determines if an item is read only, read/write, or write only (single-line fields only).
filename and mimetype	Specifies the filename and MIME type.
fontinfo and labelfontinfo	Defines the typeface, point size, and bold, italics, or underline for an item or label.
format	Uses subelements to provide field validation for items.
group	Associates groups of radio buttons, and cells with lists, popups, and comboboxes.

Table 12-2 Continued

Option	Description
help	Associates help with an item.
image	Identifies a data item containing an image for a button or label.
itemlocation, size and thickness	Defines the location and size of an item.
justify	Used to left, center, or right justify text.
label	Gives a text label to an item.
mimedata	Stores large binary data blocks encoded in Base-64 format.
next and previous	Defines tab order for items on a page.
printsettings	Sets print properties.
saveformat and transmitformat	Saves or submits a form in either UFDL, XFDL, or HTML.
scrollhoriz and scrollvert	Sets horizontal and vertical scrollbars. Also can be used to control word-wrap, vertical sliding, and so on.
signature, signdatagroups, signer, signformat, signgroups, signitemrefs, signitems, signoptionrefs and signoptions	Provides a full-featured system for digital signatures.
triggeritem	Used in form globals to identify which action, button, or cell was last selected or activated.
type	Specifies whether the action, button, or cell item will perform a network operation, print, save, digitally sign, etc.
url	Specifies the address for a page jump, link or submit.
value	The text associated with an item.
visible	Determines whether the item should be shown to the user or made invisible.

12.2 | The <compute> Element

If XFDL was just a reformulation of HTML forms, it would not be especially useful. After all, you could simply combine HTML with CSS within an XSL transformation to achieve much of the functionality we have described so far. Of course, the ability to support binary objects using MIME (Base 64) encoding coupled with extended support for actions within GUI objects makes XFDL very attractive to forms developers.

However, one of the features that truly adds value to XFDL is the ability to define computational expressions using the <compute> element. For example:

```
<str_length content="compute">
      <compute>strlen("This is a literal string")</compute>
</str_length>
```

The <compute> element defines a full set of computation functions that include string manipulation, mathematical functions, time and date functions, and various utility functions. Table 12-3 summarizes these features.

Table 12-3   List of functions supported in XFDL

Option	Description
String Functions	
countlines	Returns the number of lines a string will take up.
replace	Replaces a substring within a string.
strlen	Returns the length of a string.
strmatch	Used to match wild cards strings.
strpbrk	Takes a substring and returns the position it occupies in the original string.
strrstr	Returns the last occurrence within a string.
strstr	Returns the first occurrence within a string.

Table 12-3   Continued

Option	Description
substr	Takes a start and end position within a string and returns a substring.
tolower	Converts a string to lower case.
toupper	Converts a string to upper case.
trim	Returns a string with leading and trailing white space removed.
URLDecode	Decodes a URL string and returns the result.
URLEncode	Encodes a URL string.
Math Functions	
abs	Computes the absolute value.
acos	Calculates the arc cosine of a value.
annuity	Given an interest rate and period, computes the present value annuity.
asin	Computes the arc sine of a number.
atan	Generates the arc tangent of a value.
ceiling	Returns the ceiling of a number.
compound	Given a period and rate, computes the compound interest.
cos	Cosine function.
deg2rad	Converts degrees to radians.
exp	Returns the exponentiation of a numeric value.
fact	Computes the factorial of an integer value.
floor	Returns the floor of a value.
ln	Natural log function.
log	Calculates the log base 10.
mod	Modulo function.
pi	Calculates the value of pi.
power	Raises a value to a specified power.
rad2deg	Converts radians to degrees.
rand	Generates a random number.
round	Returns the round of a floating-point value.
sin	The sine function.

Table 12-3   Continued

Option	Description
sqrt	Returns the square root of a number.
tan	Computes the tangent of a number.

Utility Functions

Option	Description
applicationName	Returns the name of the currently running application.
applicationVersion	Gets the version of the currently running application.
applicationVersionNum	Retrieves the decimal version number of the currently running application.
decimal	Converts a number to its decimal representation.
formatString	Returns a formatted string.
isValidFormat	Returns a Boolean value indicating whether the specified format is valid.
set	Sets the value of a form option.
toggle	Detects when an option is toggled and returns the result.

Time/Date Functions

Option	Description
date	Returns the date in yyyymmdd format.
dateToSeconds	Calculates the number of seconds since 00:00:00 GMT, January 1st, 1970.
day	Takes a date and returns the numeric day of the month.
dayOfWeek	Takes a date and returns the numeric day of the week.
endOfMonth	Returns the difference between the number of seconds since 00:00:00 GMT, January 1st, 1970 and the current time on the last day of the month.
hour	Takes a date/time string and returns the hour.
minute	Takes a date/time string and returns the minute.
month	Takes a date/time string and returns the month.
now	Returns the number of seconds since 00:00:00 GMT, January 1st, 1970.
second	Takes a date/time string and returns the second.
time	Returns the current time in hh:mm:AM format.
year	Takes a date/time string and returns the year.

Finally, it is worth noting that vendors can extend or replace XFDL functions with their own expression language. In such cases, you would use the `format` attribute within `<compute>` to specify other expression languages. However, no such languages were available at the time of this writing.

12.3 | XML Forms Architecture

The XML Forms Architecture, or XFA, is another proposal that would provide support for forms in XML. The proposal, which was submitted by JetForm Corporation, has been "acknowledged" by the W3C. However, no comment was forthcoming from the consortium and the status of this proposal was still pending at the time of this writing.

The architecture proposes many of the same things included in XFDL. The specification describes a GUI model for the layout of controls. XFA also provides for an extensible scripting language that includes string and date/time handling, mathematical functions, and so on. In addition, XFA defines a simple box model that allows for positioning of elements and finer control over borders. This allows for more flexible layout, which might allow you to flow text around images and objects. The proposal defines a "pluggable" architecture that allows third-party controls and languages to be specified from within the markup language.

XFA defines a collection of "container" elements that can contain various "UI" subelements. Some of these UI elements may be defined as `<ExObject>`s, which are externally developed user interface controls. Presumably, these controls could be packaged as Java Beans or ActiveX controls.

As a brief example, the following, which was borrowed from the XFA proposal, shows how to create a form:

```
<Subform X="0" Y="0" W="3in" H="2in">
  <Border>
```

```
      <Margin TopInset=".1in" RightInset=".1in"
             BottomInset=".1in" LeftInset=".1in"/>
      <Edge Thickness="6pt">
        <Color Value="0,0,255"/>
      </Edge>
    </Border>

    <Draw X=".5in" Y=".5in" W="1in" H=".5in">
      <Border>
        <Margin TopInset=".05in" RightInset=".05in"
               BottomInset=".05in" LeftInset=".05in"/>
        <Edge Thickness="3pt">
          <Color Value="0,128,0"/>
        </Edge>
      </Border>
      <Margin TopInset=".1in" RightInset=".1in"
             BottomInset=".1in" LeftInset=".1in"/>
      <Align HAlign="Left" VAlign="Top"/>
      <Value>
        <Text>XFA Forms Architecture</Text>
      </Value>
    </Draw>

    <Draw X="2.7in" Y="1.2in" W="1in" H=".5in">
      <Border>
        <Margin TopInset=".05in" RightInset=".05in"
               BottomInset=".05in" LeftInset=".05in"/>
        <Edge Thickness="3pt">
          <Color Value="0,128,0"/>
        </Edge>
      </Border>
      <Margin TopInset=".1in" RightInset=".1in"
             BottomInset=".1in" LeftInset=".1in"/>
      <Align HAlign="Center" VAlign="Middle"/>
      <Value>
        <Ellipse>
          <Edge Thickness="1pt">
            <Color Value="0,128,0"/>
          </Edge>
          <Fill>
            <Color Value="128,128,128"/>
          </Fill>
        </Ellipse>
      </Value>
    </Draw>
  </Subform>
```

XFA includes several other features that are not directly supported by XFDL. These include support for digital signatures and internationalization. Of course, the W3C provides for both of these features in other draft specifications. Presumably, the W3C would prefer that these features remain as separate proposals, allowing all XML technologies to take advantage of these important features.

12.4 | Conclusion

When you assemble a form in HTML, you encapsulate the essence of an "interactive user interface." The interface may include edit fields for collecting and presenting information, radio buttons and checkboxes to select and set options, and submit buttons for posting data to the server. But when all is said and done, what you are left with is just the interface.

If there were some way you could turn the interface around and expose its back side, you might find a collection of wires hanging out the back, each waiting to be connected in some way. Your job as the developer is to bring your scripts and use them to wire that interface to server-side components, controls, applications, and programs.

XML has no such notion of a form. So, proposals like XFDL and XFA are attempting to bridge this gap by providing the ability to describe things like computations and digital signatures that go above and beyond the simple description of the user interface. Unfortunately, progress has been slow in this area. Nevertheless, we as Web developers yearn for the day when true forms support arrives.

Schemas in XML

ne subject that this book has carefully side-stepped is that of Document Type Definitions (DTDs). DTDs are one of the fundamental building blocks that allow you to define element types, attributes, entities, and the other pieces of XML. In addition, DTDs constrain the ways in which you can structure a document. More importantly, they help to give meaning to the elements and attributes you create. Without such a definition, others would not be able to interpret and use your documents. So why would we side-step such an important topic, one that has been used productively for a dozen years in SGML document management systems.

Unfortunately, DTD syntax differs from XML instance markup. While DTD syntax can be mastered with some effort, it can appear daunting to the uninitiated. And, given that DTDs are primarily used by software programs to validate documents, not much has been said about their construction in this book.

However, there is a far more significant reason for deferring such an important subject. That reason is schemas. Over the past two years, several languages for defining schemas have been proposed in many forms by the members of the W3C. These proposals include Document Content Description (DCD), XML-Data, DDML, and SOX. After much reviewing of these specifications, the W3C is developing a two-part specification known as "XML Schema."

The most prominent feature of a schema definition language is that it allows you write document type definitions using XML instance syntax. Therefore, it allows you to "define, describe, and catalog XML vocabularies for classes of XML documents." However, schema definition languages also introduce another feature critical to the maturity of XML, data types. Because of the use of XML instance syntax and additional features like data typing, it is my belief that schema definition language will eventually replace DTD syntax. However, the W3C has not finalized schemas as of this writing, and as DTDs are in use, I include a quick summary of DTD syntax in Appendix B.

The remainder of this chapter walks you through the development of schemas using the Microsoft XML schema definition language that is supported by Microsoft in Internet Explorer 5.

13.1 | What Exactly Are Schemas?

If you have ever worked with database schemas, you know that a schema represents, in some way, the structure and organization of something. In the relational database community, that involves the way in which tables are defined and the manner in which they are combined to produce a relational structure.

In XML, you infer a schema any time you combine a set of elements to create a new document. Without some formal definition, however, your document is just a collection of elements. The elements can be parsed into a DOM tree, and you can access them programmatically. You can even apply transformations to any element in the document.

But, your document lacks the formal definitions that define how others can use your element types.

So, a "schema" is a set of constraints that control how documents may be structured. There are two standard means for describing a schema. The first is the document type definitions (DTD) as described in the XML 1.0 specification, and the other is the XML Schema specification, which currently holds the status of a W3C Working Draft.

The W3C XML Schema specification defines a schema instance as "an XML document whose structure conforms to some schema." The draft specification also defines a schema definition as "an XML document that defines a schema... The term 'Schema Definition' may also be abbreviated to 'schema' where no confusion is likely." As you can see, the schema terminology is like walking through a minefield.

Be that as it may, schemas are important for all the same reasons that DTDs are important. They allow you to validate documents and provide documentation for your vocabularies. They can even be embedded as metadata that software agents can use to better process a document.

13.2 | Defining Schemas

The implementation of the schema definition language that ships with Internet Explorer 5 is actually based on two earlier W3C proposals. The first, called XML-Data, was submitted to the W3C in January 1998 by Microsoft, DataChannel, ArborText, and others. The second proposal, which was edited by Tim Bray and others, is called Document Content Description (DCD). DCD defines document constraints in an XML syntax and provides additional properties, including basic data types. Similar functionality is now appearing in the latest W3C draft proposal. However, this specification has yet to reach Recommendation status. Therefore, this section focuses on Microsoft's implementation. Be aware that the functionality described here is specific to Internet Explorer and will likely change as new software becomes available.

Because an XML Schema document is also an XML document, the first step is to write the document prolog. Then you can create the root <Schema> element. This first example shows the general structure for your schema documents:

```
<?xml version="1.0"?>
<Schema name="myschema"
        xmlns="urn:schemas-microsoft-com:xml-data"
        xmlns:dt="urn:schemas-microsoft-com:datatypes>

   <!-- schema definitions go here -->

</Schema>
```

The <Schema> element is the root element and includes a name attribute so that you can identify your schema. The first namespace declaration, which is required in IE5, includes a namespace for the schema elements. You could provide a prefix for this namespace. However, this example makes Schema the default namespace. This means we don't have to include the prefix in every XML Schema element, thus simplifying the syntax a bit. The second namespace declaration sets up a namespace for the inclusion of data types. We will discuss data types in a moment.

The <Schema> element provides several element types you can use to create schema definitions. The most commonly used one, <elementType>, allows you to define new element types for your documents. The general form for <elementType> is:

```
<ElementType
    content="{empty | textOnly | eltOnly | mixed}"
    dt:type="datatype"
    model="{open | closed}"
    name="name"
    order="{one | seq | many}" >
```

```
<!-- content model goes here -->

</elementType>
```

`<ElementType>`'s attributes tell the XML processor what goes inside of your elements. When you assign values to these attributes, you are defining properties of the element's "content model."

Elements may contain data, other elements, a combination of elements and data, or be empty. So, the `content` attribute allows you to specify what content is allowed. Mixed content is the most flexible since it allows you to mix elements and character data. You can constrain your content to just elements using the `eltOnly` value, or just text data using the `textOnly` value. If your element will always be an empty element, then assign the value `empty` to the content attribute.

The next line defines a data type. The `dt` prefix signifies the data type namespace, which is created in the `<Schema>` start-tag. The type attribute takes any one of several data types, including an int, number, date, or a char. The basic data types were summarized in Table 6-5 in Chapter 6.

Microsoft includes a `model` attribute that provides an added level of flexibility. By setting this value to `open`, your documents may contain content other than what is specified in the content model. For example, you could include mixed content in an element of your document even if the content attribute was set to `eltOnly`. This allows documents to pass validation even though they don't conform to this part of the schema. Setting the model attribute to `closed` forces elements to follow the content model.

The `name` attribute names your element type. This name will also be used when you use the element type in a content model with `<element>`. Finally, the order attribute allows you to specify whether the element types in the content model of this element type may occur in any order (`many`), only one may occur (`one`), or that they must occur in sequence (`seq`).

To see how this works, consider the following XML document fragment, which describes an invoice record:

```
<invoice>
    <clientName>ACME Programming Company</clientName>
    <contact>Kris Butler</contact>
    <clientAdrress>123 Fourth Street,
                   Sometown, USA
    </clientAddress>
    <descriptionOfServices>
        XML Training
    </descriptionOfServices>
    <costOfServices>1000</costOfServices>
</invoice>
```

The `<invoice>` element contains `clientName`, `contact`, `clientAd-
dress`, `descriptionOfServices`, and `costOfServices` elements. In
XML Schema, we can define the following:

```
<elementType name="invoice"
             content="eltOnly"
             order="many" model="closed>
    <element name="clientName" />
    <element name="contact" />
    <element name="clientAddress" />
    <element name="descriptionOfServices" />
    <element name="costOfServices" />
</elementType>
```

All we are doing at this point is defining the content that is allowed
in an `<invoice>` element. That is, we are specifying the content
model for the `<invoice>` element. In this case, we are allowing only
`<invoice>` to contain elements. You specify the names of the allowed
subelement types with `<element>`.

To define the subelement types, you must add the following:

```
<elementType name="clientName"
             content="textOnly" />
<elementType name="contact"
             content="textOnly" />
<elementType name="clientAddress"
             content="textOnly" />
<elementType name=" descriptionOfServices"
             content="textOnly" />
<elementType name=" costOfServices"
             content="textOnly" />
```

13.2.1   *Refining the Content Model*

You can refine your content model using the `<group>` element, which allows you to organize your subelements into groups. The general form for `<group>` is:

```
<group
    maxOccurs="{1 | *}"
    minOccurs="{0 | 1}"
    order="{one | seq | many}" >
</group>
```

For instance, the invoice example above defined a single element type for a client's address. It would be more useful to break the address out into a street address, city, state, zip code, and country. We might also want to group these elements together and specify that they occur in a particular order, as shown here:

```
<elementType name="invoice"
            content="eltOnly"
            order="many" model="closed>

  <element name="clientName" />
  <element name="contact" />

  <group order="seq>
     <element name="streetAddress" minOccurs="1"
            maxOccurs="*" />
     <element name="city" />
     <element name="state" />
     <element name="zip" />
     <element name="province" />
     <element name="country" />
  </group>

  <element name="descriptionOfServices" />
  <element name="costOfServices" />
</elementType>

...

<elementType name="streetAddress"
            content="textOnly" />
<elementType name="city"
```

```
                          content="textOnly" />
<elementType name="state"
                          content="textOnly" />
<elementType name="zip"
                          content="textOnly" />
<elementType name="province"
                          content="textOnly" />
<elementType name="country"
                          content="textOnly" />
```

The <group> element specifies the order as a sequence. Each element must occur in the order "it is specified within the <group> element." Note that the street address can occur more than once, allowing the user of this document to include additional information, such as a suite number. All other elements are required and may occur only once.

The <group> element also provides attributes that allow you to control the number of occurrences for a group. The minOccurs attribute allows you to specify a minimum number of occurrences, while maxOccurs allows you to indicate the maximum number of times the group may appear. For example, you may want to allow for a billing address and a second address indicating where you performed the services. Since the structure of the data is the same, you can reuse the group definition to include both addresses by specifying the following:

```
<group order="seq" minOccurs="1" maxOccurs="2>

    ...

</group>
```

Finally, setting minOccurs to 0 makes the group optional. You can also allow for an unlimited number of occurrences by setting maxOccurs="*".

13.2.2 *Defining Attributes*

Creating attributes is similar to defining element types. The element for defining an attribute takes the form:

```
<AttributeType
    default="default-value"
    dt:type="primitive-type"
    dt:values="enumerated-values"
    name="idref"
    required="{yes | no}" >
```

The first thing you will notice is that you can set a default value for an attribute. Also, you can define a list of possible values by setting `dt:type="enumeration"` and setting `dt:values` equal to the values in your list. Finally, you can specify whether an attribute is required or optional using the `required` attribute.

As an example, let's create a set of attributes for the `<invoice>` element. We may want to include an invoice number, a date, and possibly a status code indicating whether the invoice was paid. The attribute defintions for the `<invoice>` element type might look something like this:

```
<AttributeType name="invoiceNum" dt:type="int"
               required="yes" />
<AttributeType name="status"
               default="unpaid" required="no" />
<AttributeType name="invoiceDate"
               dt:type="date required="yes" />
```

Now, to use these attributes, all you need to do is include an `<attribute>` reference within the invoice element type.

```
<elementType name="invoice"
             content="eltOnly"
             order="many" model="closed>

<attribute type="invoiceNum" />
<attribute type="status" />
<attribute type="invoiceDate" />


...

</elementType>
```

13.2.3   *Putting It All Together*

Before looking at the finished schema definition, there is one more element you can use to provide documentation for your schemas. The <description> element allows you to place comments within your element type and attribute definitions in order to document them. Note that these comments are not included in the result tree when a document instance is processed. Our final schema makes ample use of the <description> element.

```
<?xml version="1.0"?>
<Schema name="myschema"
        xmlns="urn:schemas-microsoft-com:xml-data"
        xmlns:dt="urn:schemas-microsoft-com:datatypes">

<Description>
   Main element       : invoice
   content            : elements only
   Multiple instances : yes
   Attributes         : invoiceNum, status, invoiceDate
   Subelements        : clientName, contact,
                        client address [group],
                        descriptionOfServices,
                        costOfServices
</Description>

<elementType name="invoice"
             content="eltOnly"
             order="many" model="closed">

   <attribute type="invoiceNum" />
   <attribute type="status" />
   <attribute type="invoiceDate" />

   <element name="clientName" />
   <element name="contact" />

   <group order="seq">
      <element name="streetAddress" minOccurs="1"
               maxOccurs="*" />
      <element name="city" />
      <element name="state" />
      <element name="zip" />
```

```
      <element name="province"
      <element name="country" />
   </group>

   <element name="descriptionOfServices" />
   <element name="costOfServices" />
</elementType>

<AttributeType name="invoiceNum" dt:type="int"
               required="yes" />
<AttributeType name="status"
               default="unpaid" required="no" />
<AttributeType name="invoiceDate"
               dt:type="date required="yes" />
<elementType name="clientName"
             content="textOnly" />
<elementType name="contact"
             content="textOnly" />
<elementType name="streetAddress"
              content="textOnly" />
<elementType name="city"
             content="textOnly" />
<elementType name="state"
             content="textOnly" />
<elementType name="zip"
             content="textOnly" />
<elementType name="province"
             content="textOnly" />
<elementType name="country"
             content="textOnly" />
<elementType name=" descriptionOfServices"
             content="textOnly" />
<elementType name=" costOfServices"
             content="textOnly" />
</Schema>
```

13.3 | Conclusion

Of all the schema definition language implementations available, Microsoft's is by far the most stable. Its implementation of XML Schema includes a majority of the key features you will eventually see in the W3C specification, and it allows you to experiment with schemas now. There are, of course, some syntactic differences, and the W3C proposal adds features not currently available in the Microsoft implementation. However, you should be able to easily migrate your schemas as the standard stabilizes, while gaining the benefits of schemas over DTDs.

13.4 | References

XML-Data: W3C Note 05 Jan 1998.
http://www.w3.org/TR/1998/NOTE-XML-data-0105/

Document Content Description for XML. (NOTE-dcd-19980731)
http://www.w3.org/TR/NOTE-dcd

An XML-Based
Web Site

In this final chapter, we bring together all of the technologies discussed throughout this book to create a Web site based on XML. This example Web site is implemented on IIS. So, you will need to be running Windows NT with IIS (or Personal Web Server) and have Active Server Pages installed. You must also enable your server with the XML components as described in Chapter 11.

Rather than devising some sample Web site, I have chosen to use a real-world Web site. That is, I will be showing how my Web site at BeyondHTML.com can be recreated using XML. All of the source files for this project are available on the CD that accompanies this book. Therefore, you can use these files as templates for creating your own XML-based Web site.

14.1 | Site Design

In designing the overall site, it is helpful to examine both conceptual and structural views of the planned site. The conceptual view will be helpful in designing and building the user interface for your site, while the structural view can be helpful with decisions about the site's physical layout. As it turns out, you can use this physical structure to design an XML document that represents the structure of your site. That, in turn, could be used to create a Web site navigation system, such as the one described in Chapter 10.

The Web site presented here is based on an online magazine that presents articles, news, and product reviews that can be viewed online. The site also includes a database that users can use to search for XML tools. Conceptually, the site looks like Figure 14-1.

To keep the site simple, the site provides five main areas that may be of interest to visitors. The Presentation area provides articles related to user-interface design, style sheet presentation, and so on. The Markup section covers markup languages like HTML and XML, and the Scripting section discusses techniques for using JavaScript, Perl, Python, and VBScript. Finally, the Archives section contains back issues while the database contains the searchable database of XML tools, as described in Chapter 11.

Likewise, the directory structure strives for simplicity, providing just two directory levels: the root directory and one level of subdirectories. This should be enough to demonstrate the overall structure. You can extend the structure to any number of levels you wish. The structural view of the Web site is shown in Figure 14-2.

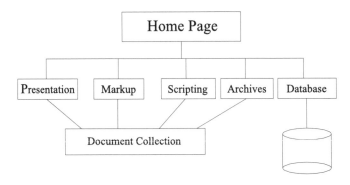

Figure 14–1   Conceptual view of the Web site.

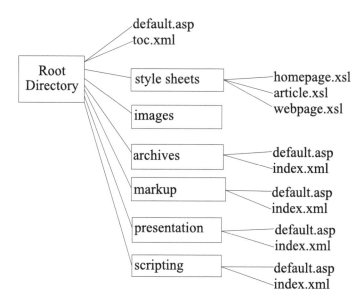

Figure 14–2   Structural view of the Web site.

As you look over Figure 14-2, note that directory names are contained in a box while file names are not. As you can see from this figure, the subdirectories roughly match the key areas of the Web site. Two additional subdirectories have been added. The images subdirectory contains all images for the Web site, and the stylesheets directory is a repository for the XSL style sheets that your XML documents reference.

Next, there are two files in the root directory: default.asp and toc.xml. The default.asp file is the server page that is invoked when visitors point their browsers to www.BeyondHTML.com. The purpose of this server page is to determine browser support and select a method for serving XML content. The toc.xml file is an XML representation of the Home page. The style sheet for this Home page is homepage.xsl, which is located in the stylesheets directory.

The subdirectories for the markup, presentation, archives, and scripting areas of the site each contains two files. Again, one is an Active Server Page to perform browser detection, and the other is an XML representation of the index file for that subdirectory. (HTTP servers generally

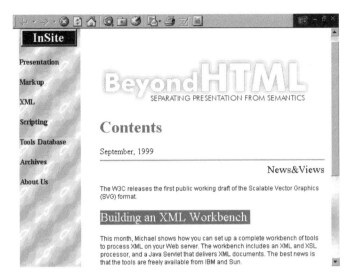

Figure 14–3   The result of serving toc.xml. In this view, the default.asp page detects that the request was made by Internet Explorer 5 and therefore redirects the client to toc.xml. Thus, this document is processed in IE5 rather than on the server.

default to a standard Web page file name, such as index.html, when no page name is provided in the URL. Although there is no such provision for XML pages, I choose to follow this same file-naming convention.) Each index.xml file provides a listing of the articles in that subdirectory. The style sheet used to transform index.xml is webpage.xsl, which is again located in the style sheets subdirectory.

The result of serving toc.xml is shown in Figure 14-3. The method for serving this page depends upon the browser making the request. That is the subject of the next section.

14.2 | Serving It Up

The next consideration is to decide how pages should be served: Should they be formatted on the server, or processed in the browser? The approach I take is to use Active Server pages to detect the "user agent." If the browser is a Microsoft Internet Explorer 5.0 browser, then the server page redirects the user agent to the XML page. Since the page contains a reference to its style sheet, the browser can collect the necessary resources and process the document on the client.

If, on the other hand, the user agent is something other than an IE5 browser, the server page processes the document on the server. The following shows the code for default.ASP, which is the server page for the site's Home page:

```
<%@ LANGUAGE=JScript %>

    <%
    var testAgent = Request.ServerVariables
                ("HTTP_USER_AGENT");

    if ( testAgent =
        "Mozilla/4.0 (compatible; MSIE 5.0; Windows NT")
      Response.Redirect("toc.xml");

    else {
      Response.Write(testAgent);
      var xmlDocument =
        Server.CreateObject("Microsoft.XMLDOM");
      var xslDocument =
        Server.CreateObject("Microsoft.XMLDOM");

      xmlDocument.load(Server.MapPath("toc.xml"));
      xslDocument.load(Server.MapPath("homepage.xsl"));
      Response.Write
        (xmlDocument.transformNode(xslDocument));
    }

    %>
</BODY>
</HEAD>
</HTML>
```

The first step is to call `Response.ServerVariables()` to determine the browser's type and version. If the `HTTP_USER_AGENT` contains the string "MSIE 5", then we can redirect the browser to the XML version of the document. There are more elegant methods for detecting browsers that you may want to employ, particularly if you plan to customize HTML for various clients. However, the goal in this example is to simply determine whether the browser has the ability to process XML on the client side. Since at publication time IE5 was the only commercial browser capable of processing XML documents, this code suffices.

In any case, if the user agent turns out to be some other browser, the remaining portion of the ASP script kicks in. This portion of the script is similar to that presented in Chapter 11. First, the DOM objects representing the XML document and XSL style sheet are created. After that, toc.xml and homepage.xsl are loaded into their respective objects. Finally, the style sheet is applied to toc.xml using `TransformNode()` and the result is sent back to the client.

14.2.1   *Toc.xml*

The layout of the Home page includes a logo for the Web site, which should appear at the top of the screen. The site also includes a common navigation bar that allows the user to get around the site. For completeness, there should also be a text-based navigation at the bottom of the screen. All of this can be handled through a style sheet template, so the XML file is free to represent only the items that change on the Home page.

The changing elements on the Home page are represented in a table of contents. Each entry in the table represents a feature story that the user can link to. The entries must include a headline for the story and an abstract summarizing it. Without having to worry about layout, the XML document is really quite simple. Here is the marked up version of toc.xml:

```
<?xml version="1.0"?>
<?xml-stylesheet type="text/xsl" href=
"http://localhost/homepage.xsl"?>

<homepage>
   <title>BeyondHTML.com Home Page</title>
   <H1>Contents</H1>
   <pubDate>September, 1999</pubDate>
   <contents>
      <headline href="news.xml">
```

```
      News&amp;Views
    </headline>

    <abstract>
    <para>
    The W3C releases the first public working draft of the
Scalable Vector Graphics (SVG) format.
    </para>
    </abstract>

    <headline2 href="workbench.xml">
        Building an XML Workbench
    </headline2>
    <abstract2>
    <para>This month, Michael shows how you can set up a
complete workbench of tools to process XML on your Web
server. The workbench includes an XML and XSL processor, and
a Java Servlet that delivers XML documents. The best news is
that the tools are freely available from IBM and
Sun. </para>
    </abstract2>

    <headline3 href="frames.xml">
       Frames With Style
    </headline3>
    <abstract3>
    <para>Because of excessive abuse, frames have gotten a
bad "rep" from Web designers and developers. But used
properly, frames can enhance navigation while easing
maintenance of your site. Michael shows you how.</para>
    </abstract3>
  </contents>

  <notes>Interested in a topic? Drop us a line at
editors@beyondHTML.com</notes>

</homepage>
```

14.2.2   *Homepage.xsl*

Next, let's take a look at the style sheet for the Home page. Like the style sheets presented throughout this book, this one performs an HTML transformation. The style sheet's root template begins by generating the CSS style rules for the Home page, then creates the <BODY> of the document.

One trick to note here involves the creation of hyperlinks. For example, the Home page references three stories in its table of contents. Each contains a headline, which is formatted using the CSS style rules, and a summary of the story. If users want to read that story, they click on the headline, which is a link to the actual story. In the XML document, the <headline> element uses an href attribute to maintain the URL. In your style sheet, you must create an anchor tag to make the headline linkable. Normally, you would write something like:

```
<A href="news.xml">Today's Top News Story
</A>
```

In your XSL style sheet, you can get the value for the attribute using the pattern headline[@href] and the content of the anchor element from the pattern article/headline. So, you might write something like:

```
<A href="
   <xsl:value-of select=" headline[@href]" />
>
   <xsl:value-of select="article/headline" />
</A>
```

You probably have already noticed the problem with this code. As soon as the style sheet processor sees the opening angle bracket for the xsl:value-of start-tag, it generates an error because there was no closing angle bracket for the anchor element start-tag. Therefore, the style sheet uses <xsl:element> to create the anchor element, like this:

```
<xsl:element name="A">
   <xsl:attribute name="href">
      <xsl:apply-templates
         select="article/headline[@href]"/>
   </xsl:attribute >
</xsl:element>
```

Following this, the content of the anchor element is generated using `<xsl:value-of>` with the article/headline pattern. To close the anchor element, an `xsl:element` end-tag is created. Here is the complete style sheet:

```
<?xml version="1.0"?>

<xsl:stylesheet
   xmlns:xsl="http://www.w3.org/TR/WD-xsl"
   xmlns="http://www.w3.org/TR/REC-html40"
   result-ns="">

  <!-- Root template -->
  <xsl:template match="/">
    <HTML>
     <HEAD>
       <META http-equiv="Content-Type" content=
       "text/html; charset=iso-8859-1"/>

        <!-- Navigation Bar Styles -->

       <STYLE TYPE="text/css">
        A:link {
           COLOR:  Navy;
           text-decoration: none }
        A:visited { COLOR: Navy }
        A:active { COLOR: blue }

       #NavText {
          font-weight: bold;
          font-size: 14px;
          text-decoration: none;
          font-family: "Times New Roman", "Garamond",
                       "serif" }

       #NavHead {
          font-weight: bold;
          text-align: center;
          font-size: 24px;
          text-decoration: none;
          font-family: "Times New Roman", "serif",
                     "Garamond"; color: white;
          display: block; background-color: navy;
                     border-style: outset;
```

```
           margin-left: 2%; margin-right: 5% }

<!-- General Styles -->
H1 {
   color: #FF0000;
     background-color: #FFFFFF;
        text-transform: Capitalize;
        text-align: Left; }

<!-- Document Styles -->

.headline {
   color: #FF0000;
   background-color: #FFFFFF;
   text-transform: Capitalize;
   text-align: Left; }

.deck {
   font-style: italic;
   font-size: 14px;
   font-weight: bold;
   color: black;
   margin-left: 64px;
   font-family: Arial, helvetica, sans-serif;}

.byline {
   color: Navy;
   font-weight: bold;
   font-size: 14px;
   font-family: Arial, helvetica, sans-serif;}

.pubDate {
   color: Red;
   font-weight: normal;
   font-size: 12px;
   font-family: Arial, helvetica, sans-serif;}

.copyright {
   color: Red;
   font-weight: normal;
   font-size: 12px;
   font-family: Arial, helvetica, sans-serif;}

 .aBody { display: block;
   font-weight: normal;
```

```
       font-size: 12px;
       font-family: "Arial", "Garamond", "serif"; }

   .dropCap { background: white;
       color: red;
       float: left;
       vertical-align: text-top;
       font-size: 24px;
       font-style: bold;
       border: none; }

   .bold { font-style: bold; }
   .ital { font-style: italic; }

   #BoxCopy { color: white;
       background-color: red;
       vertical-align: text-bottom;
       font-size: 24px;
       font-style: bold;
       font-family: "Times New Roman", "serif",
                    "Garamond"; color: white;
       padding-left: 1px;
       padding-right: 3px;
       text-decoration: none;
       border: none; }

   #BoxCopy1 { color: white;
        background-color: gray;
        vertical-align: text-top;
        font-size: 24px;
        font-style: bold;
        text-decoration: none;
        border: inset }

   #BoxCopy2 { color: navy;
        background-color: white;
        float: right;
        vertical-align: text-top;
        font-size: 20px;
        font-style: bold;
        border: none; }
</STYLE>
<TITLE>
  <xsl:value-of select="article/headline"/>
</TITLE>
```

```
    </HEAD>
    <BODY>

  <TABLE WIDTH="100%">
    <TR>
      <TD WIDTH="121" HEIGHT="211"
          BACKGROUND="gifs/navBackground.jpg"
          VALIGN="TOP">

      <Span id="NavHead">InSite</Span>

      <P>
      <A HREF="present/index.xml" TARGET="_top">
         <SPAN id="NavText">Presentation</SPAN>
      </A></P>

      <P>
      <A HREF="markup/index.xml" TARGET="_top">
         <SPAN id="NavText">Markup</SPAN>
      </A></P>

      <P>
      <A HREF="markup/xml/index.xml" TARGET="MainPane">
         <SPAN id="NavText">XML</SPAN>
      </A></P>

      <P>
      <A HREF="scripting/index.xml" TARGET="_top">
         <SPAN id="NavText">Scripting</SPAN>
      </A></P>

      <P>
      <A HREF="db/searchform.html" TARGET="_top">
         <SPAN id="NavText">Tools Database</SPAN>
      </A></P>

      <P>
      <A HREF="resources/index.xml" TARGET="_top">
         <SPAN id="NavText">Archives</SPAN>
      </A></P>

      <P>
      <A HREF="bio.shtml">
         <SPAN id="NavText">About Us</SPAN>
      </A></P></TD>
```

```
        <TD WIDTH="35" HEIGHT="211" BGCOLOR="#FFFFFF"
            VALIGN="TOP"></TD>
        <TD WIDTH="442" HEIGHT="211" BGCOLOR="#FFFFFF"
            VALIGN="TOP">


    <MAP NAME="logosmall">
       <AREA SHAPE="RECT" COORDS="0,1,199,52"
            HREF="http://www.beyondhtml.com"
            ALT="Jump to Home page"></AREA>
       <AREA SHAPE="default"
            HREF="http://www.beyondhtml.com"></AREA>
    </MAP>


    <P>
      <BR></BR> <IMG SRC="gifs/logo.gif"
               ALT="BeyondHTML Logo" ALIGN="MIDDLE"
               WIDTH="426" HEIGHT="112">
          </IMG>
    </P>
 <!-- template rules go here -->


    <H1>
       <xsl:value-of select="homepage/H1"/>
    </H1>
       <xsl:value-of select="homepage/pubDate"/>
    <HR></HR>


<!-- Create an Anchor element and a link to the headline -->
    <xsl:element name="A">
       <xsl:attribute name="href">
         <xsl:apply-templates
         select="homepage/contents/headline[@href]"/>
       </xsl:attribute >
    </xsl:element>
             <Span ID="BoxCopy2">
                <xsl:value-of
                 select="homepage/contents/headline"/>
                <xsl:apply-templates/>
             </Span><BR></BR>
    <xsl:element name="/A">
      <xsl:apply-templates />
    </xsl:element>


    <DIV Class="aBody">
      <P><xsl:value-of
```

```
            select="homepage/contents/abstract/para"/></P>


  <!-- Create an Anchor element and a link to headline2 -->
    <xsl:element name="A">
      <xsl:attribute name="href">
        <xsl:apply-templates
        select="homepage/contents/headline2[@href]"/>
      </xsl:attribute >
    </xsl:element>
                  <Span ID="BoxCopy">
                     <xsl:value-of
                       select="homepage/contents/headline2"/>
                  </Span><BR></BR>
    <xsl:element name="/A">
      <xsl:apply-templates />
   </xsl:element>


          <P><xsl:value-of
          select="homepage/contents/abstract2/para"/></P>


  <!-- Create an Anchor element and a link to headline3 -->
    <xsl:element name="A">
      <xsl:attribute name="href">
        <xsl:apply-templates
        select="homepage/contents/headline3[@href]"/>
      </xsl:attribute >
    </xsl:element>
                  <Span ID="BoxCopy1">
                     <xsl:value-of
                       select="homepage/contents/headline3"/>
                  </Span><BR></BR>
    <xsl:element name="/A">
      <xsl:apply-templates />
   </xsl:element>


                  <P><xsl:value-of
                  select="homepage/contents/abstract3/para"/>
                  </P>
                  <P><I>
                  <xsl:value-of
                        select="homepage/notes"/>
                  </I></P>
              </DIV>
          </TD></TR>
        </TABLE>
```

```
    <P ALIGN="CENTER"><FONT SIZE="-1">
      [<A HREF="/present/index.xml">Presentation</A>]
      [<A HREF="/markup/index.xml">Markup</A>]
      [<A HREF="/markup/xml/index.xml">XML</A>]
       <A HREF="/scripting/index.xml">[Scripting</A>]
      [<A HREF="/db/searchform.html">Tools Database</A>]
      [<A HREF="/archives/index.xml">Archives</A>]
      [<A HREF="/bio.shtml">About Us</A>]</FONT>
    </P>
  <HR></HR>

  <P><FONT SIZE="-1">Copyright (c) 1998, 1999.
    <A HREF="mailto:mfloyd@beyondhtml.com">
       Michael Floyd</A> . All Rights Reserved</FONT>
  </P>

  </BODY>
  </HTML>
</xsl:template>

<xsl:template match="headline[@href]">
   <xsl:value-of select="@href"/>
</xsl:template>

<xsl:template match="headline2[@href]">
   <xsl:value-of select="@href"/>
</xsl:template>

<xsl:template match="headline3[@href]">
   <xsl:value-of select="@href"/>
</xsl:template>

<xsl:template match="aBody">
   <P>
      <xsl:apply-templates/>
   </P>
</xsl:template>

<xsl:template match="dropCap">
   <DIV Class="dropCap">
      <xsl:apply-templates />
   </DIV>
</xsl:template>

<xsl:template match="bold">
```

```
      <B>
         <xsl:apply-templates/>
      </B>
   </xsl:template>

   <xsl:template match="italic">
      <I>
         <xsl:apply-templates/>
      </I>
   </xsl:template>

   <xsl:template match="byline[@Email]">
      <A HREF="mailto:mfloyd@BeyondHTML.com">
         <xsl:apply-templates/>
      </A>
   </xsl:template>

   <xsl:template match="text()">
      <xsl:value-of />
   </xsl:template>
 <!-- template rules end here -->

</xsl:stylesheet>
```

The transformed Web page contains a table of contents with three news stories (see Figure 14-3). The top of the screen includes the logo for the Web site, and the left-hand side of the screen provides a navigation bar for getting around the site. Text-based navigation is also provided at the bottom of the screen, along with a suitable copyright notice.

14.3 | Linked Pages

The rest of the site contains pages that are linked from the Home page. Each linked page resides in its own directory, which corresponds to one of the links in the navigation bar. Thus, you will find a directory called markup containing a file called index.xml. The Home page (and all other pages) include a navigation bar with a link to this page.

These linked pages all use a single style sheet webpage.xsl. The style sheet is similar to that for the Home page in that it includes a navigation bar and the same footers at the bottom of the screen. Because this style sheet is similar to homepage.xsl, I won't repeat the code here. However, there are some differences in how the style sheet lays out pages. You will find this style sheet on the disk that comes with this book, so I will leave that for you to explore. Also, maintaining just one style sheet allows for only one page type on your site. In practice, you will want to create several style sheets, each representing a different page type on your site.

14.4 | Conclusion

To run the example with the ASP pages, you must access the Home XML page through the Web server. If you have set up your server as described in Chapter 11, you should be able to access the Home page by entering the URL http://localhost/ in your browser. This will invoke the default.asp page, which either loads the appropriate document or redirects the browser, depending upon its capabilities.

If you do not have Microsoft's IIS or Personal Web Server configured on your system, you can still run the example Web site in Internet Explorer 5.0 by launching toc.xml. Of course, you lose the benefits that ASP provides, namely, the ability to perform browser detection and load different pages based on the browser's capabilities.

Finally, this Web site is provided for example purposes only. A production Web site will likely provide better layout capability, support for rich media types, and database capabilities. However, this simple Web site can serve as a template for your own development efforts. If you take the time to migrate your existing site, you will gain all the benefits that XML has to offer. Good luck.

Just Enough XML

Introductory Discussion

- Elements
- Character set
- Entities
- Markup
- Document types

This appendix is taken verbatim from The XML
Handbook, Second Edition *by Charles F. Goldfarb
and Paul Prescod. Chapter and page references within
it refer to that book.*

I n this chapter we will explore the fundamental concepts of
XML documents and XML systems. If XML were a great
work of literature then this chapter would be the Cliff Notes.
The chapter will introduce the ideas that define the language but will
avoid the nitty-gritty details (the syntax) behind the constructs. As a
result, some concepts may remain slightly fuzzy because you will not
be able to work with them "hands on." Later chapters will provide
that opportunity.

This early presentation of these ideas will allow you to see XML's
"big picture." We will do this by walking through the design process
for an XML-like language. Hopefully, by the end of the process you
will understand each of the design decisions and XML's overall
architecture.

Our objective is to equip you with "just enough" XML to appreciate the application scenarios and tool descriptions in the following
parts of the book, but being over-achievers we may go a little too
far. Feel free to leave at any time to read about XML in the real
world.

A.1 | The Goal

First we should summarize what we are trying to achieve. In short, "What is XML used for?" XML is for the *digital representation* of documents. You probably have an intuitive feel for what a document is. We will work from your intuition.

Documents can be large and small. Both a multi-volume encyclopedia and a memo can be thought of as documents. A particular volume of the encyclopedia can also be called a document. XML allows you to think of the encyclopedia whichever way will allow you to get your job done most efficiently. You'll notice that XML will give you these sorts of options in many places. XML also allows us to think of an email message as a document. XML can even represent the message from a police department's server to a police officer's handheld computer that reports that you have unpaid parking tickets.[1]

When we say that we want to *digitally represent* documents we mean that we want to put them in some kind of computer-readable notation so that a computer can help us store, process, search, transmit, display, and print them. In order for a computer to do useful things with a document, we are going to have to tell it about the structure of the document. This is our simple goal: to represent the documents in a way that the computer can "understand," insofar as computers can understand anything.

XML documents can include pictures, movies, and other multimedia, but we will not actually represent the multimedia components as XML. If you think of representation as a translation process, similar to language translation, then the multimedia components are the parts that we will leave in their "native language" because they have no simple translation into the "target language" (XML). We will just include them in their native formats as you might include a French or Latin phrase in an English text without explicit translation. Most pictures on the Web are files in formats called GIF or JPEG, and most movies are in a format called MPEG. An XML document would just

---

[1]Sorry about that.

refer to those files in their native GIF, JPEG, or MPEG formats. If you were transcribing an existing print document into XML, you would most likely represent the character-text parts as XML and the graphical parts in these other formats.

A.2 | Elements: The Logical Structure

Before we can describe exactly how we are going to represent documents, we must have a model in our heads of how a document is structured. Most documents (for example, books and magazines) can be broken down into components (chapters and articles). These can also be broken down into components (titles, paragraphs, figures, and so forth). It turns out that just about every document can be viewed this way.

In XML, these components are called *elements*. Each element represents a logical component of a document. Elements can contain other elements and can also contain the words and sentences that you would usually think of as the text of the document. XML calls this text the document's *character data*. This hierarchical view of XML documents is demonstrated in Figure A-1.

Markup professionals call this the *tree structure* of the document. The element that contains all of the others (e.g. `book`, `report`, or `memo`) is known as the *root element*. This name captures the fact that it is the only element that does not "hang" off of some other element.

The elements that are contained in the root are called its *subelements*. They may contain subelements themselves. If they do, we will call them *branches*. If they do not, we will call them *leaves*.

Thus, the `chapter` and `article` elements are branches (because they have subelements), but the `paragraph` and `title` elements are leaves (because they only contain character data).[2] The root element is also referred to as the *document element* because it holds the entire

---

[2]This arboreal metaphor is firmly rooted in computer science. However, markup experts have recently extended it with the term "grove." This term recognizes that a single document may best be viewed as multiple trees.

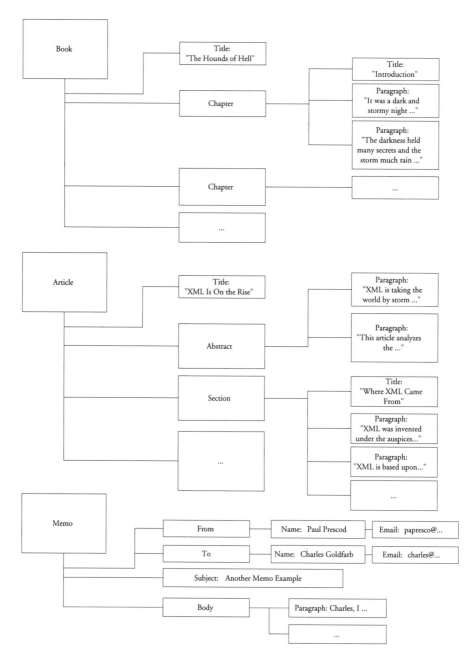

Figure A-1   Hierarchical views of documents.

logical document within it. The terms *root element* and *document element* are interchangeable.

Elements can also have extra information attached to them called *attributes*. Attributes describe properties of elements. For instance a `CIA-record` element might have a security attribute that gives the security rating for that element. A CIA database might only release certain records to certain people depending on their security rating. It will not always be clear which aspects of a document should be represented with elements and which should be represented with attributes, but we will give some guidelines in Chapter 54, "Creating a document type definition," on page 748.

Real-world documents do not always fit this *tree* model perfectly. They often have non-hierarchical features such as cross-references or hypertext links from one section of the tree to another. XML can represent these structures too. In fact, XML goes beyond the powerful links provided by HTML. More on this in A.8, "Hyperlinking and addressing," on page 36.

A.3 | Unicode: The Character Set

Texts are made up of characters. If we are going to represent texts, then we must represent the characters that comprise them. So we must decide how we are going to represent characters at the bits and bytes level. This is called the *character encoding*. We must also decide what characters we are going to allow in our documents. This is the *character set*. A particularly restrictive character set might allow only upper-case characters. A very large character set might allow Eastern ideographs and Arabic characters.

If you are a native English speaker you may only need the 52 upper- and lower-case characters, some punctuation, and a few accented characters. The pervasive *7 bit ASCII character set* caters to this market. It has just enough characters (128) for all of the letters, symbols, some accented characters, and some other oddments. ASCII is both a character set *and* a character encoding. It defines what set of characters are available and how they are to be encoded in terms of bits and bytes.

XML's character set is *Unicode*, a sort of ASCII on steroids. Unicode includes thousands of useful characters from languages around the world.[3] However the first 128 characters of Unicode are compatible with ASCII, and there is a character encoding of Unicode, *UTF-8*, that is compatible with 7 bit ASCII. This means that at the bits and bytes level, the first 128 characters of UTF-8 Unicode and 7 bit ASCII are the same. This feature of *Unicode* allows authors to use standard plain-text editors to create XML immediately.

A.4 | Entities: The Physical Structure

An XML document is defined as a series of characters. An XML processor starts at the beginning and works to the end. XML provides a mechanism for allowing text to be organized non-linearly and potentially in multiple pieces. The parser reorganizes it into the linear structure.

The "piece-of-text" construct is called an *entity*. An entity could be as small as a single character or as large as all the characters of a book.

Entities have *names*. Somewhere in your document, you insert an *entity reference* to make use of an entity. The processor replaces the entity reference with the entity itself, which is called the *replacement text*. It works somewhat like a word processor macro.

For instance, an entity named "sigma" might contain the name of a Greek character. You would use a reference to the entity whenever you wanted to insert the sigma character. An entity could also be called "introduction-chapter" and be a chapter in a book. You would refer to the entity at the point where you wanted the chapter to appear.

---

[3]It also includes some not-so-useful characters—there is an entire section dedicated to "dingbats," and there is a proposal to include "Klingon," the artificial language from Star Trek™.

One of the ideas that excited Ted Nelson, the man who coined the word *hypertext*, was the idea that text could be reused in many different contexts automatically. An update in one place would propagate across all uses of the text. The feature of XML that allows text reuse is called the *external entity*. External entities are often referred to merely as entities, but the meaning is usually clear from context. An XML document can be broken up into many files on a hard disk or objects in a database, and each of them is called an entity in XML terminology. Entities could even be spread across the Internet. Whereas XML elements describe the document's logical structure, entities keep track of the location of the chunks of bytes that make up an XML document. We call this the *physical structure* of the document.

Note   *The unit of XML text that we will typically talk about is the entity. You may be accustomed to thinking about files, but entities do not have to be stored as files.*

For instance, entities could be stored in databases or generated on the fly by a computer program. Some file formats (e.g. a *zip* file) even allow multiple entities to reside in the same file at once. The term that covers all of these possibilities is entity, *not* file. Still, on most Web sites each entity will reside in a single file, so in those cases external entities and files will functionally be the same. This setup is simple and efficient, but will not be sufficient for very large sites.

Entities' bread and butter occupation is less sexy than reusing bits of text across the Internet. But it is just as important: entities help to break up large files to make them editable, searchable, downloadable, and otherwise usable on the ordinary computer systems that real people use. Entities allow authors to break their documents into workable chunks that can fit into memory for editing, can be downloaded across a slow modem, and so forth.

Without entities, authors would have to break their documents unnaturally into smaller documents with only weak links between them (as is commonly done with HTML). This complicates document management and maintenance. If you have ever tried to print out one of these HTML documents broken into a hundred HTML files then you know the problem. Entities allow documents to be broken up into chunks without forgetting that they actually represent a single coherent document that can be printed, edited, and searched as a unit when that makes sense.

Non-XML objects are referenced in much the same way and are called *unparsed entities*. We think of them as "data entities" because there is no XML markup in them that will be noticed by the XML processor. Data entities include graphics, movies, audio, raw text, PDF, and anything else you can think of that is not XML (including HTML and other forms of SGML).[4] Each data entity has an associated *notation* that is simply a statement declaring whether the entity is a GIF, JPEG, MPEG, PDF, and so forth.

Entities are described in all of their glorious (occasionally gory) detail in Chapter 55, "Entities: Breaking up is easy to do," on page 780.

A.5 | Markup

We have discussed XML's conceptual model, the tree of elements, its strategy for encoding characters, Unicode, and its mechanism for managing the size and complexity of documents, entities. We have not yet discussed how to represent the logical structure of the document and link together all of the physical entities.

Although there are XML word processors, one of the design goals of XML was that it should be possible to create XML documents in standard text editors. Some people are not comfortable with word processors and even those who are may depend on text editors to "debug" documents if the word processor makes a mistake, or allows the user to make a mistake. The only way to allow authors convenient access to

---

[4]Actually, a data entity could even contain XML, but it wouldn't be treated as part of the main XML document.

both the structure and data of the document in standard text editors is to put the two right beside each other, "cheek to cheek."

As we discussed in the introduction, the stuff that represents the logical structure and connects the entities is called markup. An XML document is made up exclusively of markup and character data. Both are in Unicode. Collectively they are termed *XML text*.

This last point is important! Unless the context unambiguously refers to data, as in "textual data," when we say "XML text," we mean the markup and the data.

Caution   *The term XML text refers to the combination of character data and markup, not character data alone. Character data + markup = text.*

Markup is differentiated from character data by special characters called *delimiters*. Informally, text between a less-than ("<") and a greater-than (">") character or between an ampersand ("&") and a semicolon (";") character is markup. Those four characters are the most common delimiters. This rule will become more concrete in later chapters. In the meantime, Example A-1 is an example of a small document to give you a taste of XML markup.

Example A-1 A small XML document

```
<?xml version="1.0"?>
<!DOCTYPE Q-AND-A SYSTEM "http://www.q.and.a.com/faq.dtd">
<Q-AND-A>
<QUESTION>I'm having trouble loading a WurdWriter 2.0 file into
WurdPurformertWriter 7.0. Any suggestions?</QUESTION>

<ANSWER>Why don't you use XML?</ANSWER>

<QUESTION>What's XML?</QUESTION>

<ANSWER>It's a long story, but there is a book I can
recommend...</ANSWER>
</Q-AND-A>
```

The markup between the less-than and greater-than is called a *tag*. You may be familiar with other languages that use similar syntax. These include HTML and other SGML-based languages.

A.6 | Document Types

The concept of a document type is fairly intuitive. You are well aware that letters, novels, and telephone books are quite different, and you are probably comfortable recognizing documents that conform to one of these categories. No matter what its title or binding, you would call a book that listed names and phone numbers a phone book. So, a document type is defined by its elements. If two documents have radically different elements or allow elements to be combined in very different ways, then they probably do not conform to the same document type.

A.6.1 *Document Type Definitions*

This notion of a document type can be formalized in XML. A *document type definition* (or *DTD*) is a series of definitions for element types, attributes, entities, and notations. It declares which of these are legal within the document and in what places they are legal. A document can claim to conform to a particular DTD in its *document type declaration*.[5]

DTDs are powerful tools for organizational standardization in much the same way that forms, templates, and style-guides are. A very rigid DTD that only allows one element type in a particular place is like a form: "Just fill in the blanks!" A more flexible DTD is like a style-guide in that it can, for instance, require every `list` to

---

[5]The document type declaration is usually abbreviated "DOCTYPE," because the obvious abbreviation would be the same as that for document type definition!

have two or more `items`, every `report` to have an `abstract`, and could restrict `footnotes` from appearing within `footnotes`.

DTDs are critical for organizational standardization, but they are just as important for allowing robust processing of documents by software. For example, a letter document with a `chapter` in the middle of it would be most unexpected and unlikely to be very useful. Letter printing software would not reliably be able to print such a document because it is not well defined what a chapter in a letter looks like. Even worse is a situation where a document is missing an element expected by the software that processes it. If your mail program used XML as its storage format, you might expect it to be able to search all of the incoming email addresses for a particular person's address. Let us presume that each message stores this address in a `from` element. What do we do about letters without `from` elements when we are searching them? Programmers could write special code to "work around" the problem, but these kinds of workarounds make code difficult to write.

A.6.2   *HTML: A Cautionary Tale*

HTML serves as a useful cautionary tale. It actually has a fairly rigorous structure, defined in SGML, and available from the World Wide Web Consortium. But everybody tends to treat the rules as if they actually came from the World Wrestling Federation—they ignore them.

The programmers that maintain HTML browsers spend a huge amount of time incorporating support for all of the incorrect ways people combine the HTML elements in their documents. Although HTML has an SGML DTD, very few people use it, and the browser vendors have unofficially sanctioned the practice of ignoring it. Programming workarounds is expensive, time consuming, boring, and frustrating, but the worst problem is that there is no good definition of what these illegal constructs mean. Some incorrect constructs will actually make HTML browsers crash, but others will merely make them display confusing or random results.

In HTML, the `title` element is used to display the document's name at the top of the browser window (on the title bar). But what should a browser do if there are two titles? Use the first? Use the last? Use both? Pick one at random? Since the HTML standard does not allow this construct it certainly does not specify a behavior. Believe it or not, an early version of Netscape's browser showed each title sequentially over time, creating a primitive sort of text animation. That behavior disappeared quickly when Netscape realized that authors were actually creating invalid HTML specifically to get this effect! Since authors cannot depend on nonsensical documents to work across browsers, or even across browser versions, there must be a formal definition of a valid, reasonable document of a particular type. In XML, the DTD provides a formal definition of the element types, attributes, and entities allowed in a document of a specified type.

There is also a more subtle, related issue. If you do not stop and think carefully about the structure of your documents, you may accidently slip back into specifying them in terms of their formatting rather than their abstract structure. We are accustomed to thinking of documents in terms of their rendition. That is because, prior to GML, there was no practical way to create a document without creating a rendition. The process of creating a DTD gives us an opportunity to rethink our documents in terms of their structure, as abstractions.

A.6.3   *Declaring a DTD*

Example A-2 shows examples of some of the declarations that are used to express a DTD:

Example A-2 Markup declarations

```
<!ELEMENT Q-AND-A (QUESTION,ANSWER)+>
<!- This allows: question, answer, question, answer ... ->

<!ELEMENT QUESTION (#PCDATA)>
<!- Questions are just made up of text ->

<!ELEMENT ANSWER (#PCDATA)>
<!- Answers are just made up of text ->
```

Caution   *A DTD is a concept; markup declarations are the means of expressing it. The distinction is important because other means of expressing DTDs are being proposed. However, most people, even ourselves, don't make the distinction in normal parlance. We just talk about the declarations as though they are the DTD that they describe.*

Some XML documents do not have a document type declaration. That does not mean that they do not conform to a document type. It merely means that they do not claim to conform to some formally defined document type definition.

If the document is to be useful as an XML document, it must still have some structure, expressed through elements, attributes, and so forth. When you create a stylesheet for a document you will depend on it having certain elements, on the element type names having certain meanings, and on the elements appearing in certain places. However it manifests itself, that set of things that you depend on is the document type.

You can formalize that structure in a DTD. In addition to or instead of a formal computer-readable DTD, you can also write out a prose description. You might consider the many HTML books in existence to be prose definitions of HTML. Finally, you can just keep the document type in your head and maintain conformance through careful discipline. If you can achieve this for large, complex documents, your powers of concentration are astounding! Which is our way of saying: We do not advise it. We will discuss DTDs more in Chapter 54, "Creating a document type definition," on page 748.

A.7 | Well-Formedness and Validity

Every language has rules about what is or is not valid in the language. In human languages that takes many forms: Words have a particular correct pronunciation (or range of pronunciations), and they can be combined in certain ways to make valid sentences (grammar). Similarly, XML has two different notions of "correct." The first is merely that the markup is intelligible: the XML equivalent of "getting the pronunciation right." A document with intelligible markup is called a *well-formed* document. One important goal of XML was that these basic rules should be simple so that they could be strictly adhered to.

The experience of the HTML market provided a cautionary tale that guided the development of XML. Much of the HTML on the Web does *not* conform to even the simplest rules in the HTML specifications. This makes automated processing of HTML quite difficult.

Because Web browsers will display ill-formed documents, authors continue to create them. In designing XML, we decided that XML processors should actually be prohibited from trying to recover from a *well-formedness* error in an XML document. This was a controversial decision because there were many who felt that it was inappropriate to restrict XML implementors from deciding the best error recovery policy for their application.

The XML equivalent of "using the right words in the right place" is called *validity* and is related to the notion of document types. A document is *valid* if it declares conformance to a DTD in a document type declaration and actually conforms to the DTD.

Documents that do not have a document type declaration are not really *invalid*—they do not violate their DTD—but they are not valid either, because they cannot be validated against a DTD.

If HTML documents with multiple titles were changed over to use XML syntax, they would be *well-formed* and invalid (presuming the HTML DTD was also converted to XML syntax). If we remove the document type declaration, so that they no longer claim to conform to the HTML DTD, then they would become merely well-formed but neither valid nor invalid.

 Caution   For most of us, the word "invalid" means something that breaks the rules. It is an easy jump from there to concluding that an XML document that does not conform to a DTD is free to break any rules at all. So for clarity, we may sometimes say "type-valid" and "non-type-valid," rather than "valid" and "invalid."

You should think carefully before you decide to make a document that is well-formed but not valid. If the document is one-of-a-kind and is small, then making it well-formed is probably sufficient. But if it is to be part of any kind of information system (even a small one) or if it is a large document, then you should write a DTD for it and validate whenever you revise it. When you decide to build or extend your information system, the fact that the document is guaranteed to be consistent will make your programming or stylesheet writing many times easier and your results much more reliable.

A.8 | Hyperlinking and Addressing

If you have used the Web, then you probably do not need to be convinced of the importance of hyperlinking. One thing you might not know, however, is that the Web's notions of hyperlink are fairly tame compared to what is available in the best academic and commercial hypertext systems. XML alone does not correct this, but it has an associated standard called *XLink* that goes a long way toward making the Web a more advanced hypertext environment.

The first deficiency of today's Web links is that there are no standardized mechanisms for making links that are external to the documents that they are linking from. Let's imagine, for example, that you stumble upon a Web page for your favorite music group. You read it, enjoy it, and move on. Imagine next week you stumble upon a Web page with all of the lyrics for all of their songs (with appropriate copyrights, of course!). You think: There should be a link between these two pages. Someone visiting one might want to know about the other and vice versa.

What you want to do is make an *external link*. You want to make a link on your computer that appears on both of the other computers. But of course you do not have the ability to edit those two documents. XLink will allow this external linking. It provides a representation for external links, but it does not provide the technology to automatically publish those links to the world. That would take some kind of *link database* that would track all of the links from people around the world. Needless to say this is a big job and though there are prototypes, there is no standardized system yet.

You may wonder how all of these links will be displayed, how readers will select link sheets and annotations, how browsers will talk to databases, and so forth. The simple answer is: "Nobody knows yet."[6]

Before the first Web browser was developed there was no way to know that we would develop a convention of using colored, underlined text to represent links (and even today some browsers use other conventions). There was also no way to know that browsers would typically have "back" buttons and "history lists." These are just conventions that arose and browser features that became popular.

This same process will now occur with external links. Some user interface (perhaps a menu) will be provided to apply external link sheets, and there will probably be some mechanism for searching for link sheets related to a document on the Web. Eventually these will stabilize into standards that will be ubiquitous and transparent (we hope!). In the meantime, things are confused, but that is the price for living on the cutting edge. XLink moves us a notch further ahead by providing a notation for representing the links.

Another interesting feature of XML extended links is that they can point to more than one resource. For instance instead of making a link from a word to its definition, you might choose to link to definitions in several different dictionaries. The browser might represent this as a popup menu, a tiny window with the choices listed, or might even open one window for each. The same disclaimer applies: The XML Link specification does not tell browsers exactly what they must do. Each is free to try to make the most intuitive, powerful user interface for links. XML brings many interesting hypertext ideas from university research labs and high tech companies "to the masses." We

---

[6]But we've got some ideas. See Chapter 44, "Extended linking," on page 588.

still have to work out exactly how that will look and who will use them for what. We live in interesting times!

A.9 | Stylesheets

To a certain extent, the concerns described above are endemic to generalized markup. Because it describes structure, and not formatting, it allows variations in display and processing that can sometimes disturb people.

However, as the Web has evolved, people have become less and less tolerant of having browser vendors control the "look and feel" of their documents. An important part of all communication, but especially modern business communication, is the idea of style. Stylesheets allow us to attach our own visual style to documents without destroying the virtue of generalized markup. Because the style is described in a separate entity, the stylesheet, software that is not interested in style can ignore it.

For instance most search engines would not care if your corporate color is blue or green, so they will just ignore those declarations in the stylesheet. Similarly, software that reads documents aloud to the sight-impaired would ignore font sizes and colors and concentrate on the abstractions—paragraphs, sections, titles, and so forth.

The Web has a very simple stylesheet language called *Cascading Style Sheets* (CSS), which arose out of the early battles between formatting and generalized markup in HTML. Like any other specification, CSS is a product of its environment, and so is not powerful enough to describe the formatting of document types that are radically different in structure from HTML.

Because CSS is not sufficient, the World Wide Web Consortium is working on a complementary alternative called the *Extensible Stylesheet Language* (XSL). XSL will have many features from CSS, but will also borrow some major ideas from ISO's DSSSL stylesheet language. XSL will be extensible, just as XML is, so that it will be appropriate for all document types and not just for HTML. Like the linking specification, XSL is still under development so its exact shape is not known. Nevertheless, there is a general design that we will review later on.

A.10 | Programming Interfaces and Models

This subject may seem intimidating if you are not a programmer—possibly even if you are! But we are just going to take a high-level view of a few constructs that will be helpful in understanding the chapters that follow. We'll cover the XML geek-speak Top Term List: Parsing, APIs, DOM, and SAX.

A.10.1   *Parsing*

Great as XML is for representing data, eventually that data has to be processed, which requires the use of one or more programs. One of the nice things about writing XML applications is that there is an abundance of reusable component and utility software available to help.

All great programmers try to reduce their work! If every programmer reinvented the wheel when it came to basic processing of XML, no programmer would ever get around to building applications that *use* XML. Instead of implementing basic XML processing over and over again, programmers tend to download or buy packages that implement various types of XML services.

The most basic reusable service is parsing. Parsing is about ripping apart the textual representation of a document and turning it into a set of conceptual objects.

For example, a parser looking at the document in Example A-1 would recognize the characters <QUESTION> to be a start-tag and would know that they signaled the start of a QUESTION element. The tag is part of the representation; the element is the conceptual object.

If the parser were also validating the document according to the DTD in Example A-2, it would make sure that an ANSWER element followed the QUESTION element.

As a human being, you do parsing subconsciously. Because you've learned about elements and attributes, when you look at XML text you can think about the document in those conceptual terms.

But without an XML *parser*, a computer program can only see the characters. It's sort of the opposite of not seeing the forest for the trees. Without some form of parsing, an XML application cannot see the tree because of all of the characters!

A.10.2   *APIs*

There are many good XML parsers out there for use with many different programming languages. There are so many that it is hard to choose. A software developer would hate to pick one and be wedded to it forever. The programmer might want to change some day to a faster or cheaper one, or from a non-validating parser to a validating one.

Switching parsers (often also called *processors*) is easy if the two "look" the same to the programmer. You can plug in different brands and types of light bulbs into the same socket because of the standardization of the socket. The equivalent concept in software components is the standardization of *Application Processing Interfaces (APIs)*.

A.10.2.1   The DOM

The World Wide Web Consortium has standardized an API for working with XML. It is called the *Document Object Model,* and it is available in Version 5 Web browsers. If you write code for Microsoft's *DOM* implementation, it should be relatively easy to make that code also work on Netscape's DOM.

But the DOM is not only for use in browsers. It can also be used on the server side. You can use the DOM to read, write, and transmit XML on your Web server. DOM-based programs can talk to some XML content management systems. The DOM is very popular for general XML processing. It has been implemented, for example, for use with Python and Perl scripts and with the C++ and Java™ programming languages, among others. In fact, Microsoft's DOM implementation is a built-in part of Windows 2000 itself.

A.10.2.2   SAX

The DOM is popular and useful but it is not the be-all and end-all of XML parsing APIs. It is a little bit like putting a plane on automatic pilot. You point your DOM-building processor at an XML document and it returns you an object tree based on the structure of the document.

But if the document is 500 megabytes of text and resides on the "other side" of the Internet, your program will just wait. And wait. And wait. When you finally get the data, it will fill your computer's memory and some of its disk space. If you are having a bad day, it might fill up everything and then crash the computer.

In a situation like this, you would rather just get tiny bits of the data as they come in. An *event-based parser* allows this mode of operation. Event-based parsers let your application work on the bit of the data that the parser finds at each "event" in the document.

For example, each XML start-tag corresponds to a "start element" event. Each end-tag corresponds to an "end element" event. Characters and other constructs have their own events. The event-based XML parser tells the application what it sees in the document as if through a peep-hole. It does not try to describe the larger picture to the application.[7]

The most popular event-based API is the *Simple API for XML*. *SAX* was developed by XML processor users and developers in an open discussion group called *XML-DEV*. Despite the name, SAX is not actually any simpler than the DOM. It is much more efficient and low-level, however. The price for efficiency is convenience. The processor only provides you with a peep-hole view, so if your application needs more than that, you'll need to write your own code to understand the "big picture" of the parsed document.

These two APIs are pervasive in the XML processing world. There are many other services that we could envision for XML handling: link management, searching, and so forth. It is likely that these will be built either on top of or as extensions to these two popular APIs.

A.11 | Conclusion

There are a lot of new ideas here to absorb, but we'll be repeating and reemphasizing them as we move along. At this point, though, we're ready to look at where XML is going and the ways that it is being used in the real world.

---

[7]If you concluded from this description that a DOM processor in effect uses an event-based parser as it constructs the DOM, you are right.

Document Type Definitions

Document Type Definitions, or DTDs, are the rules that define the element types, attributes, and entities within your documents. Any time you markup a document using XML, you informally define these rules. To formally define these rules, you create markup declarations either internally within your XML document or in an external file, or both. Whether internal or external, this collection of declarations is also called a DTD.

DTDs allow you to create your own vocabularies; in effect, your own tagging language. They are used for validating your XML documents. While a formal DTD is never required for well-formed documents, one is useful whenever a specialized vocabulary is required.

The following sections of this appendix provide a brief reference to the various parts of a DTD. This section is not designed to teach the intricacies of DTD design, but rather to provide a quick reference to usage.

B.1 | Declaring Use of a DTD

```
<!DOCTYPE contact SYSTEM "contact.dtd"[
<!--internal markup declarations-->
     <!ELEMENT contact(name,address, phone,fax,email)*>
     <!ELEMENT name(#PCDATA)>
     ...etc. ]>

<contact>
     <name>Joe Butler</name>
     <address>some address</address>
     <phone>123-456-7890</phone>
</contact>
```

B.2 | DTD Syntax

```
<!- contact.dtd external markup declarations ->
<!ELEMENT article (headline,deck,byline,text+),
   (listing1|figure|example|table)*)>

<!ELEMENT headline #PCDATA>
<!ELEMENT deck #PCDATA>
<!ELEMENT byline (#PCDATA|emailAddr)*>
<!ELEMENT emailAddr #PCDATA>
<!ELEMENT text (#PCDATA|emph|bold|ital|underline)*)>
<!ELEMENT listing (#PCDATA|plus|multiplied|lt|gt)*)>
<!ELEMENT example(#PCDATA|plus|multiplied|lt|gt)*)>
<!ELEMENT figure (CAPTION?)>
```

B.2.1   *Element Type Declarations*

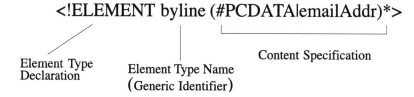

Figure B-1

B.2.2 *Content Specifications*

Value	Description
EMPTY	May not have content.
ANY	Any type of content is allowed.
Mixed	May contain either character data or a mix of character data and sub-elements.
Element	Only sub-elements are allowed.

B.2.3 *Occurrence Indicators*

Value	Description
?	Optional (0 or 1 time)
*	Optional and repeatable (0 or more)
+	Required and repeatable (1 or more)

B.2.3.1 Examples

Empty Content:
```
<!ELEMENT image EMPTY>
```

Element Content (Content Model):
```
<!ELEMENT article (headline,deck,byline,text+),
    (listing|figure|example|table)*>
```

Mixed Content:
```
<!ELEMENT headline (#PCDATA)>
<!ELEMENT byline (#PCDATA|emailAddr)*>
```

ANY Content:
```
<!ELEMENT whatever ANY>
```

B.3 | Attribute List Declarations

Rules for attribute list declarations are as follows:

- Multiple attributes can be declared in a single list.
- There can be multiple attribute list declarations for an element type.
- If the same attribute is declared more than once for the same element type, the first declaration is used.
- The same attribute name can be declared for different element types.

B.3.1   *Anatomy of an Attribute List Declaration*

<!ATTLIST byline email CDATA #fixed "beyondhtml.com"

| Element Type Name | Attribute Name | Attribute Type | Fixed Attribute | Default Value |

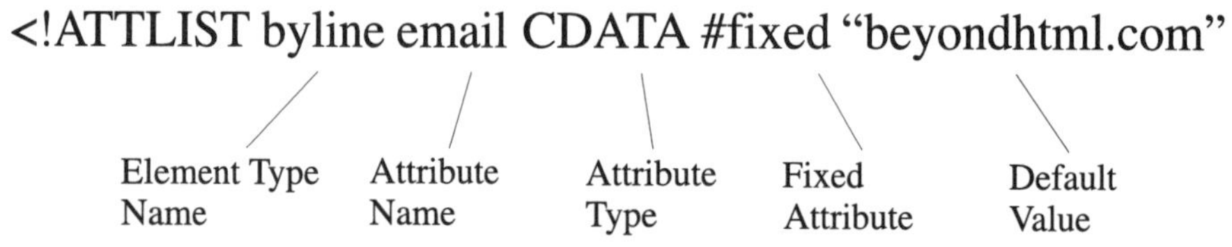

Figure B-2

B.3.2   *Attribute Defaults*

Keyword	*Description*
#IMPLIED	Processor can imply value.
#REQUIRED	Value must be supplied.
#FIXED	Can't override default.

B.3.2.1 Examples

```
<!ATTLIST contact country CDATA "USA">
<!ATTLIST image url CDATA #REQUIRED>
```

B.3.3 *Enumerated Lists*

```
<!ATTLIST list(north|south|east|west) #REQUIRED>
```

B.3.4 *Notation Attributes*

Notation attributes are used to declare that an element's data content conforms to a declared notation.

B.3.4.1 Example

```
<!ATTLIST date NOTATION (JULIAN|GREGORIAN)  #REQUIRED>
```

B.3.5 *Entity Attributes*

Entity attributes refer to external objects.

B.3.5.1 Example

```
<!ENTITY book SYSTEM "http://www.../book.pdf">
```

B.4 | Notations

Notations conform to the following:

- Notations describe how bits should be interpreted.
- They are referred to as data content notations.
- They provide an internal name for an external resource.

■ They are typically used for associating an object with a resource that can process it (a handler).

B.4.1 Example

```
<!NOTATION gif SYSTEM "draw.exe">
```

B.5 | Anatomy of an Entity

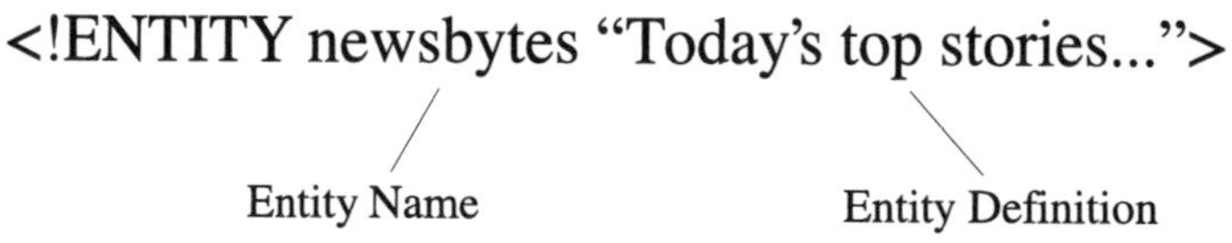

<!ENTITY newsbytes "Today's top stories...">

Entity Name   Entity Definition

Figure B-3

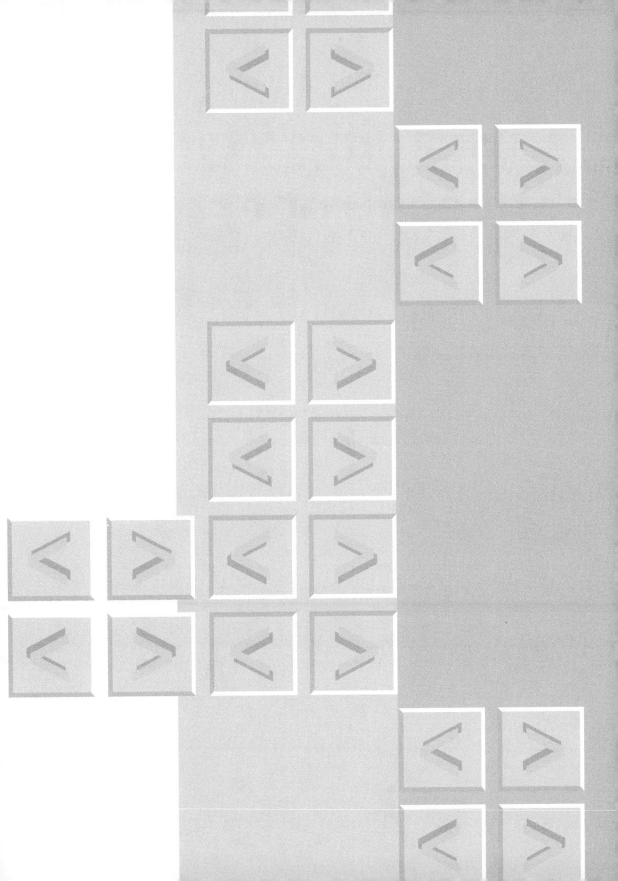

Cascading Style Sheet Properties

For the typical Web developer, presentation is everything. However, as strange as it seems, XSL is not presently the preferred method for formatting the presentation of XML documents. Rather the standard means for presenting XML in the browser rests solely on Cascading Style Sheets (CSS).

The idea is that an XML document is generally transformed to HTML for delivery over the Web. Since it is HTML that is being delivered, it only makes sense to use CSS to render it. However, even when XML is being delivered directly to the client, it is possible to link a CSS style sheet to the document. Eventually, XML clients will directly support the rendering of XML elements using XSL formatting objects. However, no such implementation currently exists. And as long as HTML is around, so will CSS be.

Following is a reference to the properties available in Cascading Style Sheets Level 2. Note that current browsers still do not fully support the Level 2 specification, so some properties will be rendered differently in various browsers, while others may not be rendered at all. This is particularly true for the properties related to aural rendering. Nevertheless, you should find this reference invaluable as you develop your own style sheets.

azimuth

Values:

<angle> | [[left-side | far-left | left | center-left | center | center-right | right | far-right | right-side] || behind] | leftwards | rightwards | inherit

Initial Value:

center

Applies to:

Aural media type

Usage:

H1 { azimuth: center }

background

Values:

[background-color || background-image || background-repeat || background-attachment || background-position] | inherit

Applies to:

Visual media type

Usage:

H1 { background: navy }

background-attachment

Values:

scroll | fixed | inherit

Initial Value:

scroll

Applies to:

Visual media type

Usage:

background-attachment: fixed;

background-color

Values:

<color> | transparent | inherit

Initial Value:

Applies to:

Visual media type

Usage:

background-color: white;

background-color: #CCFFF;

background-image

Values:

<uri> | none | inherit

Initial Value:

Applies to:

Visual media type

Usage:

BODY { background-image: url("logo.gif") }

background-position

Values:

[[<percentage> | <length>]{1,2} | [[top | center | bottom] || [left | center | right]]] | inherit

Initial Value:

0% 0%

Comments:

This element applies to block-level and replaced elements, and specifies the position for a background element such as an image. Percentages refer to the size of the box itself.

Applies to:

Visual media type

Usage:

background-position: 100% 100%;

background-repeat

Values:

repeat | repeat-x | repeat-y | no-repeat | inherit

Initial value:

repeat

Comments:

For repeat, the image is repeated both horizontally and vertically. repeat-x repeats the image vertically and repeat-y does so horizontally.

Usage:

background-repeat: repeat-y;

border

Values:

[<border-width> || <border-style> || <color>] | inherit

Initial Value:

See individual properties.

Comments:

The border property can be used to set all borders at the once. To set individual borders, see border-top, border-bottom, border-right, and border-left.

Usage:

P { border: solid blue }

border-bottom

Values:

[<border-bottom-width> || <border-style> || <color>] | inherit

Initial Value:

See individual properties.

Comments:

<border-bottom-width> refers to a border-width value. See border width for possible values.

Usage:

border-right: thick solid black;

border-collapse

Values:

collapse | separate | inherit

Initial Value:

collapse

Comments:

The border-collapse property applies to table and inline-table elements and designates the model to be used for the border. collapse selects the collapsing borders and separate chooses separated borders.

Usage:

border-collapse: collapse;

border-color

Values:

<color>{1,4} | transparent | inherit

Comments:

<color> refers to either a keyword or hex value defining a color. Refer to the color property for possible values.

Usage:

border-color: blue;
border-color: #006699;

border-left

Values:

[<border-left-width> || <border-style> || <color>] | inherit

Initial Value:

See individual properties.

Comments:

<border-left-width> refers to a border-width value. See border width for possible values.

Usage:

border-left: hidden;

border-right

Values:

[<border-right-width> || <border-style> || <color>] | inherit

Initial Value:

See individual properties.

Comments:

<border-right-width> refers to a border-width value. See border width for possible values.

Usage:

border-right: thick solid black;

border-spacing

Values:

<length> <length>? | inherit

Initial Value:

0

Comments:

The border-spacing property applies to table and inline-table elements, and is used in the separated borders model (see the border-collapse property).

Usage:

border-spacing: 10pt;

border-style

Values:

[none | hidden | dotted | dashed | solid | double | groove | ridge | inset | outset] {1,4} | inherit

Initial Value:

See individual properties.

Usage:

border-style: ridge;

border-top

Values:

[<border-top-width> || <border-style> || <color>] | inherit

Initial Value:

See individual properties.

Comments:

<border-bottom-width> refers to a border-width value. See border width for possible values.

Usage:

border-top: medium solid red;

border-top-color, border-right-color, border-bottom-color, border-left-color

Values:

<color> | inherit

Initial Value:

Value of the color property.

Comments:

The border-top-color, border-right-color, border-bottom-color, border-left-color properties can be used to set the color for the top, right, bottom, and left borders, respectively. See the color property for possible values for <color>.

Usage:

border-top-color: #CCCCCC;

border-top-style, border-right-style, border-bottom-style, border-left-style

Values:

<border-style> | inherit

Initial Value:

Comments:

The border-top-style, border-right-style, border-bottom-style, border-left-style properties can be used to set the style for the top, right, bottom, and left borders, respectively. See the border-style property for possible values for <border-style>.

Usage:

border-left-style: hidden;

border-top-width, border-right-width, border-bottom-width, border-left-width

Values:

<border-width> | inherit

Initial Value:

medium

Comments:

The border-top-width, border-right-width, border-bottom-width, border-left-width properties can be used to set the width for the top, right, bottom, and left borders, respectively. See the border width property for possible values for the <border-width>.

Usage:

border-bottom-width: thick;

border-width

Values:

[thin | medium | thick | <length>]{1,4} | inherit

Initial Value:

See individual properties.

Comments:

When a length is specified, it may be defined as em (relative to a font size), ex (relative to the height), or px (in pixels). Absolute values can also be used. Specifically, widths can be defined as in (inches), cm (centimeters), mm (millimeters), pt (points), or pc (picas).

Usage:

border-width: medium;

bottom

Values:

<length> | <percentage> | auto | inherit

Initial Value:

auto

Applies to:

positioned elements

Comments:

The bottom property applies to positioned elements. Percentages refer to the height of containing blocks. When a length is specified, it may be defined as em (relative to a font size), ex (relative to the height), or px (in pixels). Absolute values can also be used. Specifically, widths can be defined as in (inches), cm (centimeters), mm (millimeters), pt (points), or pc (picas).

Usage:

bottom: 20px;

caption-side

Values:

top | bottom | left | right | inherit

Initial Value:

top

Comments:

See table-caption.

Usage:

caption-side: bottom;

clear

Values:

none | left | right | both | inherit

Initial Value:

Usage:

clear: right;

clip

Values:

<shape> | auto | inherit

Initial Value:

auto

Comments:

The clip property applies to elements that have an overflow property with a value other than visible.

Usage:

clip: rect(5px, 10px, 10px, 5px);

color

Values:

<color> | inherit

Initial Value:

Depend upon the user agents.

Comments:

The color property describes the foreground color of an element's text content. Color can be specified as a text value, as a set of RGB values, or as a hex value. If no color is specified, the value is inherited from its parent.

Usage:

color: red;

color: rgb(255,0,0);

color: #FF0000;

content

Values:

[<string> | <uri> | <counter> | attr(X) | open-quote | close-quote | no-open-quote | no-close-quote]+ | inherit

Initial Value:

empty string

Applies to:

:before and :after pseudo-elements

Comments:

The content property is used with the :before and :after pseudo-elements to generate content in a document. Values have the following meanings:

Value	Description
<string>	Specifies text content.
<uri>	Designates an external source.
<counter>	Generates a counter or counters.
attr(x)	Returns the value of attribute x as a string.

counter-increment

Values:

[<identifier> <integer>?]+ | none | inherit

Initial Value:

Comments:

The counter-increment property takes one or more counters and increments its value. By default, the incremented value is 1. However, you can optionally specify increment value after each counter name.

Usage:

counter-increment: page;

counter-reset

Values:

[<identifier> <integer>?]+ | none | inherit

Initial Value:

Comments:

The counter-reset property allows you to reset the increment value in a counter. See counter-increment.

cue, cue-before, cue-before

Values:

<uri> | none | inherit

Initial Value:

Comments:

Applies to aural style sheets and allows you to cue an auditory sound either before or after an element.

Usage:

cue-after: url("somesound.wav");

cursor

Values:

[[<uri> ,]* [auto | crosshair | default | pointer | move | e-resize | ne-resize | nw-resize | n-resize | se-resize | sw-resize | s-resize | w-resize | text | wait | help]] | inherit

Initial Value:

auto

Comments:

The cursor property specifies the type of cursor for a pointing device. Values have the following meanings:

Value	*Description*
auto	Allows the user agent to determine the cursor to display based on the current context.
crosshair	Specifies a crosshair cursor.
default	Uses the default cursor.
pointer	Cursor indicates a link.
move	Cursor used to indicate a move operation.
e-resize, ne-resize, nw-resize, n-resize, se-resize, sw-resize, s-resize, w-resize	Cursor that indicates a direction for a move.
text	The text cursor; typically an I-beam.
wait	Indicates the system or application is busy.
help	Indicates help.
<uri>	Allows the user agent to retrieve a cursor.

Usage

P { cursor : text; }

direction

Values:

ltr | rtl | inherit

Initial Value:

ltr

Comments:

This property defines the writing direction for blocks and the direction for embeddings and overrides. Also is used to indicate the direction of table column layout, horizontal overflow, and the position of an incomplete last line in a block. The ltr value indicates a left-to-right direction and rtl indicates right-to-left.

display

Values:

inline | block | list-item | run-in | compact | marker | table | inline-table | table-row-group | table-header-group | table-footer-group | table-row | table-column-group | table-column | table-cell | table-caption | none | inherit

Initial Value:

inline

Comments:

The values of this property have the following meanings:

Value	Description
block	Generates a block box.
inline	Creates one or more inline boxes.
list-item	Creates a list item within a list box.
marker	Declares a marker either before or after a box.
none	Indicates that no boxes are to be generated.
run-in and compact	Creates either a block or inline box.
table, inline-table, table-row-group, table-column, table-column-group, table-header-group, table-footer-group, table-row, table-cell, table-caption	Cause an element to behave like a table.

Usage:

P { display: block }

elevation

Values:

<angle> | below | level | above | higher | lower | inherit

Initial Value:

level

Comments:

Used in aural style sheets to indicate special properties. See also azimuth.

empty-cells

Values:

show | hide | inherit

Initial Value:

show

Comments:

This value applies to table-cell elements and controls the rendering of borders around cells that have no visible content.

Usage:

TABLE { empty-cells: show }

float

Values:

left | right | none | inherit

Initial Value:

Comments:

The float property indicates whether a box should float to the left, right, or not at all.

Usage:

float: left;

font

Values:

[[<font-style> || <font-variant> || <font-weight>]? <font-size> [/ <line-height>]? <font-family>] | caption | icon | menu | message-box | small-caption | status-bar | inherit

Initial Value:

Depends upon the individual property.

Comments:

The font property allows you to set font-style, font-variant, font-weight, font-size, line-height, and font-family from a single property.

Usage:

P { font: bold italic medium Garamond, serif }

font-family

Values:

[[<family-name> | <generic-family>],]* [<family-name> | <generic-family>] | inherit

Initial Value:

Depends upon the user agent.

Comments:

Sets the font family to be used.

Usage:

font-family: "Times New Roman", "Garamond", "serif"

font-size

Values:

<absolute-size> | <relative-size> | <length> | <percentage> | inherit

Initial Value:

medium

Comments:

Sets the font size.

Usage:

font-size: 14px;

font-size-adjust

Values:

<number> | none | inherit

Initial Value:

Comments:

Used to reset or adjust the font size.

font-stretch

Values:

normal | wider | narrower | ultra-condensed | extra-condensed | condensed | semi-condensed | semi-expanded | expanded | extra-expanded | ultra-expanded | inherit

Initial Value:

normal

Comments:

Selects a normal, condensed, or extended face from a font family.

font-style

Values:
normal | italic | oblique | inherit

Initial Value:
normal

Comments:
Specifies a family of fonts that the user agent can select from.

Usage:
font-family: "Times New Roman", "Garamond", "serif"

font-variant

Values:
normal | small-caps | inherit

Initial Value:
normal

Comments:
Requests small cap fonts.

Usage:
H2 { font-variant: small-caps }

font-weight

Values:
normal | bold | bolder | lighter | 100 | 200 | 300 | 400 | 500 | 600 | 700 | 800 | 900 | inherit

Initial Value:
normal

Comments:
Sets the weight for a font.

Usage:
font-weight: bold;

height

Values:

<length> | <percentage> | auto | inherit

Initial Value:

auto

Comments:

The height property applies to all elements except non-replaced inline elements, table columns, and column groups.

Usage:
height: 75px;

left

Values:
<length> | <percentage> | auto | inherit

Initial Value:

auto

Comments:
Specifies the left offset for a box.

Usage:
left: 2%;

letter-spacing

Values:
normal | <length> | inherit

Initial Value:
normal

Comments:
Indicates the spacing for letters.

Usage:
letter-spacing: 0.1em

line-height

Values:

normal | <number> | <length> | <percentage> | inherit

Initial Value:

normal

Comments:

Specifies the height for a box generated by an element.

Usage:

line-height: 1.2em;

list-style

Values:

[<'list-style-type'> || <'list-style-position'> || <'list-style-image'>] | inherit

Initial Value:

not defined

Comments:

The list-style property applies to elements generated with display: list-item.

Usage:

list-style: circle outside;

list-style-image

Values:

<uri> | none | inherit

Initial Value:

Comments:

This property applies to elements defined with display: list-item and sets the image to be used for the list item marker.

Usage:

list-style-image: url("http://png.com/ellipse.png")

list-style-position

Values:

inside | outside | inherit

Initial Value:

outside

Comments:

This property sets the position of a marker box in the principal block box.

list-style-type

Values:

disc | circle | square | decimal | decimal-leading-zero | lower-roman | upper-roman | lower-greek | lower-alpha | lower-latin | upper-alpha | upper-latin | hebrew | armenian | georgian | cjk-ideographic | hiragana | katakana | hiragana-iroha | katakana-iroha | none | inherit

Initial Value:

disc

Comments:

This property specifies the appearance of a list item marker when list-style-image has the value none (or if the image pointed to by the URI cannot be displayed).

margin

Values:

<margin-width>{1,4} | inherit

Initial Value:

Not defined for individual properties.

Comments:

The margin property allows you to set margin-top, margin-right, margin-bottom, and margin-left within a single property.

Usage:

margin: 2% 4%;

margin-right, margin-top, margin-bottom, margin-left

Values:

<margin-width> | inherit

Initial Value:

0

Comments:

These properties allow you to set the individual margins.

Usage:

margin-left: 2%;

margin-right: 5em;

margin-bottom: 4px;

marker-offset

Values:

<length> | auto | inherit

Initial Value:

auto

Comments:

The marker-offset property defines the distance between the nearest border edges of a marker box and its associated principal box.

Usage:

marker-offset: 4em;

marks

Values:

[crop || cross] | none | inherit

Initial Value:

Comments:

Allows you to specify whether cross marks, crop marks, or both should be rendered outside the page box edge.

max-height, min-height

Values:

<length> | <percentage> | none | inherit

Initial Value:

Comments:

These two properties are used to constrain box heights to a certain range.

max-width, min-width

Values:

<length> | <percentage> | none | inherit

Initial Value:

Comments:

These two properties are used to constrain box widths to a certain range.

orphans

Values:

<integer> | inherit

Initial Value:

2

Comments:

The orphans property specifies the minimum number of lines of a paragraph that must be left at the bottom of a page. This property applies to block-level elements for visual and paged media types. Also see the widows property.

outline

Values:

[<'outline-color'> || <'outline-style'> || <'outline-width'>] | inherit

Initial Value:

See individual properties.

Comments:

The outline property allows you to draw an outline over a box within a single property. Note that the outline is always on top and doesn't affect the position or size of the box, or of any other boxes. Also see individual properties.

Usage:

See individual properties for settings.

outline-color

Values:

<color> | invert | inherit

Initial Value:

invert

Comments:

Sets the color for an outline.

Usage:

outline-color : red;

outline-width

Values:

<border-width> | inherit

Initial Value:

medium

Comments:

Sets the width for an outline.

Usage:

outline-width : thick;

outline-style

Values:

<border-style> | inherit

Initial Value:

Comments:

Sets the style for an outline.

Usage:

See border-style.

overflow

Values:

visible | hidden | scroll | auto | inherit

Initial Value:

visible

Comments:

The overflow property dictates whether the content of a block-level element is clipped when it overflows the element's box.

Usage:

overflow: auto;

padding

Values:

<padding-width>{1,4} | inherit

Initial Value:

Not defined for individual properties.

Comments:

The padding property allows you to set the padding-top, padding-right, padding-bottom, and padding-left properties from a single property. See individual properties for details.

padding-top, padding-right, padding-bottom, padding-left

Values:

<padding-width> | inherit

Initial Value:

0

Comments:

Allows you to set the padding for the top, right, bottom, and left edges of a containing box.

Usage:

padding-left: 2px;

page

Values:

<identifier> | auto

Initial Value:

auto

Comments:

The page property allows you to define a page type that can be used to specify a particular type of page where an element should be displayed. This property applies to both visual and paged media types.

Usage:

@page rotated {size: landscape}
@page narrow {size: 9cm 18cm}

page-break-after

Values:

auto | always | avoid | left | right | inherit

Initial Value:

auto

page-break-before

Values:

auto | always | avoid | left | right | inherit

Comments:

The page-break-before property is used to set a page break before the current element. This property applies to both visual and paged media types.

page-break-inside

Values:

avoid | auto | inherit

Initial Value:

auto

Comments:

The page-break-inside property is used to set a page break within the current element. This property applies to both visual and paged media types.

pause

Values:

[[<time> | <percentage>]{1,2}] | inherit

Initial Value:

Depends upon the user agent.

Comments:

Used in aural style sheets, this property allows you to set the pause-before and pause-after together within a single property. When both values are specified, the first value refers to pause-before and the second refers to pause-after. If only one value is given, it sets both properties.

Usage:

pause: 20ms

pause-after, pause-before

Values:

<time> | <percentage> | inherit

Initial Value:

Depends upon the user agent.

Comments:

These properties allow you to set a pause either after or before speaking an element's content.

Usage:

pause-before: 20ms

pause-after: 10ms

pitch

Values:

<frequency> | x-low | low | medium | high | x-high | inherit

Initial Value:

medium

Comments:

Used with aural style sheets, the pitch property sets the average pitch for the speaking voice.

pitch-range

Values:

<number> | inherit

Initial Value:

50

Comments:

This property is used in aural style sheets to specify the variation in average pitch.

play-during

Values:

<uri> mix? repeat? | auto | none | inherit

Initial Value:

auto

Comments:

Used in aural style sheets, this property specifies a sound to be played as a background while an element's content is spoken.

position

Values:

static | relative | absolute | fixed | inherit

Initial Value:

static

Comments:

Sets the positioning of a box. Static is a normal box, laid out according to the normal flow. The relative value allows you to set a position relative to another object. absolute allows you to set the absolute positioning of a box based on its left, right, top, and bottom properties. fixed specifies that a box's position should be calculated according to the absolute model, but additionally fixes the box with respect to a reference.

Usage:

position: fixed

quotes

Values:

[<string> <string>]+ | none | inherit

Initial Value:

Depends upon the user agent.

Comments:

This property is used to specify quotation marks for quotations.

Usage:

quotes: "" "" "" ""
quotes: "«" "»" "<" ">"

richness

Values:

<number> | inherit

Initial Value:

50

Comments:

Used in aural style sheets to specify the richness or brightness of the speaking voice. Values for number can range from 0 to 100, with lower values producing a softer voice.

right

Values:

<length> | <percentage> | auto | inherit

Initial Value:

auto

Comments:

The right property applies to positioned elements and specifies how far a box's right edge is offset relative to its containing block.

Usage:

right: 2%;

size

Values:

<length>{1,2} | auto | portrait | landscape | inherit

Initial Value:

auto

Comments:

This property sets the size and orientation of a page box.

Usage:

size: auto;

speak

Values:

normal | none | spell-out | inherit

Initial Value:

normal

Comments:

Used with aural style sheets, this speak property toggles aural rendering of text and the manner in which it should be rendered.

speak-header

Values:

once | always | inherit

Initial Value:

once

Comments:

Used in aural style sheets in connection with elements that have table header information, this property specifies whether table headers are spoken before every cell or just before a cell with a new header.

speak-numeral

Values:

digits | continuous | inherit

Initial Value:

continuous

Comments:

Used in aural style sheets to control how numerals are spoken. The digit's value instructs the processor to speak a number as individual digits. The continuous value causes the processor to voice the numeral as a full number.

speak-punctuation

Values:

code | none | inherit

Initial Value:

Comments:

This property is used in aural style sheets to control how punctuation is spoken. The code value indicates that punctuation such as semicolons is to be spoken literally. A value of none indicates that punctuation is rendered as various pauses.

speech-rate

Values:

<number> | x-slow | slow | medium | fast | x-fast | faster | slower | inherit

Initial Value:

medium

Comments:

This property is used in aural style sheets to set the speaking rate. Both absolute and relative keyword values are allowed.

stress

Values:

<number> | inherit

Initial Value:

50

Comments:

Used in aural style sheets to specify the height of local peaks in the intonation contour of a voice.

table-layout

Values:

auto | fixed | inherit

Initial Value:

auto

Comments:

Used in connection with the table and inline-table elements, this property controls the algorithm used to lay out the table cells, rows, and columns. The fixed value uses fixed-table layout, while auto allows automatic table layout.

text-align

Values:

left | right | center | justify | <string> | inherit

Initial Value:

Depends upon writing direction and user agent.

Comments:

The text-align property controls how the in-line content of a block is aligned.

Usage:

text-align: center;

text-decoration

Values:

none | [underline || overline || line-through || blink] | inherit

Initial Value:

Comments:

This property describes decorations that are added to the text of an element.

Usage:

text-decoration: underline;

text-indent

Values:

<length> | <percentage> | inherit

Initial Value:

0

Comments:

The text-indent property controls the indentation for the first line of text in a block.

Usage:

text-indent: 3em;

text-shadow

Values:

none | [<color> || <length> <length> <length>? ,]* [<color> || <length> <length> <length>?] | inherit

Initial Value:

Comments:

This property takes a comma-separated list of shadow effects and applies it to the text of an element.

Usage:

text-shadow: 3px 3px 5px red;

text-transform

Values:

capitalize | uppercase | lowercase | none | inherit

Initial Value:

Comments:

The text-transform property controls capitalization effects of an element's text.

Usage:

text-transform: capitalize;

top

Values:

<length> | <percentage> | auto | inherit

Initial Value:

auto

Comments:

This property specifies the offset for the top edge of the box.

Usage:

top: 2%;

unicode-bidi

Values:

normal | embed | bidi-override | inherit

Initial Value:

normal

Comments:

Useful with non-Latin based languages, this property specifies an embedding level.

Usage:

unicode-bidi: embed

vertical-align

Values:

baseline | sub | super | top | text-top | middle | bottom | text-bottom | <percentage> | <length> | inherit

Initial Value:

baseline

Comments:

This property applies to inline-level and table-cell elements and sets the vertical positioning inside a line box.

Usage:

vertical-align: text-bottom;

visibility

Values:

visible | hidden | collapse | inherit

Initial Value:

inherit

Comments:

The "visibility" property specifies whether the boxes generated by an element are rendered. Invisible boxes still affect layout unless you set the display property to none.

Usage:

visibility: hidden;

voice-family

Values:

[[<specific-voice> | <generic-voice>],]* [<specific-voice> | <generic-voice>] | inherit

Initial Value:

Depends upon the user agent.

Comments:

Used with aural style sheets to specify a comma-separated, prioritized list of voice family names.

volume

Values:

<number> | <percentage> | silent | x-soft | soft | medium | loud | x-loud | inherit

Initial Value:

medium

Comments:

Used in connection with aural style sheets to control the median volume of the waveform.

white-space

Values:

normal | pre | nowrap | inherit

Initial Value:

normal

Comments:

This property controls how white space is handled inside an element. The normal setting removes excess white space characters, while pre prevents user agents from removing white space.

Usage:

white-space: pre;

widows

Values:

<integer> | inherit

Initial Value:

2

Comments:

The widows property specifies the minimum number of lines of a paragraph that must be left at the top of a page. Also see the orphans property.

Usage:

widows: 4;

width

Values:

<length> | <percentage> | auto | inherit

Initial Value:

auto

Comments:

This property specifies the content width of boxes generated by block-level and replaced elements. This property does not apply to inline elements, table rows, or row groups.

Usage:

width: 20%;

word-spacing

Values:

normal | <length> | inherit

Initial Value:

normal

Comments:

This property affects the spacing between words. Under normal operation, the user agent determines word spacing.

Usage:

word-spacing: 1em;

z-index

Values:

0

auto | <integer> | inherit

Initial Value:

auto

Comments:

This property specifies the z-index for a positioned box, including the stack level of the box, and specifies whether the box establishes a local stacking context.

Usage:

z-index: 3;

Index

Symbols

#, 48
%>, 259
*, 40, 51
.., 40
|, 41
//, 40
<, 57
<%, 259
<%=, *See* ASP
   output directive, 262
<%@, *See* ASP
   processing directive, 262
<=, 57
=, 57
>, 57
>=, 57
@, 41

A

A, 124
Abort, 135
Abs, 295
Abstract, 124, 130
Acos, 295
Action, 291
Activated, 292
Active Server Pages, 225
   defined, 258
Active Server Pages, *See* ASP, 258

ActiveX Data Object, *See* ADO, 267
ActiveXObject(), 150
ADO, 267, 277
   connection to ODBC data source, 278
Allaire, 77
And, 57
And the DOM, 89
Annuity, 295
Apache JServ, 236
API, server, 215
APIs, server, 223
AppendChild, 95, 98
AppendData, 103
Application, 261
Application object
   in ASP, 260
ApplicationName, 296
ApplicationVersion, 296
ApplicationVersionNum, 296
Asin, 295
ASP
   adding script to, 262
   and the DOM, 225
   attributes for processing
         instruction in, 260
   creating, 259
   discussed, 258
   installing XML support in, 264
   introducing, 258
   output directive, 262
   page to determine browser type, 317
   processing directive in, 262
Atan, 295
Attr, 91
Attr interface, 101
<attribute>, 309
Attribute, 138
   node type, 35
   retrieving with a pattern, 322
   subnode, 35
   xml lang, 58

Attribute lists, 23
Attribute-set, 39
Attributes, 97
    defining in XML Schema attributes, 308
    selecting in patterns, 41
    versus subelements, 23, 26
Attributes property, 95
AttributeType, 138
<AttributeType>, 137, 309
Axis identifier, *See* paths, location, 50
Axis, *See* paths, location, 50

▋ B

Base 64, *See* encoding, MIME, 294
Berners-Lee, Tim, 7
BeyondHTML.com, 279
Bgcolor, 292
Bin.base64, 141
Bin.hex, 141
Bitmap graphics
    described, 69
Bluestone XML-server, 226
Bluestone XML-Server
    discussed bluestone, 226
Boilerplate
    XML document as, 182
Boolean, 141
    in expressions, 50
    in string expressions, 54
Boolean(), 57
Booleans
    in expressions
        discussed booleans, 57
Borderwidth, 292
Box, 291
Browser
    determining type, 190
Browser detection
    and the XML Enabler servlet, 251
Button, 291

▋ C

C Perl Archive Network, *See* CPAN, 218
C++
    direct DOM interfaces, 100
C/C++
    and the DOM, 89
CDATA, 92
CDATASection, 91
CDATASection interface
    in DOM, 104
CDF, 79
    as an XML vocabulary, 121
    discussed cdf, 121
    support in Internet Explorer, 111
Ceiling, 295
Ceiling(), 56
Cell, 291
CGI, 215
    described, 216
Channel, 124
Channel Definition Format, *See* CDF, 79
<Channel>, *See* CDF, 123
Char, 141
CharacterData interface char data, 102
Check, 291
ChildNodes, 96
Children collection
    in Internet Explorer 4, 175
CLASSPATH
    and the JRE, 249
    setting for Cocoon, 236
    setting for LotusXSL, 250
CloneNode, 98
Cocoon
    discussed Cocoon, 235
    drawbacks, 237
    installing, 236
Cocoon Project, 224
CODEBASE, 130
CODEPAGE, 260
Cold Fusion, 77
Combobox, 291

Comment, 91
Comment(), 44
Compound, 295
<compute>, 294
Concat(), 54
Connection Factory, 80
Contains(), 54-55
Content attribute
    in XML Schema, 305
Content model
    ANY, 121
    defining in XML Schema, 305
    refining refine, 307
Context node, 52
Coordinates, 292
Cos, 295
Count(), 53
Countline, 294
CPAN, 218
CreateAttribute, 94
CreateCDATASection, 94
CreateComment, 94
CreateDocument-Fragment, 94
CreateElement, 94
CreateEntityReference, 94
CreateProcessing-Instruction, 94
CreateTextNode, 94
CSS, 110
    style sheet generating from XSL, 190

∎ D

2-D graphics, 69
Data, 291-292
    filtering from XSL, 200
    posting using HTML form, 271
    presenting from database, 196
Data island, 199
    versus inline XML, 112
Data islands
    defined, 112

Data property, 105
Data source names, 277
Data Source Object, *See* DSO, 111
Data Source Objects
    See also, DSO, 113
Data Source Objects dso, 113
Data types, *See* schemas, 140
Database
    development and XML, 273
    flat-file, 273
    ODBC compliant, 273
    query using XML, 279
    searching, 204, 279
    XML representation of, 273
Database Access component, 260
Database, flat-file
    representing in XML, 273
Database, SQL, 277
DataChannel Rio, 225
Datagroup, 292
DATAPAGESIZE attribute,
        See DSO, 117
Datasrc attribute
    in DSO, 114
Datatype, 139
Date, 141, 296
DateTime, 141
DateTime.tz, 141
DateToSeconds, 296
Day, 296
DayOfWeek, 296
DCD, 302
DDML, 302
Decimal, 296
Deg2rad, 295
Delay, 292
DeleteData, 103
DEPENDENCY, 131
Depth-first search, 157
Description, 139
<description>, 310
DHTML, 194
DISKSIZE, 131

Div, 56
DNS, 266
Doc(), 53
Doctype, 92
<!DOCTYPE>, 92, 183
    and OSD, 129
Document
    database, 25
    discussed doc object, 92
    extended definition of, 11
    representing Web site structure, 21
    self describing, 25
Document Content Description, 302
Document object, 90-91
    accessing in Internet Explorer, 146
    creating, 150
    creating in IE5, 93
    embedding in HTML, 150
Document Object Model
    in SVG, 70
Document type definitions, *See also* DTD, 11
Document, structured
    conceptual view of, 19
    defined, 18
Document, structuring
    discussed, 20
DocumentElement, 92-93
DocumentFragment, 91
Documents
    concept of, 18
DocumentType, 91
DocumentType Interface, 104
DocumentType interface
    entities, *See* entities property, 104
DOM
    base objects implemented by, 90
    calling methods from JavaScript, 150
    core, 90
    core versus HTML, 90
    direct interfaces, 99
    extensions in Internet Explorer DOM, 134
    in XFDL, 288
    support for in XML for Java, 248
    support in Internet Explorer, 110

DOM chapter, 90
DOMString, 104
DSO, 111, 200
    assigning elements to tables, 119
    defined, 111
    instantiating, 115
    methods, 117
DSSSL, 31
DTD, 11, 301
DTDs, 10

■ E

EarliestTime, 124
ECMAScript
    direct interfaces in DOM, 99
Editstate, 292
Element, 139
<element>, 305
Element Interface
    tagName, 100
Element Interface element, 100
Element, result, 35
Elements
    matching all, 40
ElementType, 139
<ElementType>, 137, 140, 304
EltOnly, 305
Embedded devices, 76
ENABLESESSIONSTATE, 260
Encoding
    MIME, 294
Encoding, EBCDIC, 248
Encoding, ISO, 248
Encoding, UTF, 248
EndOfMonth, 296
Entities property
    in DocumentType interface, 104
Entity, 91
Entity interface, 105
EntityReference, 91-92
EXcelon XML data server, 225
Exp, 295

Expat, 218
Expressions
    and location paths, 50
    discussed expressions, 49
    numbers in, 56
    objects returned by, 50
    string, 54
Extensible Forms Description Language,
        See XFDL, 288
EXtensible Server Pages, *See* XSP, 238

F

Fact, 295
Factory methods, 93
False(), 57
FastCGI, 218
Field, 291
Filename, 292
FirstChild, 97
Fixed.14.4, 141
Float, 141
Floating-point
    numbers, 56
Floor, 295
Floor(), 56
Flow objects
    support in LotusXSL, 249
Flow objects, *See* formatting objects, 37
Focused, 292
Fontcolor, 292
Fontinfo, 292
For-each, 59
Format, 292
Format-number(), 54
FormatString, 296
Formatting objects, *See* XSL, 37
From-ancestor, 52
From-ancestors-or self, 52
From-attributes, 52
From-children, 52
From-descendants, 52
From-descendants-or-self, 52

From-following, 52
From-following-siblings, 52
From-parent, 52
From-preceeding, 52
From-preceeding-siblings, 52
From-self, 52
Functions, 39

G

Generate-id(), 53
GetAllResponseHeaders, 135
GetAttribute, 101
GetAttribute(), 166
GetAttributeNode, 101
GetElementsByTagName,
        94, 101
GetNamedItem, 99
GetResponseHeader, 135
GIF, 68
Goldfarb, Charles F., 7
Group, 139, 292
<group>, 307

H

HasChildNodes, 98
Help, 291, 293
Homepage.xsl
    style sheet for, 317
HOSTS file, 266
Hour, 296
HTML
    and Scalable Vector Graphics, 70
    frames, 162
    framing document, 162
    in relation to XML, 13
    transforming to, 321
HTTP USER AGENT, 319
HTTP-EQUIV, 124

▌ *I*

I1, 141
I2, 141
I4, 142
Id(), 53
IEEE 754
    floating-point numbers specified by, 56
IIS, 225
Image, 293
IMPLEMENTATION, 131
Implementation attribute, 92
#IMPLIED, 102
Import, 39
Include, 39
Inline, *See* XML, inline, 112
InnerHTML property, 194
    discussed innerhtml, 194
    workarounds for, 195
InsertBefore, 95, 98
InsertData, 103
Int, 141
Internet appliances, 76
Internet Information Server, *See* IIS, 225
IntervalTime, 124
ISAPI, 223
ISO 8601, 78
IsValidFormat, 296
Item, 99, 124
<Item>, *See* CDF, 123
Itemlocation, 293

▌ *J*

Java
    and the DOM, 89
    direct DOM interfaces, 100
    in XSL, 59
Java Development Kit jdk, 244
Java Development Kit, *See* JDK, 224
Java ProjectX, 252

Java Runtime Environment, 249
Java Servlet Development Kit, *See* JSDK, 246
Java Speech Markup Language, *See* JSML, 79
Java Virtual Machine
    and servlets, 234
JavaScript
    and the DOM, 89
    direct interfaces in DOM, 99
    embedding within frame, 163
    in XSL, 59
JDK, 224
    installing, 245
JPEG, 68
JScript
    loading XML documents, 116
JSDK, 246
JSML, 79
Justify, 293

▌ *K*

Kanji, 104
Key, 39
Key(), 53

▌ *L*

Label, 291, 293
Labelborderwidth, 292
Lang(), 57
LANGUAGE, 131, 260
Last(), 53
LastChild, 97
LatestTime, 124
LCID, 260
LICENSE, 131
Line, 291
List, 291
LMHOSTS file, 266
Ln, 295
Load, 268

Load method, 93
Load(), 150
LoadXML, 268
LoadXML method
    in IE5, 93
Local-part(), 53
Locale, 39
Localhost, 266
Location paths
    and patterns, 38
Location paths, *See* paths, location, 50
Log, 124, 295
Logic sheets
    in Cocoon, 239
Login, 124
Logo, 124
LogTarget, 125
LotusXSL
    and Cocoon, 236
    installing xsl, 249

▮ M

Many, 305
MapPath, 268
Match attribute, 35
MaxOccurs attribute, 308
MEMSIZE, 131
<META>, 10
Metacontent, 25
Metadata, 9
    and PICS, 10
    and RDF, 82
Microsoft Access, 279
Microsoft IIS, 258
Microsoft Internet Component
        Download, *See* MSICD, 128
Microsoft Personal Web Server, 264
Microsoft.FreeThreaded
        XMLDOM, 271
Microsoft.XMLDOM, 271
Mimedata, 293

MinOccurs attribute, 308
Minute, 296
Mod, 56, 295
Month, 296
MSICD, 128, 132
MSXML, 248, 264, 273
MusicML, 80

▮ N

Name property, *See* Attr interface, 101
NamedNodeMap, 95
    methods, 99
NamedNodeMap object, 90
Namespace
    for XML Schema, 304
    HTML, 37
    HTML result, 45
    result, 37
    XSL, 36-37
Namespace(), 53
Navigation, 21
    using XML, 159
Netdynamics, 214
Netscape Application Server, 214
Next, 293
NextSibling, 97, 101
Node
    defined, 34
    properties
        query for, 166
        retrieving properties of current, 157
Node interface
    discussed node interface, 95
Node object, 90
Node sets
    functions that operate on, 53
Node type
    attribute, 35
    child elements, 35
    determining, 35
    element, 35

Node types, 34
  converting from integer
      to string, 151
  element, 41
  root node, 34
  selecting in patterns, 42
  testing for, 43
Node(), 44
NodeList, 95
NodeList object, 90
NodeName, 96, 105
Nodes
  getting child in IE4, 175
NodeType, 96
NodeValue, 96
Normalize, 101
Normalize(), 54-55
Not(), 57
Notation interface, 105
NotationName
  property, 105
Notations
  described, 105
Now, 296
NT Server, 264
Number, 141
Number(), 56
Numbers
  in expressions, 56

ONCLICK event, 150
One, 305
Onreadystatechange, 134
Open, 135
Open Software Description, *See* OSD,
      111, 128
OpenXML
  and Cocoon, 235
Operators
  to control patterns searches, 40
Options
  setting in XFDL, 292
Or, 57
OS, 131
OSD, 111, 128
  elements included in, 130
  including in CDF, 128
OwnerDocument, 97

O

Object Design, *See* eXcelon, 225
ObjectContext, 261
ObjectContext object
  in ASP, 260
Objects, ASP
  methods, properties, events
      and collections, 261
ODBC
  access, 260

P

ParentNode, 96, 101
Parse tree
  accessing in LotusXSL, 251
Parser
  in Internet Explorer, 167
  MSXML, 264
  role in style-sheet processing, 32
Parsers, 233
  XML for Java, 248
Paths
  location
      discussed location paths, 50
Paths, location
  and patterns, 50
  axis
      defined, 50
  axis identifier in, 50
Pattern
  defined, 35, 38
  syntax, 39

Patterns
    and alternative paths, 41
    and tree traversal, 38
    discussed, 38
    in XSLT, 38
    refining results, 43
    specifying, 40
    step, 40
    syntax described, 42
    white space in, 41
Perl
    parsing XML with, 218
Pi, 295
Pi(), 42, 44
PICS
    and RDF, 83
PNG, 69
Popup, 291
Position(), 51, 53
Power, 295
Preserve-space, 39
Previous, 293
PreviousSibling, 97, 101
Printsettings, 293
Processing instruction
    <?xml>, 70
    and notations, 105
    within a
            Document node, 91
Processing, conditional
    discussed conditional, 62
ProcessingInstruction, 91
ProcessingInstruction
            interface, 105
PROCESSOR, 131
PublicID, 105
PublicId property, 105
PurgeTime, 125
Push channels
    and CDF, 79
PWS for Windows 98, 264
Python
    and the DOM, 89

Q

Qname(), 53
Quo, 56

R

R4, 142
R8, 142
Rad2deg, 295
Radio, 291
Rand, 295
Raster graphics, 69
RDF, 82
    and PICS, 83
Readystate, 134
Real Name system, 15
RealNetworks
    G2 player, 73
    SMIL presentation wizard, 74
Recursion, 157
Redirect
    performing from ASP, 319
RemoveAttribute, 101
RemoveAttributeNode, 101
RemoveChild, 98
RemoveNamedItem, 99
Replace, 294
ReplaceChild, 95, 98
ReplaceData, 103
Request, 261
Request object, 272
    in ASP, 260
Resource Description Framework rdf, 82
Response, 261
Response object
    in ASP, 260
Response.ServerVariables(), 319
Response.Write, 262
    method, 260
ResponseBody, 134

ResponseStream, 134
ResponseText, 134
ResponseXML, 134
Result elements, 48
Result tree
   defined, 35
   generating, 37
Root element
   defined, 33
Round, 295
Round(), 56
Rule, template
   components of, 35
   discussed, 35

■ S

Saveformat, 293
SAX
   support for in XML for Java, 248
Scalable Vector Graphics
   and HTML, 70
   discussed svg, 68
Scanning, *See* hacking, 8
Schedule, 125
Schema, 139
   defined, 303
   namespace, 136
<Schema>, 136, 304
Schemas
   creating, 303
   data types in datatypes, 140
   described, 302
   discussed schemas, 135
   purpose of, 11
   versus DTDs, 136
Schemas, Schemas DTDs Vocabs, 10
Scope identifier, 290
<SCRIPT>, 259
Scripting engine
   in ASP, 258

Scrollhoriz, 293
Second, 296
SelectNodes(), 207
Send, 135
Seq, 305
Server, 261
   CreateObject method, 268
Server object
   in ASP, 260
Server, Web
   methods for extending, 215-216
   running locally, 265
Server, XML
   building, 243
Servlet engine
   installing, 246
ServletRunner, 247
Servlets, 215, 224
   and multithreading, 235
   versus CGI, 234
Session, 261
Session object
   in ASP, 260
Set, 296
Set-top boxes, 76
SetAttribute, 101
SetAttributeNode, 101
SetNamedItem, 99
SetRequestHeader, 135
SGML, 7
Signature, 291, 293
Signdatagroups, 293
Signer, 293
Signformat, 293
Signgroups, 293
Signitemrefs, 293
Signitems, 293
Signoptionrefs, 293
Silverstream, 214
Simple API for XML,
       See SAX, 248
Sin, 295
Size, 293

SMIL, 73
 discussed, 73
SOFTPKG, 131
<SOFTPKG> element,
  See OSD, 129
Sorting
 in XSL sorting, 63
Source tree
 walking, 153
SOX, 302
Spacer, 291
Specified, *See* Attr interface, 102
SplitText, 103
SQL Server, 277
Sqrt, 296
Standard Generalized Markup Language,
  See SGML, 7
Starts-with(), 54-55
Status, 135
StatusText, 135
Step patterns, 51
Step patterns, *See* patterns, 40
String(), 54
Strip-space, 39
Strlen, 294
Strmatch, 294
Stroke graphics, *See* vector graphics, 69
Strpbrk, 294
Strrstr, 294
Strstr, 294
Structure
 documenting in Internet Explorer 4,
   171
 documenting, utility for, 152
Structure, documenting, 20
Structure, *See* document, 20
Structured Documents, 18
Structured Graph Format, 81
Style rules, CSS
 generating from XSL, 322
Style sheet
 as an XML document, 36
 creating, 36

<stylesheet>
 in Cocoon, 241
Substr, 295
Substring-after(), 54-55
Substring-before(), 54-55
SubstringData, 103
Sum(), 56
SVG, 69
Synchronized Multimedia Integration
  Language, *See* SMIL, 73
Syntax, DTD
 drawbacks of, 301
SystemID, 105

■ T

Table
 populating from database, 196
TagName, *See* Element interface, 100
Tan, 296
Target property, 105
TCP/IP
 configuring for IIS, 266
Template, 39
 defined, 35
Template rule
 root, 190
Template rules, *See* rule, template, 35
Templates
 discussed, 44
 within a template rule, 44
Text interface
 in DOM, 102
Text(), 44
TextOnly, 305
Threading models, 270
Time, 141, 296
Title, 125, 131
Toggle, 296
Tolower, 295
Toolbar, 291
Toupper, 295

TRANSACTION, 260
Transformation
    from XML to HTML, 46
Transformation, *See* XSL, 31
Transformations
    style-sheet generation, 32
    when converting to HTML, 37
TransformNode, 269
TransformNode(), 194, 320
TransformNodeToObject, 270
Translate(), 54
Tree model
    branches in, 33
    discussed tree model, 32
    leaves in, 33
    style-sheet processing, 32
Tree structure, *See* tree model, 32
Tree traversal
    versus list searching, 26
Triggeritem, 293
Trim, 295
True(), 57
Tutorial Markup Language, 81
Type, 293
    Document, 91

U

Ui1, 142
Ui2, 142
Ui4, 142
UML, 82
UML eXchange Format, 82
Unified Modeling Language, *See* UML, 82
Universal Time Coordinated, *See* UTC, 127
Unparsed entities
    and notations, 105
Uri, 142
Url, 293
URLDecode, 295
URLEncode, 295
Usage, 125

UserData
    as a replacement for cookies, 110
UTC, 127
Uuid, 142

V

ValidateOnParse, 134
Value, 293
Variable, 39
    scope in an ASP, 263
VBScript
    direct interfaces in DOM, 99
    in XSL, 59
Vector graphics, 69
Visible, 293
Vocabularies, 10
    Web vocabs discussed, 66
Vocabulary
    and DTDs, 68
    defined, 68
    for Web-site navigation, 160

W

WDDX
    defined, 77
    described wddx, 77
    packet element, 78
Web site
    conceptual view of, 316
    structural view of, 316
Weblogic, 214
WebMethods
    B2B, 225
White space, *See* also patterns, 41

X

XFA xfa, 297
XFDL, 289
    described, 288
XHTML
    described, 236
XHTML, 76
XML
    adding support for in Microsoft IIS,
        258
    and ASP, 264
    benefits of serving, 213
    constructing a Web site based on
        building, 315
    data stream, 196
    database in, 273
    defined, 8
    document
        loading from script, 146
    generating dynamically in Cocoon
        dynamic, 238
    in Internet Explorer, 110
    in relation to HTML, 13
    inline
        versus data island, 112
    inline inline, 111
    methods for delivering, 109
    Parser
        discussed, 218
    processing in three-tier architecture,
        214
    processing on IIS, 267
    schemas, See schemas, 135
    scripting with ASP, 266
    sending as stream, 215
    sending from client, 271
    serving from Web site, 318
    strategies for presenting strategies, 182
    support in Internet Explorer 4, 168
    supporting without installing Internet
        Explorer, 265

Tools database, 196, 273, 279
transformations, 31
translating between file formats, 9
validating, utility for, 167
in Internet Explorer 5, 112
?xml, 124
XML Database
    example of, 25
<XML> element, 114
XML Enabler, 244
    as a servlet, 251
    installing, 251
XML for Java
    and Cocoon, 236
    installing xml4j, 248
XML Forms Architecture,
        See XFA, 288, 297
XML Schema, 136
    element reference, 138
    features of, 302
XML Schema (cont.)
    see also, schemas, 140
    specification, 303
XML Working Group, 7
XML, parsing
    using Perl, 218
XML, processing
    on server versus client, 214
XML, serving
    using Java, 243
XML, XML uses, 8
XML-Data, 302
XML-Server, See Bluestone, 226
XML-Space
    Preserve attribute, 126
XMLDOMParseError, 134
XMLHttpRequest, 134, 273
    methods and properties, 134
XPointer, 248
XSL
    as a declarative language, 38
    capabilities, 182
    components of, 12

formatting, 32
formatting objects, 37, 181
style sheets
    selecting from multiple, 192
to format XML, 182
<xsl\
    apply-templates>, 36, 44
    attribute>, 48
    choose>, 62
    comment>, 49
    element>, 48
    for-each>, 60, 202
    if>, 62, 202, 204
    otherwise>, 62
    pi>, 49
    sort>, 63
    stylesheet>, 36
        using, 36
    template>, 35
    text>, 44

and white-space stripping, 48
value-of>, 190
when>, 62
XSL discussed, 31
XSL Transformations, *See* XSLT, 32
XSL Working Draft
    support in Internet Explorer, 110
XSLT, 32
XslTarget, 194
<xsp\
    eval>, 242
    logic>, 241
    structure>, 241
XSP dynamic, 238

■ Y

Year, 296

LICENSE AGREEMENT AND LIMITED WARRANTY

READ THE FOLLOWING TERMS AND CONDITIONS CAREFULLY BEFORE OPENING THIS SOFTWARE MEDIA PACKAGE. THIS LEGAL DOCUMENT IS AN AGREEMENT BETWEEN YOU AND PRENTICE-HALL, INC. (THE "COMPANY"). BY OPENING THIS SEALED SOFTWARE MEDIA PACKAGE, YOU ARE AGREEING TO BE BOUND BY THESE TERMS AND CONDITIONS. IF YOU DO NOT AGREE WITH THESE TERMS AND CONDITIONS, DO NOT OPEN THE SOFTWARE MEDIA PACKAGE. PROMPTLY RETURN THE UNOPENED SOFTWARE MEDIA PACKAGE AND ALL ACCOMPANYING ITEMS TO THE PLACE YOU OBTAINED THEM FOR A FULL REFUND OF ANY SUMS YOU HAVE PAID.

1.　　**GRANT OF LICENSE:** In consideration of your payment of the license fee, which is part of the price you paid for this product, and your agreement to abide by the terms and conditions of this Agreement, the Company grants to you a nonexclusive right to use and display the copy of the enclosed software program (hereinafter the "SOFTWARE") on a single computer (i.e., with a single CPU) at a single location so long as you comply with the terms of this Agreement. The Company reserves all rights not expressly granted to you under this Agreement.

2.　　**OWNERSHIP OF SOFTWARE:** You own only the magnetic or physical media (the enclosed software media) on which the SOFTWARE is recorded or fixed, but the Company retains all the rights, title, and ownership to the SOFTWARE recorded on the original software media copy(ies) and all subsequent copies of the SOFTWARE, regardless of the form or media on which the original or other copies may exist. This license is not a sale of the original SOFTWARE or any copy to you.

3.　　**COPY RESTRICTIONS:** This SOFTWARE and the accompanying printed materials and user manual (the "Documentation") are the subject of copyright. You may not copy the Documentation or the SOFTWARE, except that you may make a single copy of the SOFTWARE for backup or archival purposes only. You may be held legally responsible for any copying or copyright infringement which is caused or encouraged by your failure to abide by the terms of this restriction.

4.　　**USE RESTRICTIONS:** You may not network the SOFTWARE or otherwise use it on more than one computer or computer terminal at the same time. You may physically transfer the SOFTWARE from one computer to another provided that the SOFTWARE is used on only one computer at a time. You may not distribute copies of the SOFTWARE or Documentation to others. You may not reverse engineer, disassemble, decompile, modify, adapt, translate, or create derivative works based on the SOFTWARE or the Documentation without the prior written consent of the Company.

5.　　**TRANSFER RESTRICTIONS:** The enclosed SOFTWARE is licensed only to you and may not be transferred to any one else without the prior written consent of the Company. Any unauthorized transfer of the SOFTWARE shall result in the immediate termination of this Agreement.

6.　　**TERMINATION:** This license is effective until terminated. This license will terminate automatically without notice from the Company and become null and void if you fail to comply with any provisions or limitations of this license. Upon termination, you shall destroy the Documentation and all copies of the SOFTWARE. All provisions of this Agreement as to warranties, limitation of liability, remedies or damages, and our ownership rights shall survive termination.

7.　　**MISCELLANEOUS:** This Agreement shall be construed in accordance with the laws of the United States of America and the State of New York and shall benefit the Company, its affiliates, and assignees.

8.　　**LIMITED WARRANTY AND DISCLAIMER OF WARRANTY:** The Company warrants that the SOFTWARE, when properly used in accordance with the Documentation, will operate in substantial conformity with the description of the SOFTWARE set forth in the Documentation. The Company does not warrant that the SOFTWARE will meet your requirements or that the operation of the SOFTWARE will be uninterrupted or error-free. The Company warrants that the media on which the SOFTWARE is delivered shall be free from defects in materials and workmanship under normal use for a period of thirty (30) days from the date of your purchase. Your only remedy and the Company's only obligation under these limited warranties is, at the Company's option, return of the warranted item for a refund of any amounts paid by you or replacement of the item. Any replacement of SOFTWARE or media under the warranties shall not extend the original warranty period. The limited warranty set forth above shall not apply to any SOFTWARE which the Company determines in good faith has been subject to misuse, neglect, improper installation, repair, alteration, or damage by you. EXCEPT FOR THE EXPRESSED WARRANTIES SET FORTH ABOVE, THE COMPANY DISCLAIMS ALL WARRANTIES, EXPRESS OR IMPLIED, INCLUDING WITHOUT LIMITATION, THE IMPLIED WARRANTIES OF MERCHANTABILITY AND FITNESS FOR A PARTICULAR PURPOSE. EXCEPT FOR THE EXPRESS WARRANTY SET FORTH ABOVE, THE COMPANY DOES NOT WARRANT, GUARANTEE, OR MAKE ANY REPRESENTATION REGARDING THE USE OR THE RESULTS OF THE USE OF THE SOFTWARE IN TERMS OF ITS CORRECTNESS, ACCURACY, RELIABILITY, CURRENTNESS, OR OTHERWISE.

IN NO EVENT, SHALL THE COMPANY OR ITS EMPLOYEES, AGENTS, SUPPLIERS, OR CONTRACTORS BE LIABLE FOR ANY INCIDENTAL, INDIRECT, SPECIAL, OR CONSEQUENTIAL DAMAGES ARISING OUT OF OR IN CONNECTION WITH THE LICENSE GRANTED UNDER THIS AGREEMENT, OR FOR LOSS OF USE, LOSS OF DATA, LOSS OF INCOME OR PROFIT, OR OTHER LOSSES, SUSTAINED AS A RESULT OF INJURY TO ANY PERSON, OR LOSS OF OR DAMAGE TO PROPERTY, OR CLAIMS OF THIRD PARTIES, EVEN IF THE COMPANY OR AN AUTHORIZED REPRESENTATIVE OF THE COMPANY HAS BEEN ADVISED OF THE POSSIBILITY OF SUCH DAMAGES. IN NO EVENT SHALL LIABILITY OF THE COMPANY FOR DAMAGES WITH RESPECT TO THE SOFTWARE EXCEED THE AMOUNTS ACTUALLY PAID BY YOU, IF ANY, FOR THE SOFTWARE.

SOME JURISDICTIONS DO NOT ALLOW THE LIMITATION OF IMPLIED WARRANTIES OR LIABILITY FOR INCIDENTAL, INDIRECT, SPECIAL, OR CONSEQUENTIAL DAMAGES, SO THE ABOVE LIMITATIONS MAY NOT ALWAYS APPLY. THE WARRANTIES IN THIS AGREEMENT GIVE YOU SPECIFIC LEGAL RIGHTS AND YOU MAY ALSO HAVE OTHER RIGHTS WHICH VARY IN ACCORDANCE WITH LOCAL LAW.

ACKNOWLEDGMENT

YOU ACKNOWLEDGE THAT YOU HAVE READ THIS AGREEMENT, UNDERSTAND IT, AND AGREE TO BE BOUND BY ITS TERMS AND CONDITIONS. YOU ALSO AGREE THAT THIS AGREEMENT IS THE COMPLETE AND EXCLUSIVE STATEMENT OF THE AGREEMENT BETWEEN YOU AND THE COMPANY AND SUPERSEDES ALL PROPOSALS OR PRIOR AGREEMENTS, ORAL, OR WRITTEN, AND ANY OTHER COMMUNICATIONS BETWEEN YOU AND THE COMPANY OR ANY REPRESENTATIVE OF THE COMPANY RELATING TO THE SUBJECT MATTER OF THIS AGREEMENT.

Should you have any questions concerning this Agreement or if you wish to contact the Company for any reason, please contact in writing at the address below.

Robin Short
Prentice Hall PTR
One Lake Street
Upper Saddle River, New Jersey 07458

About the CD-ROM

The CD-ROM that comes with this book is divided into three areas: the XML Web site, example programs, and online resources.

The XML Web site is a template for a complete site based on XML. The template is generally described in Chapter 14. The site is fully functional and contains "skeleton" XML documents for all parts of a typical XML Web site. You can modify these files and customize them to your needs. In addition, you can add new sections by copying these templates into new directories and modifying the style sheets to reflect the new sections in menus.

To run the Web site, you should install it under a Windows NT server running IIS, as described in Chapter 11. Currently all URL references (namely, the <stylesheet> references in the <!DOCTYPE> declarations of most XML documents) point to http://localhost. This makes it easy for you to test the Web site on a development platform. If you install a development system as described in Chapter 11, the Web site will load without modification.

The second section of the CD contains the source code to many of the examples presented in this book. Readme files are included for longer projects and provide descriptions as well as instructions for running the examples.

Finally, rather than providing outdated software tools and source code, the CD provides references to many of the tools, vocabularies, and SDKs described in this book. You can find these references in two areas. The first is the XML Tools database, which is included with the sample Web site. The database includes the names, descriptions, and Web site addresses for nearly 50 XML tools. The database is in Microsoft Access format and is located in /website/db/xmltools.mdb. You can access the database through the sample Web site. However, the database records are not fully displayed within the sample site. Therefore, you will need Microsoft Access to obtain the complete records. Alternatively, you can modify the style sheets contained in the db/ directory to display the URLs and other fields for the records.

Finally, resources.html contains a list of the other tools (e.g., servlet engines) you will need to build your own XML-enabled Web site. Finally, be sure to check http://www.BeyondHTML.com for updates to the database, new resources, and errata to this book.

Technical Support

Prentice Hall does not offer technical support for this software. However, if there is a problem with the media, you may obtain a replacement copy by e-mailing us with your problem at: disc_exchange@phptr.com.